Maria D' Andrea, William Alexander Ori

With Special Introduction by Timothy Green Beckley

Also Includes Bonus Section
SECRET CIPHER OF THE UFONAUTS
by Bishop Allen Greenfield

ANGEL SPELLS

The Enochian Occult Workbook of Charms, Seals, Talismans and Ciphers

ANGEL SPELLS

The Enochian Occult Workbook of Charms, Seals, Talismans and Ciphers

Inner Light/Global Communications

Metaphysical artist Carol Ann Rodriguez renders visionary likeness of her Guardian Angel.

Angel Spells - The Enochian Occult Workbook of Charms, Seals, Talismans and Ciphers

By Maria D' Andrea, William Alexander Oribello, Sean Casteel
With Special Introduction by Timothy Green Beckley

Includes **Secret Ciphers of the UFOnauts** By Bishop Allen Greenfield

Published in the United States of America By Timothy Green Beckley
Box 753 • New Brunswick, NJ 08903

Staff Members
Timothy G. Beckley, Publisher
Carol Ann Rodriguez, Assistant to the Publisher
Sean Casteel, Editorial Consultant
William Kern, Editorial Consultant
Tim R. Swartz, Typesetting, Formatting & Cover Design

Contents

ANGEL SPELLS

THIS BOOK IS DEDICATED

TO MY LONG TIME FRIEND HELEN HOVEY

MAKE FRIENDS WITH ANGELS. . .

WHILE, THOUGH THEY ARE INVISIBLE,

THEY ARE ALWAYS THERE ALONGSIDE YOU.

SPEAKING WITH THE ANGELS - AND UTILIZING THEIR POWERS FOR GUIDANCE AND PERSONAL BENEFITS

By Timothy Green Beckley

EVEN linguistic experts disagree on this one.

Estimates of the number of languages spoken in the world vary somewhere between 6,000 and 7,000 depending on an arbitrary distinction between languages and dialects.

Language is the way we communicate with each other. Somewhere in the distant past, our grunts and utterances became intelligence as we moved out of the cave and into the world.

Is it possible, however, that we have "missed" a few languages along the way? We know today that it's possible to communicate with other species, especially the dolphin. It may only be a series of clicks, but to them it might be a form of "conversation."

But suppose beings from other worlds and realms landed upon our cosmic shores? Would they have languages that we would need to learn pretty fast? Would their language be similar to ours or totally different? If they wanted to "invite us to lunch," we should have a pretty good inkling of their true intentions.

And here is a BIG abstraction – what if there really were Angels and we could get them to assist in our lives . . . if we only knew how to speak with them?

Are Angels real, as described in the Bible? Or are they simply figments of our overly zealous spiritual imaginations?

I have to say I believe something. My Guardian Angel, perhaps, saved my life at the tender tot age of three or four. I have told the story only once or twice to listeners of such shows as "Coast to Coast AM," hosted by George Noory.

My parents were on their way to Kentucky. My mother had severe asthma and this was then known as an allergy-free state. My dad was driving. My mom was in the passenger seat and I was hunkered down in the back with a blanket and a couple of toys to keep me out of mischief.

It was on the third day of our trip that the fog started to roll in as the evening progressed.

At some point my mother insisted we stop and pull over to the side of the road as it was unsafe, she felt, to continue to drive on any further. My father, on the other hand, was anxious to get to their destination and started to apply pressure to the gas pedal.

My mother would have none of this reckless attitude and demanded that my father pull over and NOW!

He did.

A short nap was to follow until the sun finally emerged, cutting through the fog until the haze disappeared entirely, at which point it was discovered that the car we were all passengers in was poised perilously on the side of a mountain cliff.

As I understand it, another foot or two at the most and we would be bear meat.

Who told my mother to insist that my dad stop driving? Why didn't he go on another foot or two till we dropped to our doom?

Perhaps a "birdie" spoke into my mother's ear. Or maybe, just maybe, it was my Guardian Angel. Indeed, if we hadn't stopped dead on the spot, I would have been a goner. So I have to respect talk of Guardian Angels, just as you should, too.

Perhaps we can learn to speak with our angelic guides and utilize them when necessary to get through rough periods in our lives. Perhaps, for those who are a bit greedier, it might be possible to even press them into personal service. Angels are there to be utilized. We just need to learn how to communicate. This book will show you that they have their own language. It is undoubtedly too complex for the average person to understand. John Dee and his accomplice studied it for their entire lives. But there are certain shortcuts we can take that will put us in the ballpark with them anyway. There are signs, symbols, ciphers, candle colors and talismans that will nudge them. There are the Angel Spells outlined in this book that will press them into divine service for you.

Angels are our friends.

One may have saved my life.

You can learn to have them do your bidding and to keep them as spiritual friends.

"Angels hear my voice now sound,
All the way Down from the Ground,
Help me in my time of need,
Stop the foils without Heed."

Summoning Angels With Enochian Magick

Section One

The History And Philosophy Of Enochian Magick

By Sean Casteel

HAVE you ever wanted to literally speak to an angel? Would you welcome a visit from one of God's celestial servants? Are you curious as to whether there is a method to achieve that goal?

There are those who believe they can take the desire for angelic conversation out of the realm of mere tantalizing possibility and place it into a real-world setting merely by knowing the language with which angels prefer to communicate. Since medieval times, practitioners of various forms of magick have been striving to accomplish that very thing, with sometimes surprisingly dramatic results. One of the oldest such systems is called Enochian magick, and we will here give a brief but thorough history of this mysterious and controversial technique for seeing beyond everyday reality and into the heavenly abodes above us.

One Man's Journey To Enochian Magick

After even a cursory examination of the literature on Enochian magick, one quickly discovers that the subject can at times be astonishingly complicated. I therefore decided to consult an expert on the topic, Aaron Leitch, who has studied Enochian Magick for many years and written extensively about it. In February of 2014, Leitch's book, "The Essential Enochian Grimoire" was released, the fourth book he has written on occult magick and the summoning of angels.

Leitch's interest in occult matters began in high school. He started to read everything he could find on the subject, but for a suburban kid in Orlando, Florida, the available resources were very limited. He was forced to settle for watered-down mainstream books on the subject, such as the "Mysteries of the Unexplained" series from TIME-LIFE Books.

"I eventually started to delve a little deeper into the darker side of things," Leitch said, "like Satanism. That was mostly just a reaction to my environment. I grew up in a real tough neighborhood and I was a skinny white boy and an easy target. Once I started taking on this air and persona of a dark Satanist, people started giving me a little more respect. I started playing around with demonic entities and learning how to work with them. Of course, I got 'burned,' and shifted gears. I went into this completely bizarre, esoteric Christian phase where I hated churches and preachers and organized religion was just a very bad thing to me.

"But I was very into the power of prayer," Leitch continued, "and trying to make things happen around me by praying to Jesus and in Jesus' name. I used the Lord's Prayer for years as a very powerful incantation for various purposes."

Leitch graduated from high school in 1992 and moved out West, where he lived for a time with a group he characterized as "neo-pagans." Knowing of Leitch's interest in Christianity, the group gave him a book called "Modern Magic," by Donald Michael Kraig. The book is an extremely famous and popular introduction to the kind of ceremonial magick practiced by the legendary occult brotherhood the Hermetic Order of the Golden Dawn, about whom more later. Leitch devoured the book and began to study related subjects Kraig wrote about, such as the Jewish mystical work the Kabbalah and the medieval magickal texts called Grimoires.

"It just grew from there," Leitch said. "My interest was piqued and I kept on wanting to research more and more into older and older texts. I started delving into the Solomonic mysticism and eventually the Enochian as well."

Who Is The Enoch In "Enochian"?

Many people are familiar with the name of the prophet Enoch and have read the apocryphal books that bear his name. Enoch is mentioned briefly in the

Bible, and an Internet posting by Jack Zavada summarizes what the Bible says about him.

"Enoch holds a rare distinction in the Bible," Zavada writes. "He did not die. Instead, God 'took him away.' We find his story in Genesis 5, in a long list of the descendants of Adam. Only a short sentence, 'Enoch walked faithfully with God,' in Genesis 5:22 and repeated in Genesis 5:24 reveals why he was so special to his Creator."

Zavada also points out that in the Letter of Jude in the New Testament, Enoch is said to have prophesied that God would one day come to execute judgment on all and to convict all the ungodly of all their deeds. In Hebrews, Chapter 11, God commends Enoch for having pleased Him. Enoch is then taken into heaven without having to suffer the experience of death. Only the prophet Elijah, who was taken away to heaven in a whirlwind, was given a similar blessing.

The aforementioned apocryphal Book of Enoch, in contrast to the brief history given in the Bible, provides an impressive wealth of information on the prophet's life and his experiences with God and the angels. At one point, Enoch ascended into heaven and was taken on a tour by an angel guide. Another story recounts how Enoch was asked by the fallen angels to make intercession for them with God so that they might return to heaven. God denies their petition, but nevertheless blesses Enoch for his efforts. I have written more about Enoch's journey into heaven and its similarities to alien abduction in another Global Communications book, "The Heretic's UFO Guidebook."

More On The Enoch Connection

The story of how the Book of Enoch came to be written is a very interesting one, according to Leitch.

"It all goes back to the captivity in Babylon, which was about 600 B.C.," he said. "This was the time when Judaism, as we know it, solidified. The Judaism with rabbis and synagogues and studying the Torah didn't exist in ancient Israel. They had had the Temple religion there, an entirely different religion."

After the Babylonians had destroyed the Temple and taken a large number of the Hebrews into captivity, the Jews went into what Leitch said was an

Aaron Leitch

"emergency phase" in order to preserve the Torah and their traditions until such time as they could return to Israel and rebuild the Temple.

As Judaism solidified, so did new forms of Jewish mysticism, some of which borrowed extensively from Babylonian mystical beliefs about the Seven Heavens, astrology and exorcism. It was during this period of captivity that the Book of Enoch was written.

"It told the story of Enoch's travel into heaven," Leitch said. "Before he was taken permanently, he supposedly went up, was shown around and given a tour of heaven by the archangels. He was granted access to see the Tablets of Destiny, which is a record of every word God has ever spoken, and he was allowed to record material from the tablets to bring back with him.

"The book also tells, simultaneously, the story of the Watchers," he continued, "the angels who came down from heaven and defied God's orders and mated with human women, thus filling the world with giants and monsters. This was supposedly the reason for the Flood."

Leitch said this is the first reference, in any Biblical literature, to fallen angels who rebelled against God and were punished.

"They were chained under the mountains," Leitch said. "It says there is a lake of fire waiting for them and on Judgment Day they'll be thrown into the lake of fire. That's the first appearance of that lake of fire and the first time any kind of Judgment Day is mentioned. And it's the first time you see any of the messianic prophecies that would become central to both Judaism and Christianity later. So this text is the embodiment of a lot of 'firsts,' a lot of trends that we take for granted in the Abrahamic religions today. They all started right there in Babylon in what they call the Talmudic Era of Judaism."

When the Catholic Church arose hundreds of years later, the Book of Enoch was outlawed and removed from the Bible and the text was entirely lost in the West.

John Dee, The Father Of Enochian Magick

John Dee is, without question, the father of Enochian Magick. But just who was he?

"Not only could that fill books," Leitch said, "that HAS filled books. Dee was a very well-renowned scholar, inventor and scientist. He befriended Elizabeth before she was queen. Now, this is Elizabeth I, in the late 1500s. Dee was literally known as 'The Man Who Knew Everything.' All human knowledge, at that point in history, he had it in his head. His house also doubled as a lab, and scientists and researchers were constantly coming there to run experiments."

In the time before Elizabeth was on the throne and England was ruled by "Bloody Mary," Dee pushed very hard to establish a national library. When Mary refused to cooperate, he established a library in his house that drew a steady stream of scholars and travelers. England's world-dominating navy, by which the British Empire did much of its conquering, was aided by the navigation skills Dee taught. He realized it was imperative that England compete with Spain in carving up the New World that would become the Americas before it was too late and advised Elizabeth I to make haste in that regard. Dee also advised the queen's spymaster on cryptography, one of his specialties, as well as serving her court as a resident magician and alchemist.

Dee reached a point where he felt he had studied everything that the human race had to offer and that for further knowledge he must turn to God and His angels. He wrote in his journals that if Enoch, Ezekiel and Daniel and all the other prophets of old had gotten their wisdom directly from angelic sources, why couldn't he do the same? So he began to explore occultism, specifically what is called the Solomonic system. He began to read medieval Christian magickal texts such as "The Keys of Solomon," books that instructed the practitioner on how to call down angels and command demons.

"The only problem with this was that he was not a clairvoyant," Leitch explained. "He could not actually see and hear angels. So he set out to find a scryer, and he tried a couple of people that didn't quite work out. Then he was introduced to Edward Kelley, a budding alchemist who had really just developed an interest in the subject. We suspect that Kelley jumped at the chance to meet and work with John Dee, a famous alchemist."

Kelley sat down at the scrying stone and immediately the visions came.

"It was like a curtain opened and he could see and hear them like they were standing in the room," Leitch enthused. "His skill impressed Dee enough that he hired him on the spot, and for the next several years the two worked

A great scholar and alchemist, John Dee befriended Queen Elizabeth I. She found him fascinating and astute.

together pretty much every day for several hours a day, calling down angels and recording in the journal what Kelley was seeing in the crystal stone and what the angels would tell him."

Dee's Initial Contact With Angels

Remember that, at this point in history, the apocryphal Book of Enoch was entirely lost in the Western world due to its exclusion from the Bible by the early Catholic Church many hundreds of years prior to Dee's work. Dee himself did not own a copy and had never seen a copy of the book.

"But the legend of Enoch's journey into the heavens," Leitch said, "and his seeing these Tablets of Destiny had remained, even though the book itself was gone. So Dee was aware of the legend, and in his journals, when he made contact with the angels, one of the very first things he asked for was the Book of Enoch. The angels told him, 'Yes, we'll bring you that book.' The next time he called the angels, they brought a book, but it was not the lost Biblical book he had been looking for. What they brought was supposedly the book that Enoch had written when he copied the text out of the Tablets of Destiny in heaven. And they said, 'This is the book. This is the celestial book that Enoch copied.'

"That book that they showed Dee became the absolute center-pin of his entire angelic mystical system. Basically, Dee was being told by his angelic contacts that they were redelivering information to him that they had first given to Enoch but that had been lost in the Flood when all of the monsters and giants were wiped out because of what the Watchers had done."

(Leitch points out in a separate online article that Dee himself never called his system "Enochian Magick." Later historians gave it that name due to this relationship to the Biblical prophet Enoch that Leitch has been explaining here. The lost apocryphal book, called 1 Enoch or the Ethiopic Book of Enoch, was rediscovered in the 17th century and is available in various editions today.)

The Search For "The Language Of Eden"

But it is not enough to merely call down angels and make requests of them. These angels much appreciate the courtesy of being addressed in their own language.

For a quarter of a century, John Dee and Edward Kelley continued in their attempts to speak with unseen beings whom they believed to be angels.

"That's another thread a little bit separate from the Book of Enoch that runs into Dee's system," Leitch said. "And that is the search for what they call the 'Adamic Language,' or the 'Language of Eden.' This was when the Bible was taken as a source/fact absolute history book. There was this place called Eden and this first human. This human could converse freely with God and with angels and he actually named all the animals and invented all of Earth's languages. So whatever he was speaking should be the root language of all humanity. And being the root language, it should also be a very powerful and magical language. So, for a period in Europe, you had linguists and historians honestly searching for this lost root language of all humanity.

"You see this thread run through Dee's journals, too," Leitch said. "As he's talking to his angels, they're telling him the mythologies, the legends and the stories that are behind the language. What's interesting to note is that every instance in the Bible where language is the central focus of the story is included in these mythologies."

The angels told Dee that Adam "spake this great language and conversed with us freely, but he fell from Eden. When he fell, he lost the memory of the language."

Adam then reconstructed a pale reflection of the language as best he could so he could talk with his family. This language is an extremely ancient form of pre-Hebrew, according to Leitch. The angels told Dee that this was the language of mankind up until the building of the Tower of Babel, when God confounded the language of mankind to punish the hubris of trying to construct a tower tall enough to reach the gates of heaven and to make war with those who live there. Adam's pre-Hebrew, itself a weak imitation of the language of Eden, was now lost as well.

"You ended up with all the languages of the world," Leitch said, "including what we know as Biblical Hebrew. Now, of course, Biblical Hebrew is also gone and it's been replaced by Modern Hebrew. So what the angels are telling Dee was, 'Now here WE are. You guys have been searching for this original Adamic language and here it is. This is what he spoke.' And they gave him the book that they brought him, that Book of Enoch that was the celestial book and was entirely written in that language. To this day, that book has not been translated. No one can crack whatever encryption is being used to protect the text in the book. No one knows what it is."

Leitch conducted a ten-year study of the Enochian language, which resulted in two books, “The Angelical Language, Volumes One and Two.” He was attempting to catalog, categorize and cross-reference the language, or, more basically, to decipher the completely unknown tongue Dee had recorded in his journals.

“When you’re studying that material,” Leitch said, “you hear a lot of references to ‘Well, this is a full language. It has grammar. It has syntax.’ This wasn’t just something Dee cribbed together for his journals. There’s a real substance to the language. But there weren’t really any sources that explored those aspects of the language. Did it really have grammar and syntax? Was it really cohesive? Could it truly stand as a real language?”

Beyond the seemingly impossible task of translating the mysterious language, Enochian magick also involves what may seem to the uninitiated to be other impossibly complex factors, including mathematics and encrypted instructions for carrying out various rituals as the angels had directed.

But, in Leitch’s understanding, a great deal of that can be bypassed without diminishing the effectiveness of the magick at all.

“Let me explain what I mean by that,” he said. “Those things are how Dee received the magick, because he was a cryptographer. So when the angels said, ‘Here’s the text showing you the names of all these different angels and what you can use them for,’ he didn’t just get a list of angels. He would get these tables of letters. Then the angels would have to tell him how to decrypt them to get the angels’ names out of them. But we already have all of that, all the angels’ names. Dee recorded how he decrypted the tables so they don’t really play into the practice of the magick.”

Leitch said that in his latest book, “The Essential Enochian Grimoire,” he didn’t include the tables in the text because, at the heart of it, Dee’s system is very similar to what one finds in the various versions of the much earlier Solomonic system.

“Dee tells you how to set up your sacred space,” he said. “He tells you what invocations to read and when to read them. It’s just simple ritual instruction. He tells you how to build the tools. There are specific ways you have to put the tools together and you have to be ritually pure when you do it. But it’s very common, what I call Solomonic-type magickal instruction.”

Leitch added that people who do focus on the cryptographic aspects do it mainly for their own amusement or because they simply enjoy the challenge of pulling angelic names out of Dee's "squares." But the practice is not crucial to understanding the magick because, again, Dee has already provided the meanings the squares contain elsewhere in his journals. So why decode them all again?

What Was It All For?

While we may never understand the entirety of what Dee and Kelley believed they had discovered in their communications with the angels, we can ask, "Had they succeeded completely in their own terms, what would have been the result?"

Leitch responded by saying, "Dee was doing his work in the later part of a period in which Christianity was looking very hard into Judaic mysteries, specifically the Kabbalah. What was being developed is what has come to be called the Christian Kabbalah. For instance, in the Judaic Kabbalah, the highest name of God is what they call the Tetragrammaton. It's four letters, Y-H-V-H. It's where we get the name Yahweh, or, if you mistranslate, Jehovah.

"This was a central mystery of the Kabbalah, what that name means and what each letter stands for. The Christians studied this and found you could take one Hebrew letter, which is pronounced SH, and if you put that in the middle, Y-H-SH-V-H, that's Yeshua, which is Jesus' name. They were taking Jewish mysteries and reformatting them to fit into their Christian mysteries."

Dee was trying to take part in that tradition. He took a lot of his Enochian system from a Jewish practice called "Counting the Omer," or "Entering the Fifty Gates of Wisdom." There are other aspects of Dee's system that are much like Merkavah mysticism, the old Jewish mystical practice of actually entering the seven heavens like Enoch did and exploring. Dee nevertheless considered himself to be a pious, universal Christian and he disdained the split between Protestantism and Catholicism. He felt, according to Leitch, that Jesus was Jesus and there was no reason to fight over doctrines.

"So, had he achieved what he set out to do," Leitch said, "he would be known today as one of history's great Christian Kabbalists and philosophers. He had actually wanted to be a prophet."

Dee felt so strongly that he had been given the gift of prophecy by his angels that he took his magickal, angelically-inspired journals to Emperor Rudolf II, who ruled as the Holy Roman Emperor from 1576 until 1612. Rudolf II held other royal titles as well and governed a large chunk of Western Europe. When Dee told Rudolf II he had messages for him from God, the monarch basically laughed Dee off, as Leitch tells it, even though Rudolf II also fancied himself an occultist and alchemist and should have been a more sympathetic audience for Dee. Dee was forced to flee from Prague (where Rudolf II had relocated his court in 1583) under cover of darkness because of the emperor's suspicion that Dee had really approached him in the spirit of espionage and not as a prophet of God.

"So Dee did not achieve this place in history that he was looking for," Leitch said. "He went back to England and lived out the rest of his life. Although Dee never got what he was hoping for from his angels, maybe the angels got what THEY were looking for because the Enochian system is still with us."

Why Do Modern People Continue To Work With Dee's System?

The above question is not easy to answer, and Leitch replied that he could only speak for himself.

"When you come into occultism as a novice," he said, "there are certain things that you're about that people just consider horrifically dangerous, powerful things that humans probably shouldn't trifle with. As a hotheaded young kid, those are, of course, the things that I just had to seek out and play with. So I began with these Solomonic Grimoires and wanted to try these methods for calling down these massive archangels that could fry your brain out with a thought. Or, later, these Enochian entities. No one could tell me what the hell those guys were, only that they were extremely powerful. Once I got into it, it was like a calling. It just called to me and spoke to me and I've just been very wedded to the material ever since."

Leitch said that, from a higher, philosophical standpoint, he doubted that anyone ever got a better understanding of God out of the Enochian angels.

"But I really suspect that the main draw from the Enochian system, specifically, is its mystery," he continued. "It's that no one can be really sure. Up until very recently in history, the whole Enochian system was obscure. Until the 1990s, no one had even gone into Dee's journals and literally picked them apart page by page. No one had compared his magick to other systems. No one had really explored it. So there's this big mystery. What is this? What are these entities? Who are they? Why does this system exist? What are all these encrypted tablets? If I get into this, and can decrypt it and decipher it, is it going to mean something?

"So I think that's what pulls people in, and it can lead you on a merry chase for years and years of your life. And you can come out not really being sure you understand much more than what you started from."

Leitch cautioned that it would be wrong to call Enochian magick merely and only another angel summoning system, but that is technically what it is at its most basic level – a very powerful and effective form of angel communication. While the earlier Solomonic system evolved over hundreds of years from within its own culture, the Enochian system is more directly and urgently delivered straight from the angels themselves, who flatly declare, "If you want to talk to us, here's our language. Here are the designs you need to draw on your table. Here's how to do it, and we'll come."

For Leitch, the fact that Enochian magick actually works keeps him fascinated.

"The angels respond to their language," he said, "and they respond to the magick. You know, I'm an 'angel worker,' so there's no reason in the world that I wouldn't want to explore something like that."

Some Angels Can Be "Dangerous"

One wonders, given all this talk of angels and various forms of Jewish and Christian mysticism, why Enochian magick is ever thought of as evil? Why does it conjure, for some people, images of a wicked wizard calling down supernatural fiends to do his egregious bidding?

"This magick has a practical edge to it," Leitch answered. "It's not very philosophical. It's not like the Kabbalah, where you will meditate on the Tree of Life and Biblical passages to find out what it all means, the creation of the universe and how it all works. Enochian magick is a little more nuts-and-bolts. You're given angels, and these angels are given powers like healing, transmuting matter, protecting you in travel or helping you to win naval battles. Remember,

Dee was doing his magick for an entire nation, not just himself. So you really do get some guys out there who want to treat Enochian angels in this way – they want to call them down and have them do their bidding. But the thing is, the Enochian angels are . . . I'll try to describe this in a way that will make sense."

Leitch next launched into a kind of mystical history lesson, explaining that the Enochian angels are "Throne Angels" and in Hebrew they're called by a name which means "life" or "living." In the first chapter of Ezekiel, in which the prophet sees a vision of the throne of God, he reports that there are four mighty archangels uplifting the throne and holding it on their backs. These are the angels that attend directly upon the throne of God. With the earlier Solomonic system of summoning angels, one generally called upon nature spirits or known, friendly archangels like Michael, Gabriel or Raphael.

"With the Enochian material," Leitch went on, "you're dealing with the highest of the high angels, the ones that don't really care much about you, you know?"

Leitch finished that sentence with a laugh, and then said, "So people call these angels down and they think they're just going to be handed things that they desire. Then they realize they've invoked this very powerful force into their life, and it's not always for the better. There's an old adage, 'Enochian angels bite,' and they do. Even the kind angels, even Michael, Gabriel and Raphael, can be dangerous if you don't know how to work with them properly. And these Enochian angels are just that to the nth degree."

In the late 1800s, when members of the Hermetic Order of the Golden Dawn (who, again, will be dealt with in more detail later) found Enochian magick and made it the pinnacle of their magickal practices, they had only a portion of Dee's journals to base their work on, which forced them to explore the missing elements on their own. They did this by experimenting with astral projection and created their own rituals intended to call the angels. But without all of the information from Dee's journals, they didn't know how to work the magick properly and inevitably made mistakes.

"Some of them were okay," Leitch said. "Some of them had encounters with angels that were perfectly benign. But some of them did not have such good experiences and ended up in some real bad places, spiritually speaking. One or two of them later published books talking about how horrible this Enochian

John Dee's black stone or scrying mirror - as well as his other ritualistic tools - reside today in the British Museum.

system is and that it's evil. But it's not an inherent problem with the system. It's more of an inherent problem with the way these particular individuals are trying to use it.

"When they get themselves in trouble, rather than accepting responsibility for their own mistakes, it's the system's fault. 'This is evil magick. These are evil angels.' Therefore you get these horror stories that live on for generations."

Leitch compared the situation to that of an electrician.

"He's working with dangerous forces," Leitch said, "but as long as he follows what he was trained to do, he'll be fine. It's when he makes mistakes, when he doesn't follow his training, when he tries to be showy or impress people – that's when he gets electrocuted. It's the same thing when working with this kind of energy."

Meaning that a certain amount of humbleness is required.

"If you don't have it when you start," Lietch said, "you'll get it. You'll get knocked pretty hard if you don't come at this with respect."

A Brief History Of The Golden Dawn

A great deal of the present day practice of Enochian magick has its roots in a society of occultists known as the Hermetic Order of the Golden Dawn, founded in London in 1888. Several of the original members of the Golden Dawn were also followers of Helena Petrovna Blavatsky and her particular brand of Theosophy, which was a religious or semi-religious set of occult beliefs rejecting Judeo-Christian revelation and theology. Theosophy often incorporated elements of Buddhism and Hinduism and claimed to be derived from special mystical insight or superior speculation.

"But the Golden Dawn was not Theosophy," Leitch said. "The Golden Dawn was founded by Masons who were members of an order called the Societas Rosicruciana in Anglia."

That last group name translates as "The Rosicrucian Society of England," a Masonic esoteric Christian order formed by Robert Wentworth Little in 1865. As one often finds when studying the occult and even conspiracy theory, the Masons seem to have their hands in everything. Leitch said that most Masonic Rosicrucian groups were focused mainly on study and theory, but the founders of the Golden Dawn were eager to practice magick in a hands-on way and to actually perform the rituals.

"They wanted to study astrology and alchemy and angel communication," Leitch said, "and all the stuff that their Masonic brethren weren't so keen about. So they went off to the side and founded the Golden Dawn, which was very similar to the Societas Rosicruciana in Anglia, except that it was very occult. They were very into magick and they insisted on admitting women as well as men. That was the founding of the Golden Dawn. Meanwhile, Blavatsky was doing her thing and she wasn't too happy about the Golden Dawn at first."

When Blavatsky told her Theosophy members to choose one or the other group so many of them chose the Golden Dawn that she was forced to rescind her ultimatum.

But, in spite of their intense interest in Enochian magick, the Golden Dawn never really replicated Dee's original work, according to Leitch.

"They weren't medieval magicians," he said. "They were 19th century Masonic magicians, so their magick shows that. There were a lot of regalia and scepters and walking around in the hall and pronouncements, the kind of thing you would see in a Masonic lodge. They weren't really even trying to go for the kind of thing that Dee would have been doing, that Solomonic style of ritual. They were basically just taking what they had of John Dee's material and incorporating it into their own system."

Leitch considers himself to be a "Dee purist" and said there are many points on which he could quibble with the Golden Dawn's version of Enochian magick. But he acknowledged that the Golden Dawn's method has had 120 years to develop in its own right and within the context of its own system and thus has a validity that makes it at least equal to Dee's system for some practitioners.

Aleister Crowley's Version Of Enochian Magick

One of the most famous occultists to work with Enochian magick was Aleister Crowley, dubbed by the news media of his time as the "Wickedest Man in the World." Why would a person so apparently evil seek out contact with the powerful angels that spoke to John Dee?

"The first thing you have to understand," Leitch said, "is that he got the title 'Wickedest Man in the World' because he was into drugs and sex. Basically, in the late Victorian era, Crowley was into many things that wouldn't become socially acceptable until the 1960s. If he was around today, he would not be the 'Wickedest Man in the World.' He wouldn't even rate a local newspaper article anywhere. The stories about him are that he was an 'asshole' and probably not someone you really wanted to be friends with.

"But he wasn't a Satanist, he wasn't evil, he wasn't any of those things. He was just shocking to the Victorian sensibility. Remember, we're talking about people that put coverings on their piano legs because the piano legs were too sexy. So that's where he got the 'Wickedest Man in the World' appellation. And, of course, he reveled in it. He thought it was hilarious. He encouraged that whole 'Great Beast 666' thing that he got stuck with. It was just a big joke to him. Other than the way he treated people and the fact that he was an arrogant jerk, other than that, he was not the wickedest man in the world."

Crowley joined the Hermetic Order of the Golden Dawn in 1898. Samuel Liddell MacGregor Mathers, one of the original founders of the Order, initiated Crowley into the group. After becoming a member, Crowley rose up the ranks until he reached the threshold of the secret inner order but was refused admittance there simply because he was so personally disliked. When Crowley took his case to Mathers, Mathers initiated him into the inner order in a private ceremony, much to the displeasure of the rest of the adepts.

The result was a big falling out between Crowley and the Golden Dawn. This feud was reflected in Crowley's later writings as well as in the setting up of his own magickal system, which he called "Thelema." Crowley also ended up feuding with Mathers himself, and the two began to send demons back and forth at each other in what Leitch characterized as "a bunch of childish outbursts."

In spite of all this conflict, Crowley's Thelema is very much influenced by what he learned from the Golden Dawn. Crowley felt that he could take their system and make it better, thus making it his own as well. When he reformatted what he had been taught into Thelema, the Enochian material came with it.

"Like I said before, the draw for a lot of people to the Enochian system," Leitch reiterated, "is its purported danger, its power, the complexity of the word squares where all the angels' names are encrypted. So I think that drew Crowley as well."

Crowley wrote a book called "Liber LXXXIV vel Chanokh," or "The Book of Enoch." The name "Chanokh" is an older Hebrew form of the name Enoch. The Roman numerals in the title represent the number 84, which is the numeration for Enoch in the Kabbalah. The book consisted of Crowley's version of the Enochian system, which Leitch says is almost word for word the same as the Golden Dawn's version.

A later book by Crowley called "The Vision and the Voice" recorded Crowley's contact with his own version of the Enochian angels. He would write down what the angels told him, as the earlier practitioners of the art had done, and these sessions also formed much of the root structure of Thelema. He practiced meditation, saw visions, and journeyed up to the heavens, where he met the Thelemic deities with names like Nuit, Hadit, and Ra-Hoor-Khuit. There is also a lesser deity named Babalon, the goddess of pleasure, who is nicknamed "the Virgin Whore" and sits astride another lesser deity named Therion.

"That's really Crowley's main contribution," Leitch said. "There are probably thousands that are practicing his version of the Enochian system, as there are probably also thousands practicing the Golden Dawn's version of the system. There are probably several hundred that are practicing John Dee's version of the system. They're all different and they're all valid within the context of their own systems. But they don't really mix too well."

Can Enochian Magick Conjure Physical Entities?

When a person summons the angels through Enochian magick, do they manifest physically?

"It really depends on who you ask," Leitch replied. "A lot of people have made a lot of claims, but I always tell people this: it depends on your ability to perceive them. There's never going to be a time when your door's going to open and something is going to walk in and sit in a chair and you can take a picture of it and share it on Facebook. 'This is the angel. Here he is.' These beings don't exist here. Their bodies don't reflect light. Their voices don't vibrate the air. When you see and hear them, it's clairvoyance, it's clairaudience. Some people are wired to be very good at that. Like my wife, for instance. She can see them as if they really are standing in the room. Literally. She can't tell the difference. But I could be standing in the room with her and NOT see anything. You know what I'm saying?"

Leitch explained that this was why John Dee employed Edward Kelley as a scryer and why Leitch himself often relies on help from his wife, who can sit and hold conversations with the Enochian angels and assist Leitch in conversing with them as well.

But the attendant danger can still be very real.

"Just because these entities aren't physical," Leitch warned, "doesn't mean they're not here. These guys represent, they embody, the forces of nature. So if you summon an angel of the sun here into your room, you are also bringing the power of the sun into your room. You're not going to be sunburned. It's not sun-LIGHT. But everything the sun represents, and everything that is mystically associated with the sun, you are bringing into your life. The sun, for instance, burns away darkness. It reveals things. If you're hiding things, those things can be revealed. It's true of any natural force that you bring in: whatever the force CAN do to you, it's going to do to you. That's the danger."

The only precautions one can take are to follow the rituals and protocols precisely as they are laid out. As with the analogy of the electrician given earlier, when working with dangerous forces, one must follow the instructions exactly as taught.

Crowley's Gray Alien

Speaking of summoning physical entities, Leitch told the somewhat famous story of when Aleister Crowley was working his Enochian magick, repeatedly and over a long period of time, and found himself in contact with a small, impish creature.

"He drew a picture of it," Leitch recounted, "and it looks every bit like a gray alien. Now, remember, when Crowley drew that picture, there were no such things as gray aliens. No one had ever heard of such a thing. I don't think that concept came along until the 1970s. People picked up on Crowley's story and this rumor or idea has gotten started that the Enochian angels are, in fact, aliens. And

Aleister Crowley drew heavily upon Enochian Magick in his rituals. He claims to have conjured up numerous celestial beings, including one that closely resembles an ultra-terrestrial being commonly known as a "Gray" in the modern age of UFOs.

that all the technology that Dee was given was alien technology that we can use to build a radio to contact them."

Leitch said he finds the whole idea silly for various reasons. One reason is that Dee had contacted known Biblical angels, such as Michael and Gabriel, and later the four archangels that had forwarded and transmitted the angelic materials. So unless one makes the leap of faith that all the Hebrew and Biblical angels are aliens, there is no connection between what Leitch calls the UFO cult and what Dee was doing. While he does not discount the fact that aliens do likely exist and have even visited the Earth, he does not believe they are the same beings said to populate the various magickal texts of all the different angel-summoning systems.

"It's only generations later that people are looking at Crowley's drawing," Leitch said, "and saying, 'Oh, it must have been a gray alien.' In a way, that's putting words into Crowley's mouth. He never claimed it was a UFO person. It was just a little creature, a little spiritual entity, that he contacted by using the Enochian formulas."

[We will deal later with opposing points of view that argue for a definite connection between Enochian magick and the UFO occupants.]

Celebrities And Enochian Magick

Did you know that Jack Parsons, the inventor of the solid rocket fuel that made the American space program possible, practiced Crowley's Thelemic version of Enochian magick? It is also believed that rock superstar David Bowie practiced Thelema for a while, making it at least a possibility that he was exploring Crowley's brand of Enochian magick as well.

The legendary poet, playwright and essayist, William Butler Yeats, headed the Golden Dawn for 20 years after Samuel Mathers left the order, so there is no question that he practiced Enochian magick. Other writers, artists and actors who were famous in the late 19th and early 20th century were also members of the Golden Dawn and students of Enochian magick.

"And remember," Leitch said, "you had this strange period in the 1960s, right after Anton LaVey founded the Church of Satan in California, when some of the celebrities were kind of messing around with that. Sammy Davis, Jr., actually attended some of the ceremonies at the local Church of Satan. LaVey played around with Thelemic Enochian magick a little, so maybe some of the stars were introduced to some of that there. There are names, but none that would be famous specifically for Enochian magick outside of, obviously, Jack Parsons. He did some really whacky stuff."

Leitch referred to a brief time when stars like Madonna and Roseanne Barr followed a kind of watered-down, Hollywood version of the Kabbalah.

"But I don't think any of those guys," he said, "would even touch Enochian magick or even know what it was if they were to see it."

What Is A Grimoire?

The term "grimoire" comes up frequently when one explores the topic of Enochian magick, and it may be helpful to offer an overview of the word's meaning.

"Technically," Leitch explained, "it's the French word for 'grammar,' as in 'grammar school.' It means the basics, a primer. You're talking about books that were written during the medieval or renaissance era, mostly in Europe. They are what contain and transmit to us what I've been referring to as the Solomonic tradition and which were basically, to put it briefly, used by the Catholic exorcists of the day. It wasn't like the movie 'The Exorcist.' They were more like faith healers. If you got sick, you would go to the exorcist to have the demon of sickness cast out."

In the effort to discover increasingly more effective methods of healing, these exorcists would often rebel against what the Catholic Church said was acceptable. The exorcists were very interested in occultism and sought to learn the healing secrets of local witches. They consulted all the written material they could get their hands on, such as ancient Greek and Egyptian occult texts and even older cuneiform writings. This happened to be the period when bound books were being introduced into Europe, so these exorcists and faith healers were the first mystics in Western history that had the luxury of recording all of their learning into nice, neat little volumes – the grimoires.

"Those are also the books that launched the Inquisition," Leitch added. "The Church found out about these books and raised hell. They started hanging people and burning books. Fortunately, the Church wasn't able to burn them all. We have a rather large, large body – and more appearing every day – of these old medieval and renaissance European magickal texts. Those are the old Solomonic grimoires and the Enochian material."

Aaron Leitch has a website at

http://kheph777.tripod.com/indexaol.html

The Sigillum Dei Aemaeth

THE Sigillum Dei Aemaeth is crucial to performing John Dee's Enochian magick. The meaning of the first two Latin words is "Seal of God," and it existed by that name for many years before Dee began to make use of it. Dee later added the word "Aemaeth," which is Hebrew for "truth," to the symbol's name. It has been pointed out that when one removes the first syllable, the "Ae," it becomes "maeth," which is the Hebrew word for "death." Perhaps it was Dee's belief that truth and death are inevitably linked; just as God created all life, so can He just as easily take it back to himself.

In any case, the Sigillum Dei consists of two circles, a pentagram, and three heptagons, and is labeled with the name of God and His angels. Its magickal function was to permit the initiated practitioner to have power over all creatures, except archangels, and was usually reserved only for those who can achieve the blessed vision of God and His heavenly servants and attendants, the angels.

The earliest description of the Sigillum Dei is found in a 14th century book called "Liber iuratus," or "Sworn Book," attributed to Honorius, the son of Euclid. The instructions begin: "Make first a circle whose diameter is three fingers, because of the three cross-nails of the Lord, or five fingers because of the five wounds of Christ, or seven for the seven sacraments, or nine for the nine orders of angels, but usually five fingers will suffice. Then make a second circle within this circle. Let it be a distance from the first two grains because of the two Tablets of the Law of Moses, or three grains because of the persons of the Trinity."

The circular band made according to these instructions will be at the top of a small cross, and from this starting point one finds written, from left to right, 72 individual Latin letters, which vary according to tradition. The sum of all the letters represents the word "Shemhamephorasch," the ineffable name of God and a clear link to Jewish tradition.

Next to the circular band is a pentagram that focuses on a Greek Tau, which is the nineteenth letter of the Greek alphabet and whose English equivalent is "t."

This is surrounded by the five letters of the name of God ("El" or "Ely") and five other pairs of letters.

Inside the pentagram is a heptagon drawn in such a way that its top side touches the center tip of the pentagram. The heptagon should be labeled with the names of seven angels and archangels: Cafziel, Satquiel, Amael, Raphael, Anael, Michael and Gabriel. From this first heptagon are made a second and a third drawing, which have been subject to various interpretations, but usually involve seven key points with crosses labeled with two rows of God's names, to include a first series of seven names of God, each in three syllables or components disassembled and connected to the first and final syllables of the last names of angels. The mathematics and interconnections of the names of God and the angels get very complex, but it should suffice to say that nearly every possible known name for God and his attendant heavenly servants are present in the intricate patterns of the Sigillum Dei.

A copy of the "Liber iuratus" is housed in the British Museum and is believed to have been partly owned by John Dee, who based his writing "Five Books of Mystical Exercises" on the Sigillum Dei and added his suffix "Aemaeth" at that time.

While the illustration provided here gives one at least some inkling on how to start practicing Enochian magick, one must nevertheless create a Sigillum Dei Amaeth with which the central section can be rotated clockwise and counter-clockwise so that the proper alignments of holy names can be adjusted to suit the needs of the moment. It must also be large enough so that one's scrying instrument, whether it is a crystal ball or obsidian mirror, can fit in the center and permit one to see visions simultaneous to the holy names being visible.

PUBLISHERS NOTE: For the purpose of getting the most out of this Workbook and Study Guide, we recommend using a copy of the Sigillum Dei Aemaeth as your angelic altar "place mat." Simply print it on cover stock or parchment and place on a large enough table so that you can center it. Place a candle at each of the four corners of the table (white for purity, green for prosperity, red for love, etc). Place your scrying mirror or black stone bowl directly in the middle of the Sigillum Dei Aemaeth. Put your chosen angel symbol upside down in it (see section on summoning angels by Maria D' Andrea) as you attempt to establish communications with an angelic being. You can also use the bowl as a means to see spirits by filling it partially with water and gazing into its depths.

THE SIGILLUM DEI ÆMETH, A PANTACLE
MADE BY DR. JOHN DEE
Figure V

Section Two

Enochian Magick and the Alien Connection

By Sean Casteel

HAVING presented Aaron Leitch's fascinating and through overview of the history and practice of Enochian magick, we now make a leap of faith that Leitch was unwilling to make: that there is a connection between the angels who abducted, or "took aloft," the prophet Enoch and the angels John Dee contacted many centuries later. We also offer the opinion that those same Enochian angels still leave their heavenly abode to work in our world today – often employing what we call UFOs as their means of conveyance. We will begin with an analysis of portions of the Books of Enoch that bolster our alien abduction take on the matter.

Enoch Rises From His Couch

The apocryphal Books of Enoch are a marvelous addendum to the Bible as we more commonly know it. We share in Enoch's wondrous adventure as he travels to both heaven and hell, bearing witness to the innumerable mysteries and testifying always for the sake of the righteous as they battle, suffer and endure the wicked. The fall of the evil angels called The Watchers, who take earthly wives and breed a horrifying race of giants; the birth of Noah as a strange and supernatural child of the great unknown who utterly terrifies his father; the creation story told by God, which begins with God as a solitary figure creating the visible from the invisible, all combine to fascinate and enthrall the reader who takes up the Books of Enoch and joins the prophet on his fearsome ride through the cosmos. Space and time melt away, and the promise of an eventual paradise where there is no time becomes the goal of Enoch's journey and our own as well.

While much has been written about the first Book of Enoch, it is perhaps more appropriate here to discuss the lesser-known Enoch Two: The Secrets of Enoch. Enoch is introduced as a wise man, much beloved by God, who is given to see the wonders of the heavenly realm, including the "inexpressible singing of the host of the cherubim and of the boundless light." Enoch's story begins when he is 165 years old and begets Methuselah. Enoch then lived another 200 years, for a total of 365 years. As he lies on his couch asleep, he begins to cry – still in his sleep – completely at a loss to explain his distress.

Two men appear to him, so large there is nothing like them on earth. Their faces, eyes and lips all shine and burn with fire, and they have the telltale wings of angels. They call Enoch by name, and he is roused from his sleep to see that the two "men" are indeed really there. Enoch salutes them and is seized with fear. The angels tell him to have courage. They are sent by God to take him into heaven. Enoch is instructed to tell his sons that he will be gone for a while and that they are not to look for him until he returns.

The angels bear Enoch on their wings to the first heaven and place him on the clouds. He is shown how angels control the houses of the snow and dew. On to the second heaven, where he is shown rebellious angels being punished as prisoners in a terrible darkness. Enoch pities them, and they ask him to pray to God on their behalf. On to the third heaven. Enoch is shown an idyllic garden with a wondrous fragrant tree. He states that paradise "is between corruptibility and incorruptibility." The garden is guarded over by three hundred angels.

Enoch is told the paradise is prepared for the righteous that suffer greatly yet do good works in the world. Next, Enoch is shown a place of darkness and torture for the punishment of sinners who practice sodomy and witchcraft and oppress the poor. The fourth heaven is taken up by an astronomical lesson on the goings of the sun and the moon. In the fifth heaven, Enoch sees a race of giant soldiers, called the Grigori, with withered faces and silent mouths. The angels tell him the Grigoris fell with Satan and impregnated the daughters of men to produce the familiar race of giants who "befouled the earth with their deeds."

After being questioned by Enoch, the giant soldiers break into song, asking God to pity them. In the sixth heaven, Enoch sees seven bands of angels who guard the sun and moon and stars and regulate events on earth, including world governments and the natural world of rivers and forests, as well as recording all the deeds of mankind. In the seventh heaven, Enoch sees a "very great light and fiery troops of great archangels." These fearsome soldiers serve God with joyful singing. After showing Enoch the seventh heaven, the two angels leave him alone, which causes Enoch great fear and he cries out for help. Gabriel comes to him. "Gabriel caught me up, as a leaf caught up by the wind." Enoch sees the eighth and ninth heavens, which include the twelve signs of the Zodiac. Finally, in the tenth heaven, Enoch sees the face of God, "like iron made to glow in fire," and emitting sparks. The Lord's face is "ineffable, marvelous, and very awful, and very, very terrible. And who am I to tell of the Lord's unspeakable being and of his very wonderful face?" The Lord instructs the Angel Michael to dress Enoch in "the garments of glory." Enoch is then taught the ways of heaven and earth and writes 366 books of the knowledge that he is given.

God tells Enoch that He was alone before He made creation. Then He made light from the darkness and the visible from the invisible. There follows a wonderful creation story where God speaks in surprising detail and frankness, a much more direct, "first-person" account than is found in Genesis. It begins with the creation of angels as troops with fiery weapons. The Genesis pattern of seven days of creation is also used here in Enoch's version, with man again being created on the sixth day. But there are fascinating differences, namely the "seven consistencies" from which man was made.

First, his flesh was made from the earth. Second, his blood from the dew. Third, his eyes from the sun. Fourth, his bones from stone. Fifth, his intelligence from the swiftness of the angels and the clouds. Sixth, his veins and his hair from the grass of the earth. And seventh, his soul from the breath of God and from the wind.

As in Genesis, God then rests on the seventh day. But God also talks of an eighth day, a day without time or the measurement of time. "A time of not counting, endless, with neither years nor months nor weeks nor days nor hours."

Enoch Returns To Tell His Tale

Enoch is then told to return to earth for thirty days to tell his household what he has seen and to write down his journey for the sake of future generations. Enoch is returned to the couch on which he slept at the book's beginning, where

The Biblical prophet Enoch is the basis for the Enochian philosophy, which was later developed into a magickal system.

his son Methuselah has been keeping watch for him and is amazed to see his return. Enoch, with weeping, tells of how being in the Lord's presence is "endless pain." Enoch also tells his son he now knows everything, being shown the utter and complete truth of mortal and universal existence by God.

Again, details of the workings of astronomy and the natural world are recited, which are then followed by exhortations to be righteous and to give no unclean gifts to God. Enoch tells his sons that the fate of man's soul is fixed even before he is born. God bids us to be meek, to endure attacks and insults, and not to offend widows and orphans. Enoch instructs his sons to pass along his books to others and then begins to speak of how it is important to treat the poor well. The moral injunctions Enoch speaks of are all familiar from the Old Testament, but there is an urgency and intensity to Enoch's version that stems mostly from the strangeness of his journey and the fact that he will be taken again by the angels, this time for good.

The word of Enoch's impending departure into heaven becomes widely known, and two thousand men arrive to kiss him goodbye and ask his blessing. Enoch again prophesies a world where time is not measured, a paradise that cannot be corrupted, and says those gathered to see him off must walk before the Lord in "terror and trembling."

The Lord sends darkness on the earth. Enoch is taken up, and the light returns. Enoch's sons erect an altar at the place where Enoch has been taken up and make sacrifices there. The people and the elders gather together for a great feast with his sons and they make merry for three days, praising God, who had favored them with the sign of Enoch's heavenly departure, the story of which is to be handed down from generation to generation and from age to age.

Some Familiar UFO Elements

The events described in Enoch Two are very similar to what we read in modern day UFO abduction accounts. We see the standard scenario in which the abductee finds himself partially awake but in a dreamlike state. He is then taken up from his bed and transported into another world very different from the normal waking world, accompanied by angels or the now familiar gray aliens.

When Enoch says that being in the Lord's presence is "endless pain," one is reminded of the stress factor in the alien abduction experience. In an early interview I did with "Communion" author Whitley Strieber, who was among the first to popularize the abduction experience, he quite flatly told me, "You cannot imagine how awful it is." Some abductees, such as New England housewife Betty Andreasson Luca, believe the alien abductors are angels sent to announce the Second Coming of Christ. But Luca also recalled some genuinely frightening moments onboard the UFOs. Strieber, meanwhile, acknowledged that alien abduction can be a beautiful experience, but rarely in the sense of "sweetness and light."

Perhaps all of that is a testimony to the authenticity of what Enoch, Strieber and Luca and many others have undergone. Alien abduction can be seen to be linked to Enoch Two as part of a tradition stretching back thousands of years. The spiritual mysteries of one age are continued in the next, and maybe we can draw comfort from believing that the Eighth Day that God speaks of in Enoch Two, a day when no time is measured, may be just around the corner on the Cosmic Calendar.

The Leap Of Faith To Enochian Aliens

The major point to be understood here is that if one can make the connection between the angels who took Enoch away and the present day aliens that regularly abduct a portion of Earth's population that the aliens have said they regard as "Chosen Ones," then it would seem to follow that those are the same entities with whom John Dee, the Hermetic Order of the Golden Dawn, and even Aleister Crowley were in contact.

Aaron Leitch, who emphatically stated that he feels this leap of faith to Enochian "aliens" is mere silliness, also said that Dee was in contact with the same Hebrew, Biblical angels who upheld the throne of God in the vision described in the first chapter of Ezekiel. While Leitch is certainly entitled to have his doubts, it's basically a cherished article of faith for most UFO/ancient astronaut believers that Ezekiel witnessed the appearance of a UFO. It is also a strongly held belief that the radiance of God manifests to us mortals, on some level, as the brightness and awe of what some call "flying saucers" and the mysterious occupants, gray or otherwise, residing within these ships.

While no one denies that this is a controversial belief and is hotly debated within the UFO community, it serves quite neatly our purposes here. There are

many contrasting proponents of the ancient astronaut theory, from Erich von Daniken to Zechariah Sitchin to Brinsely Le Poer Trench, but nevertheless they all involve this primal principle that our creators came to the Earth in ships and taught us the ways of civilization.

Allen Greenfield, Aleister Crowley And Alien Occultism

Allen Greenfield holds the title of bishop in the Gnostic Church. He has a long history of active – and contentious – membership in many occult organizations, including the Ordo Templi Orientis, established by Aleister Crowley. Along with his esoteric pursuits, Greenfield has also studied the UFO phenomenon for many decades.

Greenfield is the author of “Secret Cipher of the UFOnauts,” a provocative grimoire for the modern age that has come to be regarded as a classic in the field of paranormal literature and one which might be considered to have a particularly hip cachet. It was at one time a rare and difficult book to track down, but we have included it here, in full, at the end of this book.

“Secret Cipher of the UFOnauts” contains Greenfield’s theory that much of the UFO phenomenon can be “decoded” by using a method that draws on the Kabbalah, especially the numerology aspects of its Jewish mysticism, as well as other similar ancient systems. Greenfield believes the UFO occupants are an eternal race that has always reached out to certain human adepts by using hidden, obscure linguistic and mathematical symbolism.

Greenfield’s method also relies on elements taught by Aleister Crowley. Greenfield, like many others, vehemently denies that Crowley was a Satanist, black magician or sexual pervert. He quotes one of Crowley’s biographers as saying that Crowley was a man “intoxicated” with God.

Chapter Two of “Secret Cipher of the UFOnauts” opens with a portion of a letter Crowley wrote to one of his students in California in 1944, near the end of Crowley’s life.

“My observation of the Universe,” Crowley wrote, “convinces me that there are beings of intelligence and power of a far higher quality than anything we can conceive of as human . . . the one and only chance for mankind to advance as a whole is for individuals to make contact with such beings.”

On October 15, 2013, at the Sacramento, California, USA, Blue Star Lodge, Allen Greenfield was ritually conferred to the 4º Degree in the Kabbalistic Order of the Rose+Croix, Knight Beneficent of the Holy City (CBCS), 8º Grand Master Elu Cohen, and 4º Free Initiator in the Martinist Order of Unknown Philosophers.

Crowley's Enochian Contact

While on vacation with his wife in Cairo in April 1904, Crowley received a surprising response to his many years of practicing Enochian magick: the appearance of "Aiwass," or "Aiwaz," a being Crowley regarded as a super-human intelligence. The being then dictated to Crowley what became "The Book of the Law," or "Liber AL vel Legis."

"Although primarily associated with the Law of the New Aeon or Age of Aquarius," Greenfield writes, "'The Book of the Law' predicts and contains the complete cipher of the UFOnauts. As far as is known, although not fully decoded until the 1970s even in the classical form, this cipher seems to have been in use among the UFOnauts themselves for some time prior to the appearance of Aiwass."

Was this UFOnaut cipher the same as the Enochian language the angels taught to John Dee? Or something similar to the Adamic Language, also called the Language of Eden, sought by many medieval Jewish and Christian mystics and scholars? There is an obvious repeated pattern here. A mere mortal seeks contact with the angels and is told he must first learn certain protocols and methods of communication that require the ability to speak to these higher beings in their own language.

Perhaps this accounts for why most abductees recall very little actually being spoken to them – telepathically or otherwise – by the alien abductors. The literature on the subject reveals time and again that the aliens often remain stonily silent when abductees ask them questions about the procedures being performed on them or what the overall purpose of the abduction program really is. This refusal to inform abductees of the aliens' intent is a primary reason the phenomenon remains so mysterious. The late abduction research pioneer, Budd Hopkins, once said that we are not dealing with an intelligence we can call into the room and interview.

Is the problem that we are simply not speaking to the aliens in their own language? Did John Dee and Aleister Crowley take the right approach when they began to compile what they felt was a directly revealed method of speaking to their angels in words the angels could respect?

Greenfield's book also includes the drawing Crowley made of Aiwass, and the creature's resemblance to a gray alien is immediate and unmistakable. Given

At center (l-r) are Timothy Green Beckley, Author of UFO Silencers and CEO of Inner Light Publications and T Allen Greenfield, author of Secret Cipher of the UFOnauts and Secret Rituals of the UFOnauts. 32nd National UFO Conference. (Photo by J. Moseley)

that Aiwass showed up after Crowley had practiced for many years with his version of the Enochian system for "summoning angels," one is hard-pressed not to draw the conclusion that John Dee was most likely working with these same beings and that overcoming the language barrier was a vital part of the process.

Greenfield writes that Crowley "wrestled all his adult life with the nature of the Higher Beings he contacted," including Aiwass. Crowley died in poverty in 1947. Under his deathbed was found a considerable sum of money belonging to the Ordo Templi Orientis, which Crowley had declined to spend, even on medicines that might have saved his life. Little understood, even by many of his followers, his death in the same year that the UFO phenomenon came to public attention seems more than coincidental, according to Greenfield.

Exploring The Actual Practice Of Enochian Magick

The reader is by now aware that Enochian magick is not a method whereby the magician can say "Abracadabra," wave a wand and conjure up anything he desires. Enochian magick is instead an astonishingly complicated means of contacting angels and receiving divine revelation, most often through visions and otherworldly voices.

Nevertheless, it is possible to describe some of the basics. As is often the case, the online encyclopedia Wikipedia offers a brief breakdown, the kind of thing that can be squeezed into a few pages for some quick edification on the subject.

The essence of the Enochian system, Wikipedia says, depends on the utilization of eighteen "Calls" or "Keys" in the Enochian language. These are a series of rhetorical exhortations, or spoken appeals, which function as evocations or to "call forth" the angels. There is a nineteenth key known as the Call or Key of the Thirty Aethyrs. The Aethyrs are the "heavens" of the system. The calls are used to enter the various Aethyrs in visionary states. The Aethyrs are conceived of as forming a map of the entire universe in the form of concentric rings which expand outward from the innermost to the outermost Aethyr.

The Enochian "map" of the universe, Wikipedia continues, is depicted by John Dee as a square made up of and containing within it various symbols surrounded by the thirty concentric circles of the Aethyrs. The Aethyrs are numbered from 30, which is called TEX and is the lowest number in the system, up to 1, which is called LIL, the highest point in the system and regarded as the Supreme Attainment. Practitioners then record their impressions and visions within each of the succeeding Enochian Aethyrs. The system is comparable but not equivalent to working with the Tree of Life in the Kabbalah, which employs 32 Sephira or paths as opposed to the Thirty Aethyrs in Enochian magick.

Each of the Thirty Aethyrs is populated by "Governors." There are three for each Aethyr, except for TEX, which has four, making for a total of 91 Governors. The list of Enochian angels also includes The Three Holy Names, the Great Elemental King, the Six Seniors (also known as "Elders"), the Two Divine Names of the Calvary Cross, the Kerubim, and the Sixteen Lesser Angels. In addition, the names of various archangels and angels who govern different aspects of the cosmic whole are part of the package. In this way, the entire universe, both visible and invisible, is depicted as teeming with living intelligences.

Certain kinds of furniture are also required to perform Enochian magick. For example, the Holy Table. The tabletop must be engraved with a hexagram surrounded by a border of Enochian letters. A twelve-fold cell engraved with further individual Enochian letters is to be placed in the middle of the tabletop. One also needs the Seven Planetary Talismans, made of tin with the names of the Goetia (a term for the demons or angels – take your pick – typically summoned by magicians) engraved on them. The equipment must also include a way of "scrying" (or gazing into an object in order to obtain visions) such as the concave obsidian mirror used by Dee and Kelley. Crowley habitually held a large topaz mounted upon a wooden cross to his forehead. Other methods include gazing into crystals, ink, fire or even a blank TV screen. A magician's ring engraved with the god-name "Pele" is also essential.

The complexities of the mathematics and the dividing of the numerous angels into their assigned places among the five elements of Earth, Air, Fire, Water and Spirit and into their various designated squares can be mind-boggling, and there have been a slew of books written to try to simplify the process for the uninitiated. The original working title for one of Aaron Leitch's books was "Enochian Magick for Beginners." But when he discovered that that title had already been used, he changed it to "The Essential Enochian Grimoire." Leitch said he wrote the book to "explain it to someone who's never even heard of it before and provide a good overview." The Wikipedia entry quoted above also recommends obtaining a text with the Enochian symbols and Calls provided in some detail before attempting to practice the magick on a do-it-yourself basis.

Even invoking the angels by merely speaking their names requires some study and effort. Practitioners see the correct pronunciation of the Enochian letters, words and Calls to be integral to using the system successfully. The letters must be memorized and their pronunciations learned.

Fortunately, there have been several compilations of Enochian words made to form Enochian dictionaries, and Leitch's two-volume set "The Angelical Language" is one of them. Sound recordings exist that feature authentic pronunciations of the words, such as the set of instructional CDs that give the Hermetic Order of the Golden Dawn's version of how to correctly speak the invocations. There are also the famous wax cylinder recordings made by Aleister Crowley in 1922 in which, among other things, he reads aloud the First and Second Calls of the Aethyrs in both English and Enochian. Crowley's recordings can serve as a guide to the correct pronunciation of at least some of the Enochian invocations and are widely available on CD.

A writer and researcher named John DeSalvo, who holds a Ph.D. in biophysics and scientifically studied the Shroud of Turin for more than thirty years, has also written extensively about Enochian magick. He calls Enochian magick a "powerful, ancient system for opening portals to the heavenly realms and enabling the ascent to God." DeSalvo says that he was able to decipher the original phonetic notations in the margins of Dee's 16th century diaries. Employing Dee's instructions on pronunciation made it possible to properly reproduce the Enochian Calls, which he says are intended to act like mantras in revealing higher dominions and invoking angels.

The most orthodox users of the Enochian language will tell neophytes just starting out that you must enunciate and articulate the words and Calls correctly or you will not be granted the same benefits as those who have studied long and hard to speak the language of the angels. There are many others – trustworthy adepts themselves – who scoff at this idea and say that summoning an angel has more to do with your determination and the energy you devote to your preparation for doing a spell or ritual.

"Pidgin-Enochian" will suffice for the majority, as one recognizes that the pronunciation of Hebrew words or other lesser known dialects are best left to the rabbi and the scholar. Of course, it wouldn't hurt to do a bit of practicing. As stated above, the Golden Dawn provides several audio presentations which can be obtained on Amazon. For those reading this in electronic, e-book format (i.e. Kindle), you can listen to a brief track at this link of the Enochian language spoken out loud. This will allow you to try and imitate what you hear or at least get the general gist of how the pronunciations go.

http://www.originalfalcon.com/cd-gd_enochian_magick.php

Proceed With Caution

Should you begin your own efforts to perform Enochian magick, hopefully with the aid of a truly complete text on the detailed rituals, remember Aaron Leitch's warning to follow those rituals exactly as instructed. If you succeed in summoning an angel or two into your presence, you may find yourself in the company of something much more powerful than you ever imagined, an entity who is no respecter of persons and whose concerns and priorities are very different from your own.

As Leitch cautioned, his voice betraying the awestruck recollection of someone who has been there, some of these angels can "fry your brain out with a thought." But you may also experience ecstatic visions comparable to those of the prophet Enoch himself and draw inexpressibly nearer to God in the process. The decision as to whether to take the risk is entirely your own.

The Enochian Keys

The Enochian Keys are given in the original Enochian Language (transliterated into English), Aleister Crowley's Phonetic version, and a Modern English Translation, based on John Dee's Old English versions. The Enochian Keys were received through Edward Kelley, circa 1584, in Krakow, Poland. The Keys comprise 48 poetic verses, which John Dee called Claves Angelicae, or Angelic Keys. The Enochian Keys correspond to various functions within the Enochian Magic system. John Dee intended to use the Enochian Keys to *"open the 49 Gates of Wisdom/Understanding"* represented by the 49 magic squares in Liber Loagaeth. Dee wrote: *"I am therefore to instruct and inform you, according to your Doctrine delivered, which is contained in 49 Tables. In 49 voices, or callings: which are the Natural Keys to open those, not 49 but 48 (for one is not to be opened) Gates of Understanding, whereby you shall have knowledge to move every Gate..."* And: *"But you shall understand that these 19 Calls are the Calls, or entrances into the knowledge of the mystical Tables. Every Table containing one whole leaf, whereunto you need no other circumstances."*

Pronunciation for the Phonetic version of the Enochian Keys

This phonetic guide to the pronunciation of the Enochian Keys is based on that given by Aleister Crowley, who derived his knowledge of the Keys from the Hermetic Order of the Golden Dawn. All letters are sounded as in English with these exceptions:

A	ah	as in "fAther"
C	k	as in "Cake"
E	eh	as in "grEy"
I	ee	as in "fEEt"
O	long o	as in "smOke"
Q	k	as in "Qabalah"
U	long u	as in "fOOl"

The First Enochian Key

Ol sonf vorsg, goho Iad balt, lansh calz vonpho: sobra z-ol ror i ta Nazpad Graa ta Malprg Ds hol-q Qaa nothoa zimz Od commah ta nobloh zien: Soba thil gnonp prge aldi Od vrbs oboleh grsam Casarm ohorela caba pir Od zonrensg cab erm Iadnah Pilah farzm zurza adna Ds gono Iadpil Ds hom Od toh Soba Ipam lu Ipamis Ds loholo vep zomd Poamal Od bogpa aai ta piap piamo-i od vaoan ZACARe c-a od ZAMRAM Odo cicle Qaa Zorge, Lap zirdo Noco MAD Hoath Iaida.

Phonetic Translation

Ol sonuf vaoresaji, gohu IAD Balata, elanusaha caelazod: sobrazod-ol Roray i ta nazodapesad, Giraa ta maelpereji, das hoel-qo qaa notahoa zodimezod, od comemahe ta nobeloha zodien; soba tahil ginonupe pereje aladi, das vaurebes obolehe giresam. Causarem ohorela caba Pire: das zodonurenusagi cab: erem Iadanahe. Pilahe farezodem zodenurezoda adana gono Iadapiel das home-tohe: soba ipame lu ipamis: das sobolo vepe zodomeda poamal, od bogira aai ta piape Piamoel od Vaoan! Zodacare, eca, od zodameranu! odo cicale Qaa; zodoreje, lape zodiredo Noco Mada, Hoathahe I A I D A!

Modern English Translation

I reign over you, says the God of Justice, in power exalted above the firmaments of wrath: in whose hands the Sun is as a sword and the Moon as a through thrusting fire: which measures your garments in the midst of my vestures, and trussed you together as the palms of my hands: whose seats I garnished with the fire of gathering, and beautified your garments with admiration. To whom I made a law to govern the holy ones and delivered you a rod with the ark of knowledge. Moreover you lifted up your voices and swore obedience and faith to him that lives and triumphs, whose beginning is not, nor end can not be, which shines as a flame in the midst of your palace, and reigns amongst you as the balance of righteousness and truth. Move, therefore, and show yourselves: open the Mysteries of your Creation: Be friendly unto me: for I am the servant of the same your God, the true worshipper of the Highest.

The Second Enochian Key

Adgt v-pa-ah zongom fa-a-ip Sald vi-i-v L sobam I-al-prg I-za-zaz pi-adph cas-arma abramg ta talho paracleda Q-ta lors-l-q turbs ooge Baltch Giui chis lusd orri Od mi-calp chis bia ozongon Lap noan trof cors tage o-q manin Ia-i-don Torzu gohel ZACAR ca c-no-qod, ZAMRAN micalzo Od ozazm vrelp Lap zir Ioiad.

Phonetic Translation

Adagita vau-pa-ahe zodonugonu fa-a-ipe salada! Vi-i-vau el! Sobame ial-pereji i-zoda-zodazod pi-adapehe casarema aberameji ta ta-labo paracaleda qo-ta lores-el-qo turebesa ooge balatohe! Giui cahisa lusada oreri od micalapape cahisa bia ozodonugonu! lape noanu tarofe coresa tage o-quo maninu IA-I-DON. Torezodu! gohe-el, zodacare eca ca-no-quoda! zodameranu micalazodo od ozodazodame vaurelar; lape zodir IOIAD!Adagita vau-pa-ahe zodonugonu fa-a-ipe salada! Vi-i-vau el! Sobame ial-pereji i-zoda-zodazod pi-adapehe casarema aberameji ta ta-labo paracaleda qo-ta lores-el-qo turebesa ooge balatohe! Giui cahisa lusada oreri od micalapape cahisa bia ozodonugonu! lape noanu tarofe coresa tage o-quo maninu IA-I-DON. Torezodu! gohe-el, zodacare eca ca-no-quoda! zodameranu micalazodo od ozodazodame vaurelar; lape zodir IOIAD!

Modern English Translation

Can the wings of the winds understand your voices of wonder, O you the second of the first, whom the burning flames have framed within the depth of my Jaws; whom I have prepared as Cups for a Wedding, or as the flowers in their beauty for the Chamber of righteousness. Stronger are your feet than the barren stone, and mightier are your voices than the manifold winds. For you are become a building such as is not, but in the mind of the All Powerful. Arise, says the First: Move therefore unto his Servants: Show yourselves in power: And make me a strong seething: for I am of him that lives for ever.

The Third Enochian Key

Micma goho Piad zir com-selh a zien biab Os Lon-doh Norz Chis othil Gigipah vnd-l chis ta-pu-im Q mos-pleh teloch Qui-i-n toltorg chis i chis ge m ozien dst brgda od torzul i li F ol balzarg, od aala Thiln Os ne ta ab dluga vomsarg lonsa cap-mi-ali vors cla homil cocasb fafen izizop od mi i noag de gnetaab vaun na-na-e-el panpir Malpirgi caosg Pild noan vnalah balt od vooan do o-i-ap MAD

Goholor gohus amiran Micma Iehusoz ca-ca-com od do-o-a-in noar mi-ca-olz a-ai-om Casarmg gohia ZACAR vniglag od Im-ua-mar pugo plapli ananael Q a an.

Phonetic Translation

Micama! goho Pe-IAD! zodir com-selahe azodien biabe os-lon-dohe. Norezoda cahisa otahila Gigipahe; vaunudel-cahisa ta-pu-ime qo-mos-pelehe telocahe; qui-i-inu toltoregi cahisa i cahisaji em ozodien; dasata beregida od toreodul! Ili e-Ol balazodareji, od aala tahilanu-os netaabe: daluga vaomesareji elonusa cape-mi-ali vaoresa CALA homila; cocasabe fafenu izodizodope, od miinoagi de ginetaabe: vaunu na-na-e-el: panupire malapireji caosaji. Pilada noanu vaunalahe balata od-vaoan. Do-o-i-ape mada: goholore, gohus, amiranu! Micama! Yehusozod ca-ca-com, od do-o-a-inu noari micaolazoda a-ai-om. Casarameji gohia: Zodacare! Vaunigilaji! od im-ua-mar pugo pelapeli Ananael Qo-a-an.

Modern English Translation

Behold, says your god, I am a Circle on whose hands stand 12 Kingdoms: Six are the seats of Living Breath: the rest are as sharp sickles or the horns of death, wherein the Creatures of your earth are to are not, except mine own hand which sleep and shall rise. In the first I made you Stewards and placed you in 12 seats of government. giving unto every one of you power successively over 456, the true ages of time: to the intent that from your highest vessels and the corners of your governments you might work my power, pouring down the fires of life and increase continually on the earth: Thus you are become the skirts of Justice and Truth. In the Name of the same your God, lift up, I say, your selves. Behold his mercies flourish and Name is become mighty amongst us. In whom we say: Move, Descend, and apply yourselves unto us, as unto the partakers of the Secret Wisdom of your Creation.

The Fourth Enochian Key

Othil lasdi babge od dorpha Gohol G chis ge auauago cormp pd dsonf vi v-di-v Casarmi oali Map m Sobam ag cormpo c-rp-l Casarmg cro od zi chis od vgeg dst ca pi mali chis ca pi ma on Ionshin chis ta lo Cla Torgu Nor quasahi od F caosaga Bagle zi re nai ad Dsi od Apila Do o a ip Q-a-al ZACAR od ZAMRAN Obelisong rest-el aaf Nor-mo-lap.

Phonetic Translation

Otahil elasadi babaje, od dorepaha gohol: gi-cahisaje auauago coremepe peda, dasonuf vi-vau-di-vau? Casaremi oeli MEAPEME sobame agi coremepo carep-el: casaremeji caro-o-dazodi cahisa od vaugeji; dasata ca-pi-mali cahisa ca-pi-ma-on: od elonusahinu cahisa ta el-o CALAA. Torezodu nor-quasahi od fe-caosaga: Bagile zodir e-na-IAD: das iod apila! Do-o-a-ipe quo-A-AL, zodacare! Zodameranu obelisonugi resat-el aaf nor-mo-lapi!

Modern English Translation

I have set my feet in the south and have looked about me, saying, are not the Thunders of increase numbered 33 which reign in the Second Angel? Under whom I have placed 9639 whom none hath yet numbered but one, in whom the second beginning of things are and wax strong, which also successively are the number of time: and their powers are as the first 456. Arise, you Sons of pleasure, and visit the earth: for I am the Lord your God which is, and liveth. In the name of the Creator, Move and show yourselves as pleasant deliverers, that you may praise him amongst the sons of men.

The Fifth Enochian Key

Sa pah zimii du-i-v od noas ta-qu-a-nis adroch dorphal Ca osg od faonts peripsol tablior Casarm amipzi na zarth af od dlugar zizop z-lida caosagi tol torg od z-chis e si asch L ta vi u od iaod thild ds peral hubar Pe o al soba cormfa chis ta la vis od Q-co-casb Ca nils od Darbs Q a as Feth-ar-zi od bliora ia-ial ed nas cicles Bagle Ge iad i L.

Phonetic Translation

Sapahe zodimii du-i-be, od noasa ta qu-a-nis, adarocahe dorepehal caosagi od faonutas peripeso ta-be-liore. Casareme A-me-ipezodi na-zodaretahe AFA; od dalugare zodizodope zodelida caosaji tol-toregi; od zod-cahisa esiasacahe El ta-vi-vau; od iao-d tahilada das hubare PE-O-AL; soba coremefa cahisa ta Ela Vaulasa od Quo-Co-Casabe. Eca niisa od darebesa quo-a-asa: fetahe-ar-ezodi od beliora: ia-ial eda-nasa cicalesa; bagile Ge-iad I-el!

Modern English Translation

The mighty sounds have entered in your 3rd Angle and are become as olives in your olive mount, looking with gladness upon the earth and dwelling in the brightness of the heavens as continual comforters. Unto whom I fastened pillars of gladness 19 and gave them vessels to water the earth with her creatures: and they are the brothers of the first and second and the beginning of their own seats which are garnished with continually burning lamps 69636 whose numbers are as the first, the ends, and your contents of time. Therefore come you and obey your creation: visit us in peace and comfort: Conclude us as receivers of your mysteries: for why? Our Lord and Master is all One.

The Sixth Enochian Key

Gah s di u chis em micalzo pil zin sobam El harg mir babalon od obloc samvelg dlugar malprg arcaosgi od Acam canal so bol zar f-bliard caosgi od chis a ne tab od miam ta vi v od d Darsar sol peth bi en B ri ta od zacam g mi calzo sob ha hath trian Lu ia he odecrin MAD Q a a on.

Phonetic Translation

Gahe sa-div cahisa EM, micalazoda Pil-zodinu, sobam El haraji mir babalonu od obeloce samevelaji, dalagare malapereji ar-caosaji od ACAME canale, sobola zodare fabeliareda caosaji od cahisa aneta-na miame ta Viv od Da. Daresare Sol-petahe-bienu Be-ri-ta od zodacame ji-micalazodo: sob-ha-atahe tarianu luia-he od ecarinu MADA Qu-a-a-on!

Modern English Translation

The spirits of your 4th Angle are Nine, Mighty in the firmament of waters: whom the first has planted a torment to the wicked and a garland to the righteous: giving unto them fiery darts to winnow the earth and 7699 continual Workmen whose courses visit with comfort the earth and are in government and continuance as the second and the third. Wherefore hearken unto my voice: I have talked of you and I move you in power and presence: whose Works shall be a song of honour and the praise of your God in your Creation.

The Seventh Enochian Key

R a as isalman para di zod oe cri ni aao ial purgah qui in enay butmon od in oas ni para dial casarmg vgear chirlan od zonac Lu cif tian cors to vaul zirn tol ha mi Soba Londoh od miam chis tad o des vmadea od pibliar Othil rit od miam C no quol Rit ZACAR, ZAMRAN oecrimi Q a dah od o mi ca olz aaiom Bagle pap nor id lugam lonshi od vmplif vgegi Bigliad.

Phonetic Translation

Ra-asa isalamanu para-di-zoda oe-cari-mi aao iala-piregahe Qui-inu. Enai butamonu od inoasa NI pa-ra-diala. Casaremeji ujeare cahirelanu, od zodonace lucifatianu, caresa ta vavale-zodirenu tol-hami. Soba lonudohe od nuame cahisa ta Da o Desa vo-ma-dea od pi-beliare itahila rita od miame ca-ni-quola rita! Zodacare! Zodameranu! Iecarimi Quo-a-dahe od I-mica-ol-zododa aaiome. Bajireje papenore idalugama elonusahi–od umapelifa vau-ge-ji Bijil–IAD!

Modern English Translation

The East is a house of virgins singing praises amongst the flames of first glory wherein the Lord hath opened his mouth: and they are become 28 living dwellings in whom the strength of man rejoices, and they are apparelled with ornaments of brightness such as work wonders on all creatures. Whose Kingdoms and continuance are as the Third and Fourth Strong Towers and places of comfort, The seats of Mercy and Continuance. O you Servants of Mercy: Move, Appear: sing praises unto the Creator and be mighty amongst us. For to this remembrance is given power and our strength waxes strong in our Comforter.

The Eighth Enochian Key

Bazmelo i ta pi ripson oln Na za vabh ox casarmg vran Chis vgeg dsa bramig bal to ha goho i ad solamian trian ta lol cis A ba i uo nin od a zi agi er rior Ir gil chis da ds pa a ox bufd Caosgo ds chis odi puran teloah cacrg isalman loncho od Vouina carbaf Niiso Bagle auauaga gohon Niiso bagle momao siaion od mabza Iad o i as mo mar poilp Niis ZAMRAN ci a o fi caosgo od bliors od corsi ta a bra mig.

Phonetic Translation

Bazodemelo i ta pi-ripesonu olanu Na-zodavabebe OX. Casaremeji varanu cahisa vaugeji asa berameji balatoha: goho IAD. Soba miame tarianu ta Iolacis Abaivoninu od azodiajiere riore. Irejila cahisa da das pa-aox busada Caosago, das cahisa od ipuranu telocahe cacureji oisalamahe lonucaho od Vovina carebafe? NIISO! bagile avavago hohon. NIISO! bagile momao siaionu, od mabezoda IAD oi asa-momare poilape. NIIASA! Zodameranu ciaosi caosago od belioresa od coresi ta a beramiji.

Modern English Translation

The Midday, the first, is as the third heaven made of Hyacinth Pillars 26: in whom the Elders are become strong which I have prepared for my own righteousness says the Lord: whose long continuance shall be as bucklers to the stooping Dragon and like unto the harvest of a Widow. How many are there which remain in the glory of the earth, which are, and shall not see death, until this house fall and the Dragon sink? Come away, for the Thunders have spoken: Come away, for the Crowns of the Temple and the coat of him that is, was, and shall be crowned, are divided. Come, appear to the terror of the earth and to our comfort and of such as are prepared.

The Ninth Enochian Key

Mica oli bransg prgel napta ialpor ds brin efafafe P vonpho o l a ni od obza Sobca v pa ah chis tatan od tra nan balye a lar lusda so boln od chis hol q C no quo di cial v nal aldon mom caosgo ta las ollor gnay limlal Amma chiis Sobca madrid z chis ooanoan chiis auiny dril pi caosgin od od butmoni parm zum vi C nila Daziz e thamz a-childao od mirc ozol chis pi di a i Collal Vl ci nin a sobam v cim Bagle Iab baltoh chirlan par Niiso od ip ofafafe Bagle acosasb icorsca unig blior.

Phonetic Translation

Micaoli beranusaji perejala napeta ialapore, das barinu efafaje PE vaunupeho olani od obezoda, soba-ca upaahe cahisa tatanu od tarananu balie, alare busada so-bolunu od cahisa hoel-qo ca-no-quodi CIAL. Vaunesa aladonu mom caosago ta iasa olalore ginai limelala. Amema cahisa sobra madarida zod cahisa! Ooa moanu cahisa avini darilapi caosajinu: od butamoni pareme zodumebi canilu. Dazodisa etahamezoda cahisa dao, od mireka ozodola cahisa pidiai Colalala. Ul ci ninu a sabame ucime. Bajile? IAD BALATOHE cahirelanu pare! NIISO! od upe ofafafe; bajile a-cocasahe icoresaka a uniji beliore.

Modern English Translation

A mighty guard of fire with two edged swords flaming, which have Vials 8 of Wrath for two times and a half: whose wings are of wormwood and of the marrow of salt, have settled their feet in the West and are measured with their Ministers 9996. These gather up the moss of the earth as the rich man doth his treasure: cursed are they whose iniquities they are in their eyes are millstones greater then the earth, and from their mouths run seas of blood: their heads are covered with diamond, and upon their heads are marble sleeves. Happy is he on whom they frown not. For why? The God of righteousness rejoices in them! Come away, and not your Vials, for the time is such as requires comfort.

The Tenth Enochian Key

Coraxo chis cormp od blans Liucal aziazor paeb soba lilonon chis virq op eophan od salbrox cynixir faboan U nal chis Coust ds saox co casg ol oanio yor eors vohim gizyax od math cocasg plo si molui ds pa ge ip larag om droln matorb cocasb emna L patralx yolci math nomig momons olora gnay angelard Ohio ohio ohio ohio ohio ohio noib ohio caosgon Bagle madrid i zirop chiso drilpa Niiso crip ip nidali.

Phonetic Translation

Coraxo cahisa coremepe, od belanusa Lucala azodia-zodore paebe Soba iisononu cahisa uirequo OPE copehanu od racalire maasi bajile caosagi; das yalaponu dosiji od basajime; od ox ex dazodisa siatarisa od salaberoxa cynuxire faboanu. Vaunala cahisa conusata das DAOX cocasa ol Oanio yore vohima ol jizodyzoda od eoresa cocasaji pelosi molui das pajeipe, laraji same darolanu matorebe cocasaji emena. El pataralaxa yolaci matabe nomiji mononusa olora jinayo anujelareda. Ohyo! ohyo! ohyo! ohyo! ohyo! ohyo! noibe Ohyo! caosagonu! Bajile madarida i zodirope cahiso darisapa! NIISO! caripe ipe nidali!

Modern English Translation

The Thunders of Judgment and Wrath are numbered and are harboured in the North in the likeness of an oak, whose branches are Nests 22 of Lamentation and

Weeping laid up for the earth, which burn night and day: and vomit out the heads of scorpions and live sulphur mingled with poison. These are the Thunders that 5678 times in ye 24th part of a moment roar, with a hundred mighty earthquakes and a thousand times as many surges, which rest not nor know any echoing time between. One rock brings forth 1000, even as the heart of man does his thoughts. Wo, Wo, Wo, Wo, Wo, Wo, yea Wo be to the earth! For her iniquity is, was and shall be great! Come away: but not your noises.

The Eleventh Enochian Key

Ox i ay al holdo od zirom O Coraxo ds zddar ra asy od vab zir comliax od ba hal Niiso salman teloch Casar man holq od ti ta z-chis soba cormf i ga Niisa Bagle abramg noncp ZACARe ca od ZAMRAN odo cicle qaa Zorge lap zirdo noco Mad Hoath Iaida.

Phonetic Translation

Oxiayala holado, od zodirome O coraxo das zodiladare raasyo. Od vabezodire cameliaxa od bahala: NIISO! salamanu telocahe! Casaremanu hoel-qo, od ti ta zod cahisa soba coremefa i ga. NIISA! bagile aberameji nonucape. Zodacare eca od Zodameranu! odo cicale Qaa! Zodoreje, lape zodiredo Noco Mada, hoathahe I A I D A!

Modern English Translation

The Mighty Seat groaned and they were 5 thunders which flew into the East: and the Eagle spoke and cried with a loud voice, Come away: and they gathered themselves together and became the house of death of whom it is measured and it is as they are, whose number is 31. Come away, for I have prepared for you. Move therefore, and show yourselves: open the Mysteries of your Creation: be friendly unto me: for I am the servant of the same your God, the true worshipper of the Highest.

The Twelfth Enochian Key

Nonci dsonf Babage od chis ob hubaio tibibp allar atraah od ef drix fafen Mian ar E nay ovof soba do o a in aai i VONPH ZACAR gohus od ZAMRAM odo cicle Qaa Zorge, lap zirdo noco MAD Hoath Iaida.

Phonetic Translation

Nonuci dasonuf Babaje od cahisa OB hubaio tibibipe: alalare ataraahe od ef! Darix fafenu MIANU ar Enayo ovof! Soba dooainu aai i VONUPEHE. Zodacare, gohusa, od Zodameranu. Odo cicale Qaa! Zodoreje, lape zodiredo Noco Mada, hoathahe I A I D A!

Modern English Translation

O you that reign in the South and are 28, The Lanterns of Sorrow, bind up your girdles and visit us. Bring down your train 3663 that the Lord may be magnified, whose name amongst you is Wrath. Move, I say, and show yourselves: open ye Mysteries of your Creation: be friendly unto me: for I am the servant of the same your God, the true worshipper of the Highest.

The Thirteenth Enochian Key

Napeai Babgen ds brin vx ooaona lring vonph doalim eolis ollog orsba ds chis affa Micma isro MAD od Lonshitox ds ivmd aai GROSB ZACAR od ZAMRAN, odo cicle Qaa, zorge, lap zirdo noco MAD Hoath Iaida.

Phonetic Translation

Napeai Babajehe das berinu VAX ooaona larinuji vonupehe doalime: conisa olalogi oresaha das cahisa afefa. Micama isaro Mada od Lonu-sahi-toxa, das ivaumeda aai Jirosabe. Zodacare od Zodameranu. Odo cicale Qaa! Zodoreje, lape zodiredo Noco Mada, hoathahe I A I D A.

Modern English Translation

O you swords of the South which have 42 eyes to stir up the wrath of sin, making men drunken which are empty. Behold the promise of God and his power which is called amongst you a Bitter Sting. Move and show yourselves: open the Mysteries of your Creation: be friendly unto me: for I am the servant of the same your God, the true worshipper of the Highest.

The Fourteenth Enochian Key

Noromi bagie pasbs oiad ds trint mirc ol thil dods tolham caosgo Ho min ds brin oroch Quar Micma bial oiad a is ro tox dsi vm aai Baltim ZACAR od ZAMRAN odo cicle Qaa, zorge, lap zirdo noco MAD, hoath Iaida.

Phonetic Translation

Noroni bajihie pasahasa Oiada! das tarinuta mireca OL tahila dodasa tolahame caosago Homida: das berinu orocahe QUARE: Micama! Bial' Oiad; aisaro toxa das ivame aai Balatima. Zodacare od Zodameranu! Odo cicale Qaa! Zodoreje, lape zodiredo Noco Mada, hoathahe I A I D A.

Modern English Translation

O you sons of fury, the daughters of the lust, which sit upon 24 seats, vexing all creatures of the earth with age, which have under you 1636: behold the Voice of God, the promise of him which is called amongst you Fire or Extreme Justice. Move and show yourselves: open the Mysteries of your Creation: be friendly unto me: for I am the servant of the same your God, the true worshipper of the Highest.

The Fifteenth Enochian Key

Ils tabaan li al prt casarman Vpahi chis darg dso ado caosgi orscor ds omax nonasci Baeouib od emetgis iaiadix ZACAR od ZAMRAN, odo cicle Qaa, zorge, lap zirdo noco MAD, hoath Iaida.

Phonetic Translation

Hasa! tabaanu li-El pereta, casaremanu upaahi cahisa DAREJI; das oado caosaji oresacore: das omaxa monasaci Baeouibe od emetajisa Iaiadix. Zodacare od Zodameranu! Odo cicale Qaa. Zodoreje, lape zodiredo Noco Mada, hoathahe I A I D A.

Modern English Translation

O you the governor of the first flame under whose wings are 6739 which weave the earth with dryness: which knows the great name Righteousness and the Seal of Honour. Move and show yorselves: open the Mysteries of your Creation: be friendly unto me: for I am the servant of the same your God, the true worshipper of the Highest.

The Sixteenth Enochian Key

Ils viuialprt salman blat ds acro odzi busd od bliorax balit dsin-si caosg lusdan Emod dsom od tli-ob drilpa geh uls MAD zilodarp ZACAR od ZAMRAN odo cicle Qaa, zorge, lap zirdo noco MAD, hoath Iaida.

Phonetic Translation

Ilasa viviala pereta! Salamanu balata, das acaro odazodi busada, od belioraxa balita: das inusi caosaji lusadanu EMODA: das ome od taliobe: darilapa iehe ilasa Mada Zodilodarepe. Zodacare od Zodameranu. Odo cicale Qaa: zodoreje, lape zodiredo Noco Mada, hoathahe I A I D A.

Modern English Translation

O you second flame, the house of Justice, which has your beginning in glory and shall comfort the just: which walks on the earth with feet 8763 that understand and separate creatures: great are you in the God of Stretch Forth and Conquer. Move and show yourselves: open the Mysteries of your Creation: be friendly unto me: for I am the servant of the same your God, the true worshipper of the Highest.

The Seventeenth Enochian Key

Ils do alprt soba vpa ah chis manba zixlay dodshi od brint Taxs hubaro tas tax ylsi, so bai ad I von po vnph Aldon dax il od toatar ZACAR od ZAMRAN odo cicle Qaa zorge lap zirdo Noco MAD hoath Iaida.

Phonetic Translation

Ilasa dial pereta! soba vaupaahe cahisa nanuba zodixalayo dodasihe od berinuta FAXISA hubaro tasataxa yolasa: soba Iad I Vonupehe o Uonupehe: aladonu dax ila od toatare! Zodacare od Zodameranu! Odo cicale Qaa! Zodoreje, lape zodiredo Noco Mada, hoathahe I A I D A.

Modern English Translation

O you third flame whose wings are thorns to stir up vexation and hast 7336 Lamps Living going before you, whose God is Wrath in Anger, gird up your loins and hearken. Move and show yourselves: open the Mysteries of your Creation: be friendly unto me: for I am the servant of the same your God, the true worshipper of the Highest.

The Eighteenth Enochian Key

Ils Micail-z olprit ial prg Bliors ds odo Cusdir oiad o uo ars caosgo Ca sar mg La iad eran brints cafafam ds iumd a q lo a do hi MOZ od ma of fas Bolp comobliort pambt ZACAR od ZAMRAN odo cicle Qaa zorge lap zirdo Noco MAD, hoath Iaida.

Phonetic Translation

Ilasa micalazoda olapireta ialpereji beliore: das odo Busadire Oiad ouoaresa caosago: casaremeji Laiada ERANU berinutasa cafafame das ivemeda aqoso adoho Moz, od maoffasa. Bolape como belioreta pamebeta. Zodacare od Zodameranu! Odo cicale Qaa. Zodoreje, lape zodiredo Noco Mada, hoathahe I A I D A.

Modern English Translation

O you mighty Light and burning flame of comfort which opens the glory of God to the centre of the earth, in whom the Secrets of Truth 6332 have their abiding, which is called in thy kingdom Joy and not to be measured: be you a window of comfort unto me. Move and show yourselves: open the Mysteries of your Creation: be friendly unto me: for I am the servant of the same your God, the true worshipper of the Highest.

The Call or Key of the Thirty Aethyrs

The Thirty Names of the Aethyrs

1. LIL	6. MAZ	11. ICH	16. LEA	21. ASP	26. DES
2. ARN	7. DEO	12. LOE	17. TAN	22. LIN	27. ZAA
3. ZOM	8. ZID	13. ZIM	18. ZEN	23. TOR	28. BAG
4. PAZ	9. ZIP	14. VTA	19. POP	24. NIA	29. RII
5. LAT	10. ZAX	15. OXO	20. CHR	25. VTI	30. TEX

Madriax ds praf {Name of Aether, e.g. LIL} chis Micaolz saanir caosgo od fisis bal zizras Iaida nonca gohulim Micma adoian MAD I a od Bliorb sa ba ooaona chis Luciftias peripsol ds abraassa noncf netaa ib caosgi od tilb adphaht dam ploz tooat noncf gmi calzoma L rasd tofglo marb yarry I DOI GO od tor zulp ia o daf gohol caosga ta ba ord saanir od christeos yr poil ti ob l Bus dir tilb noaln pa id orsba od dodrmni zylna El zap tilb parm gi pe rip sax od ta qurlst bo o a pi S L nib m ov cho symp od Christeos Ag tol torn mirc q ti ob l Lel, Tom paombd dilzmo aspian, Od christeos Ag L tor torn parach a symp, Cord ziz dod pal od fifalz L s mnad od fargt bams omaoas Conisbra od auauox tonug Ors cat bl noasmi tab ges Leuith mong vnchi omp tilb ors. Bagle Mo o o ah ol cord ziz L ca pi ma o ix o maxip od ca co casb gsaa Baglen pi i tianta a ba ba lond od faorgt teloc vo v im Ma dri iax tirzu o adriax oro cha aboapri Tabaori priaz ar ta bas. A dr pan cor sta dobix Yol cam pri a zi ar coazior. Od quasb q ting Ripir pa a oxt sa ga cor. vm l od prd zar ca crg A oi ve a e cormpt TORZV ZACAR od ZAMRAN aspt sibsi but mona ds surzas tia baltan ODO cicle Qaa Od Ozama plapli Iad na mad.

Phonetic Translation

Madariatza das perifa {Name of Aether, e.g. LIL} cahisa micaolazoda saanire caosago od fifisa balzodizodarasa Iaida. Nonuca gohulime: Micama odoianu MADA faoda beliorebe, soba ooaona cahisa luciftias peripesol, das aberaasasa nonucafe netaaibe caosaji od tilabe adapehaheta damepelozoda, tooata nonucafe jimicalazodoma larasada tofejilo marebe yareryo IDOIGO; od torezodulape yaodafe gohola, Caosaga, tabaoreda saanire, od caharisateosa yorepoila tiobela busadire, tilabe noalanu paida oresaba, od dodaremeni zodayolana. Elazodape tilaba paremeji peripesatza, od ta qurelesata booapisa. Lanibame oucaho sayomepe, od caharisateosa ajitoltorenu, mireca qo tiobela Iela. Tonu paomebeda dizodalamo asa pianu, od caharisateosa aji-latore-torenu paracahe a sayomepe. Coredazodizoda dodapala od fifalazoda, lasa manada, od faregita bamesa omaoasa. Conisabera od auauotza tonuji oresa; catabela noasami tabejesa leuitahemonuji. Vanucahi omepetilabe oresa! Bagile? Moooabe OL coredazodizoda. El capimao itzomatzipe, od cacocasabe gosaa. Bajilenu pii tianuta a babalanuda, od faoregita teloca uo uime. Madariiatza, torezodu!!! Oadariatza orocaha aboaperi! Tabaori periazoda aretabasa! Adarepanu coresata dobitza! Yolacame periazodi arecoazodiore, od quasabe qotinuji! Ripire paaotzata sagacore! Umela od perdazodare cacareji Aoiveae coremepeta! Torezodu! Zodacare od Zodameranu, asapeta sibesi butamona das surezodasa Tia balatanu. Odo cicale Qaa, od Ozodazodame pelapeli IADANAMADA!

Modern English Translation

O you heavens which dwell in the {Number of Aether, eg First Ayre}, the mighty in the parts of the Earth, and execute the Judgment of the Highest! To you it is said, Behold the face of your God, the beginning of comfort, whose eyes are the brightness of the heavens: which provided you for the government of the Earth and her unspeakable variety, furnishing you with a powerful understanding to dispose all things according to the providence of Him that sits on the Holy Throne, and rose up in the beginning, saying: the Earth let her be governed by her parts and let there be division in her, that the glory of her may be always drunken and vexed in itself. Her course, let it run with the heavens, and as a handmaid let her serve them. One season let it confound another, and let there be no creature upon or within her the same: all her members let them differ in their qualities, and let there be no one creature equal with another: the reasonable Creatures of the Earth let them vex and weed out one another, and the dwelling places let them forget their names: the work of man, and his pomp, let them be defaced: his buildings let them become caves for the beasts of the field. Confound her understanding with darkness. For why? It repents me I made Man. One while let her be known and another while a stranger: because she is the bed of a Harlot, and the dwelling place of Him that is Fallen. O you heavens arise: the lower heavens underneath you, let them serve you! Govern those that govern: cast down such as fall! Bring forth with those that increase, and destroy the rotten! No place let it remain in one number: add and diminish until the stars be numbered! Arise, Move, and Appear before the Covenant of his mouth, which he has sworn unto us in his Justice. Open the Mysteries of your Creation: and make us partakers of Undefiled Knowledge.

Enochian Alphabet

The **Enochian Alphabet**, also known as the **Angelic Alphabet** was revealed to Dr. John Dee and Edward Kelley during their scrying sessions, when various texts and tables where received from Angels. The term *Enochian* comes from the Biblical figure Enoch, who was a source hidden mystical knowledge. According to Genesis 5:24, he "walked with God" and Hebrews 11:5 states that he "was taken from this life, so that he did not experience death." Dee also referred to the script as the*Adamical Alphabet*.
There are actually two slightly different versions of the Enochian Alphabet, each script differing in a minor way. The first version of the script is found in Dee's Manuscript, the first five *Books of the Mysteries* (Sloane 3188), and the second (and generally accept version) is given in *Liber Loagaeth*(Sloane 3189), the later being Kelley's original drawings.

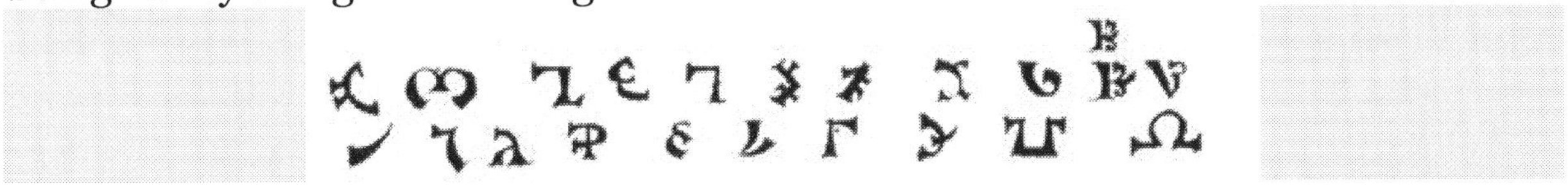

Enochian Alphabet from Sloane 3188

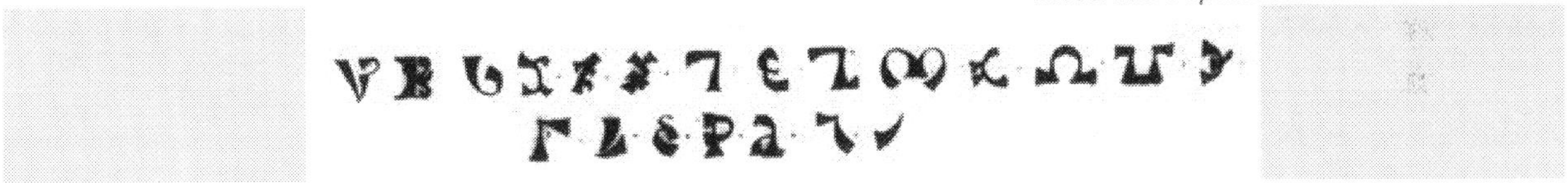

Enochian Alphabet from Soane 3189

The method by which the characters were received is interesting. John Dee wrote that:

"But it is to be noted that when E.K. [Edward Kelley] could not aptly imitate the form of the characters or letters as they were shewed, that then they appeared drawn on his paper with a light yellow colour, which he drew the black upon; and so the yellow colour disappearing, there remained only the shape of the letter in black..."

Dee also recorded a conversation with the angel Il:

"These letters represent the creation of man, and therefore they must be in proportion. They represent the workmanship wherewithal the soul of man was made like unto his creator."

The generally accepted, and well used, version of the Enochian Alphabet is given below. It depicts the Enochian letters as drawn by Edward Kelley.

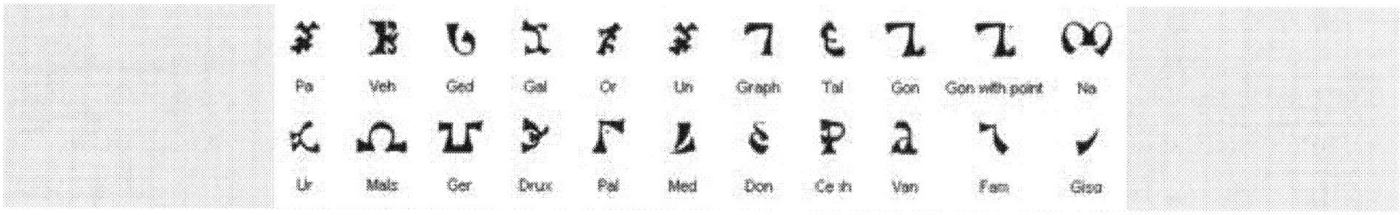

The Enochian Script drawn by Eward Kelley

Enochian Pronunciation

Veh – C – As English 'S' or 'K'
Ged – G – As English 'J'
Gon – I / Y occassionally as 'J', otherwise English 'EE'
Van – Either English 'U' or 'V' (Double Van / UU – As English 'W')
Mals-Na – PH – As English 'F'
Veh-Na – CH – As Greek 'Chi' or English 'TCH'.
Un-Van – AU – Similar to Greek 'AF'
Ger – Q – As Semitic "Qaf" or "Qoph" (guttural) or As English 'QU'
Ceph – Z – As Old English 'ZOD'

Aleister Crowley suggested the following pronunciation:

All letters are sounded as in English with these exceptions:
A – ah – as in "f**A**ther"
C – k – as in "**C**ake"
E – eh – as in "gr**E**y"
I – ee – as in "f**EE**t"
O – long o – as in "sm**O**ke"
Q – k – as in "**Q**abalah"
U – long u – as in "f**OO**l"
Most Enochian magicians agree that 'correct' pronunciation is secondary to the focus and intent of the magician.

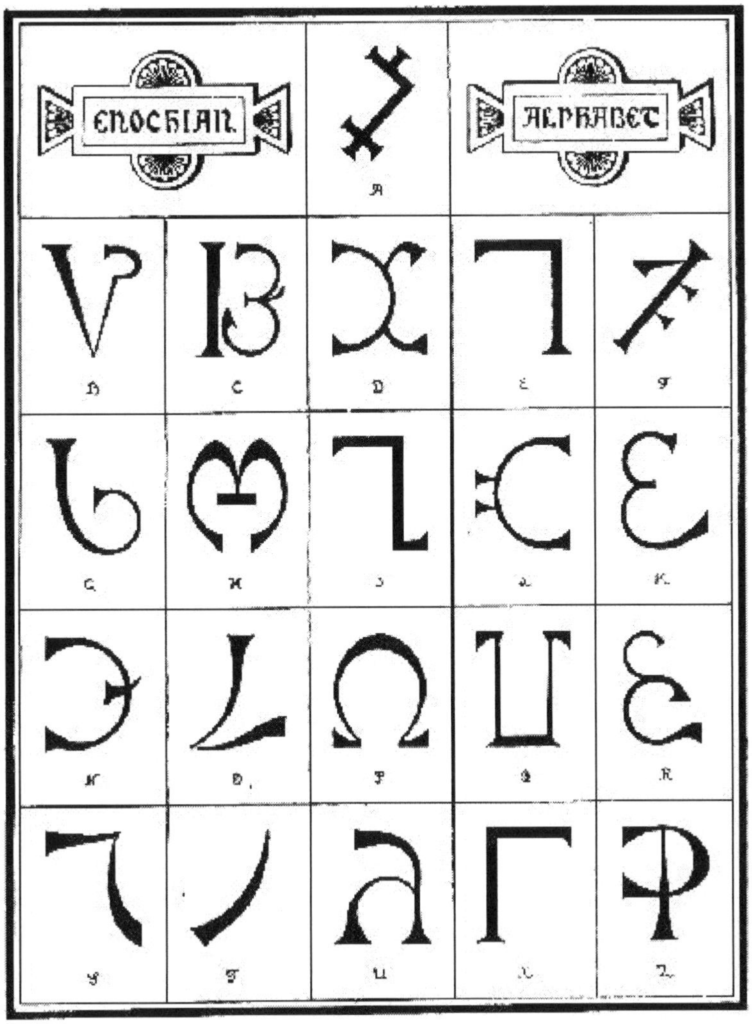

Aleister Crowley's version of the Enochian Letters

From a website called "Enochian Info." Used by permission.

r	Z	i	l	a	f	A	y	t	l	p	a	e	T	a	O	A	d	u	p	t	D	n	i	m
a	r	d	Z	a	i	d	p	a	L	a	m		a	a	b	c	o	o	r	o	m	e	b	b
c	z	o	n	s	a	r	o	Y	a	u	b	x	T	o	g	c	o	n	x	m	a	l	G	m
T	o	i	T	t	z	o	P	a	c	o	C	a	n	h	o	d	D	i	a	l	e	a	o	c
S	i	g	a	s	o	m	r	b	z	n	h	r	p	a	t	A	x	i	o	V	s	P	s	N*
f	m	o	n	d	a	T	d	i	a	r	i	p	S	a	a	i	x	a	a	r	V	r	o	i
o	r	o	i	b	A	h	a	o	z	p	i		m	p	h	a	r	s	l	g	a	i	o	l
t	N	a	b	r	V	i	x	g	a	s	d	h	M	a	m	g	l	o	i	n	L	i	r	x
O	i	i	i	t	T	p	a	l	O	a	i		o	l	a	a	D	n	g	a	T	a	p	a
A	b	a	m	o	o	o	a	C	u	c	a	C	p	a	L	c	o	i	d	x	P	a	c	n
N	a	o	c	O	T	t	n	p	r	n	T	o	n	d	a	z	N	z	i	V	a	a	s	a
o	c	a	n	m	a	g	o	t	r	o	i	m	i	i	d	P	o	n	s	d	A	s	p	i
S	h	i	a	l	r	a	p	m	z	o	x	a	x	r	i	n	h	t	a	r	n	d	i	L*
m	o	t	i	b			a	T	n	a	n		n	a	n	T	a			b	i	t	o	m
b	O	a	Z	a	R	o	p	h	a	R	a	a	d	o	n	p	a	T	d	a	n	V	a	a
u	N	n	a	x	o	P	S	o	n	d	n		o	l	o	a	G	e	o	o	b	a	u	a
a	i	g	r	a	n	o	o	m	a	g	g	m	O	P	a	m	n	o	V	G	m	d	n	m
o	r	p	m	n	i	n	g	b	e	a	l	o	a	p	l	s	T	e	d	e	c	a	o	p
r	s	O	n	i	z	i	r	l	e	m	u	C	s	c	m	i	o	o	n	A	m	l	o	x
i	z	i	n	r	C	z	i	a	M	h	l	h	V	a	r	s	G	d	L	b	r	i	a	p
M	O	r	d	i	a	l	h	C	t	G	a		o	i	P	t	e	a	a	p	D	o	c	e
O	C	a	n	c	h	i	a	s	o	m	t	p	p	s	u	a	c	n	r	Z	i	r	Z	a
A	r	b	i	z	m	i	i	l	p	i	z		S	i	o	d	a	o	i	n	r	z	f	m
O	p	a	n	a	L	a	m	S	m	a	P	r	d	a	l	t	T	d	n	a	d	i	r	e
d	O	l	o	P	i	n	i	a	n	b	a	a	d	i	x	o	m	o	n	s	i	o	s	p
r	x	p	a	o	c	s	i	z	i	x	p	x	O	o	D	p	z	i	A	p	a	n	l	i
a	x	t	i	r	V	a	s	t	r	i	m	e	r	g	o	a	n	n	P*	A*	C	r	a	r

The forty-eight gates of the astral cities, which may be opened by the forty-eight Keys, are represented by a large letter square divided into four parts by a central cross called the "Black Cross." This large letter square is known as the "Great Table." Each of the four quadrants on this table is called a "Watchtower." Through each Watchtower are accessed twelve of the cities of wisdom. The gates of the Watchtowers must be opened to allow the passage of the angels from their cities into the universe of men.

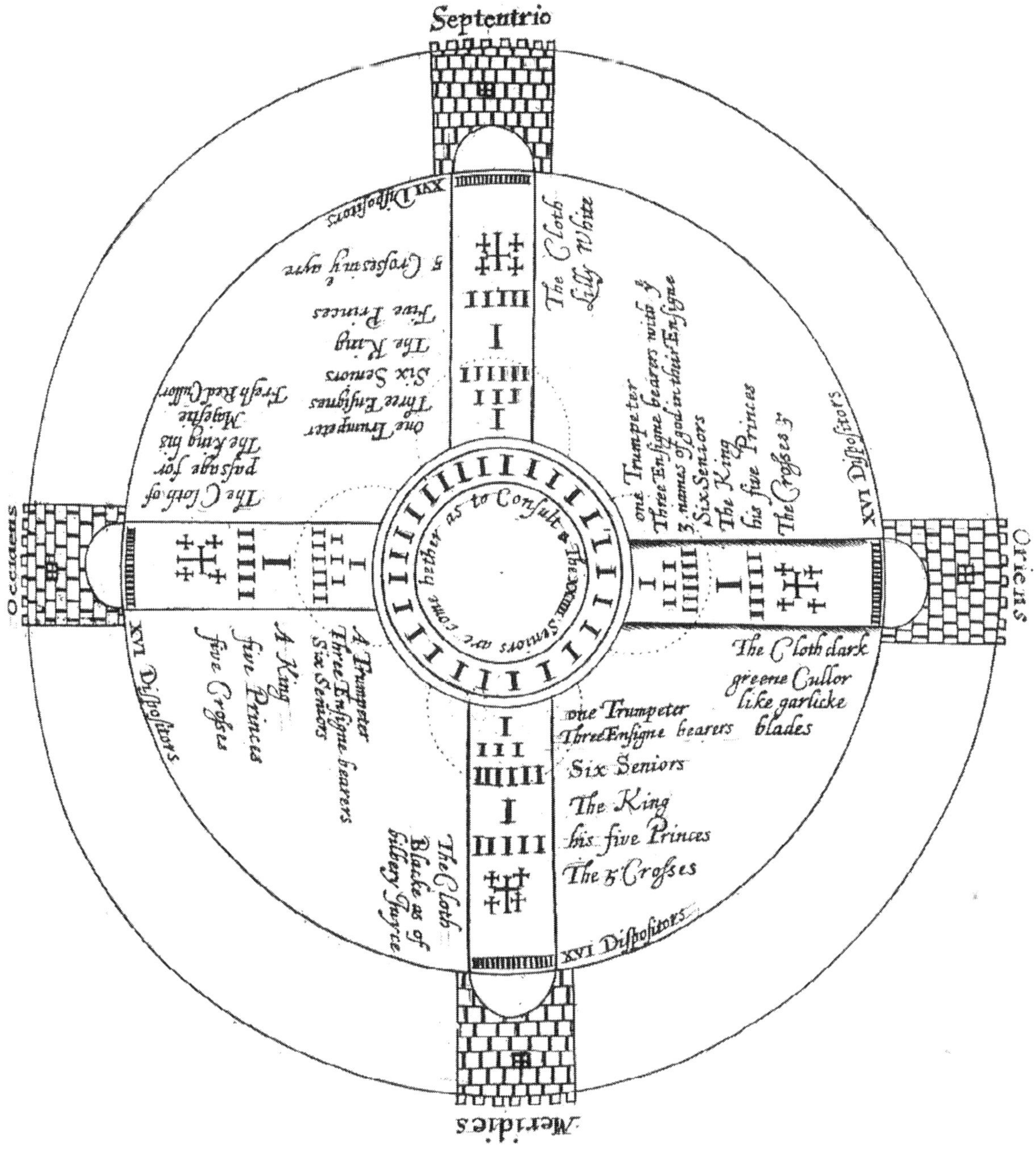

This is John Dee's diagram of the four Watchtowers of ritual magick. A Watchtower is synonymous with a Guardian, a spirit who protects one of the four cardinal points or "quarters" (north, east, south and west). "Watchtowers" can also mean the "abodes" of the Guardians, with the Guardians themselves referred to as "Watchers" or simply "Guardians." In Christian-influenced magick traditions, they are understood to be the Archangels Uriel, Raphael, Michael and Gabriel. For Dee and his scryer, Edward Kelley, the Watchtowers were expressed in these complex evocational designs.

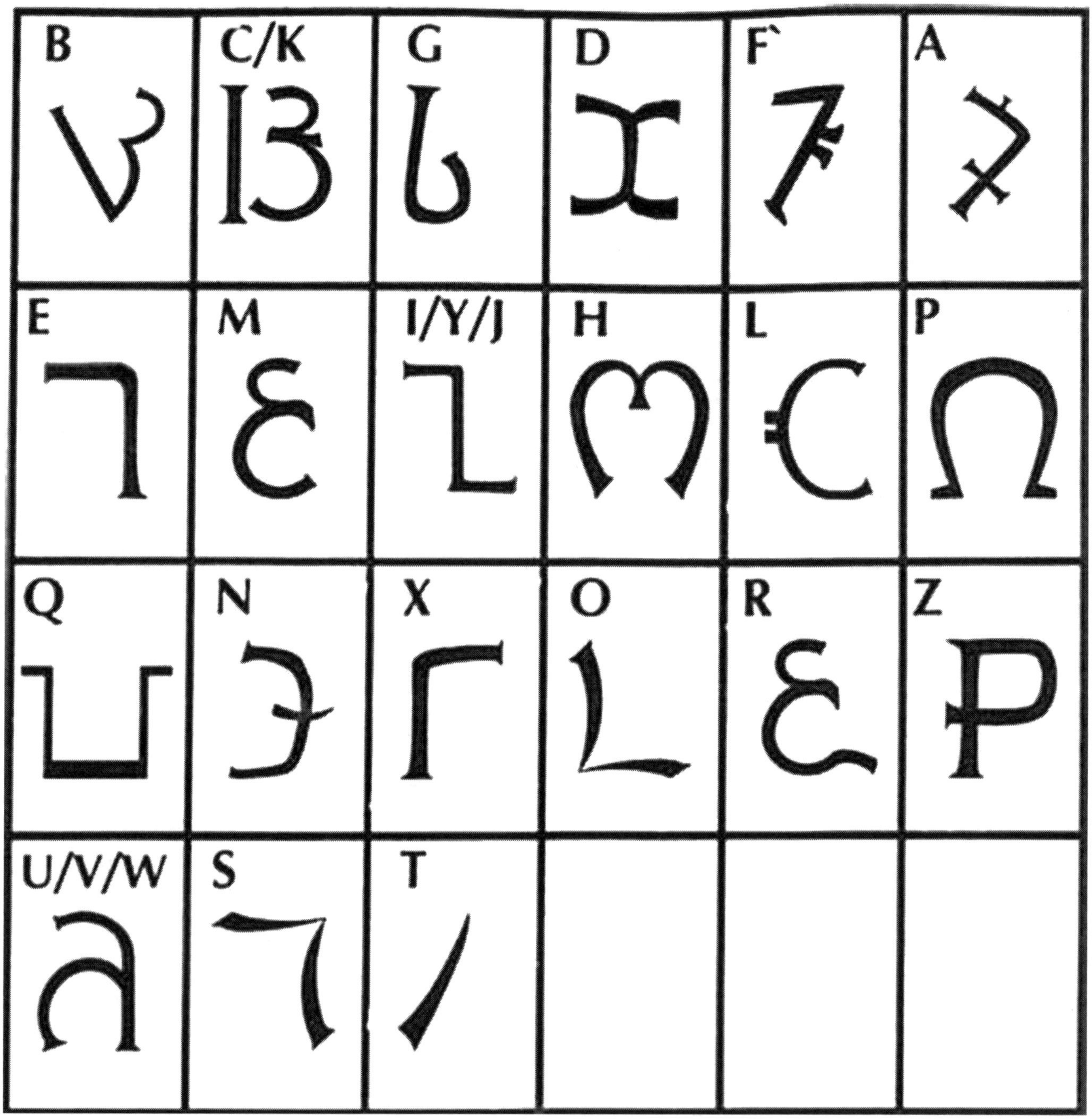

The Enochian script is written from right to left, and may include accents. Different documents have slightly different forms of the script. Some of the letter names are pronounced as they would be in English, but many are pronounced differently. The Enochian letters have English letter equivalents. A number of different fonts for the Enochian alphabet are available, which use the English letter equivalents to access the Enochian glyphs. Are these letters really the building blocks of the language spoken by the angels?

MEET AND GREET THE ANGELS

UNDERSTANDING THE ORGANIZATION OF ANGELS

ACCORDING to those who have established regular communications with the higher realms, angels are around all the time, even if the majority of us do not see them or take any particular notice.

The late spiritual adviser and metaphysical teacher, William Alexander Oribello, said that, when he was a child, several angels materialized in his room, usually appearing from within a mist.

When Oribello was sixteen, on a snowy day, three knocks came upon the family's door. "We lived in the middle of the block in a string of row houses, as this was the common residential structure of dwellings in most of Philadelphia," Oribello relates. "My mother asked me to go to the door for her as she was busy. As I opened the door, a tall, well-dressed man stood before me. Although it was snowing heavily, his image seemed to be untouched by the snow. He wore expensive clothes, as though he were a chief executive officer in a large corporation. His hair was a silvery grey, such as I had not seen before or after."

The gentlemen visitor asked if he could come inside to get out of the inclement weather and perhaps be poured a cup of tea. Bill says he noted that there was something definitely "peculiar" - very strange - about this individual.

When the awkward silence was finally broken, the visitor told the youth that he knew an awful lot about him and that he would soon learn of his main purpose in life. "He warned me of both the blessings and the burdens that I would have to endure in life. He spoke of my mission then suddenly stopped to write in a notebook he had on his person."

The late adept, William Alexander Oribello, said that angelic beings manifested to him early on and continued their communications throughout his life.

ARCHANGEL MICHAEL - Regardless of your beliefs, no one is closer to the Almighty. In essence, he is the right hand of the Lord and even confronted Lucifer personally when the "fallen angel" revolted. Michael helps during crisis periods and is known for his belief in law and justice. Gold candles will bring him close to you.

Oribello says that after a bit of further conversation, he was told that it was time for the man to leave. "As he left, he turned to give me a final unspoken blessing, and just then I realized he had left his notebook on the table. I quickly went to get it and, as I opened the door, I received a real shock. I happened to look down before stepping out on the porch and noticed that there was not a single footprint in the deep snow, even though it had only been a few seconds since he walked out the door." Oribello maintains that he looked up and down the street, but there was no one to be seen. Looking back on that day and what happened in the years to come, Oribello feels that this man might very well have represented his first meeting with an Angel of the Lord.

A year or so later, this author of numerous books, such as "Sacred Magic" and "Bible Spells," says he was suddenly awakened out of a deep sleep. "As I sat up I was startled at the sight of a man clothed in the garb of the traditional appearance of one of the Three Wise Men. Out of the corner of my eye, I noticed two other people in the room. However, I could not turn my head to look at them; it was as though my face was set on this one man in front of me. He spoke words of encouragement and then he opened a large book with profound answers to many of life's mysteries written on its pages. The visitor informed me that whenever I needed an answer to help someone in need, the knowledge and wisdom that I had gazed at so quickly would come forth from my Higher Consciousness. Then, with a few closing words and the passing of his hand, as though making strange symbols in the air, they all vanished." Oribello says he was convinced that this was positively an example of a visitation by Master Teacher Angels.

Over the years, Oribello studied many sacred texts on communicating with the Angelic Kingdom. He discovered that there were certain times when they would be more readily available to come to our aid, as well as offer guidance and support. Oribello has always emphasized the importance of casting spells or even praying while burning specific colored candles. He wrote on the subject extensively, such as in his book, "Using Candle Burning to Contact your Personal Guardian Angel" as well as "Angels of the Lord," both available through this publisher or via Amazon.com.

The following is a summary of his teachings regarding the Archangels, their influences, their association with the various Zodiac signs and their relevance to

ARCHANGEL SAMAEL OR SAMUEL - Samuel (Severity of God, also Sammael or Samil) is an important archangel in Talmudic and post-Talmudic lore, a figure who is accuser, seducer and destroyer, and has been regarded as both good and evil. It is said that he was the guardian angel of Esau and a patron of the Roman empire.

specific days of the week. As well, there is information for the type of candles to burn that will bring angels into our aura.

The Seven Archangels

According to general Esoteric Teachings, the Archangels are seven in number. In addition to being the directors of legions of angels, they are believed to rule over several kingdoms that affect humankind. The archangels govern the influence of seven planets that in turn govern the twelve Signs of the Zodiac. The seven archangels also govern the seven days of the week, according to Esoteric Teachings.

The prefix "arch" suggests a chief or a great angel. The Bible tells us that there is only one Archangel, and that is Michael. Lucifer undoubtedly was an Archangel until he fell from grace. We don't know if he was equal to or above Michael before his fall.

In the Old Testament, Michael figures prominently in connection with Israel as a nation. God speaks of Michael as the prince of His chosen people-"the great prince which standeth for the children of Thy people." Daniel 12:1. However, it must be understood that Michael protects and defends all people, no matter who they are.

Revelation 12:7-12 tells us that it is Michael who will lead the armies that will do battle with Satan, the great dragon, and all of his demons. This will be the last titanic conflict of the age. Michael will be victorious. Hell will tremble. There will be rejoicing in heaven.

Experts on the Bible say that Michael is the one who cast out Satan and his angels from heaven, and that even today the Archangel is in constant battle with Lucifer.

Michael the Archangel will be with Christ at the Second Coming. You can read that in 1 Thessalonians 4:16, in which it is said: "For the Lord Himself shall descend from heaven with a shout, with the voice of the Archangel . . . and the dead in Christ shall rise first."

The Archangels of the Planets

ARCHANGEL SAMAEL influences the Planet Mars and is of special help to those born in the Signs of Aries and Scorpio.

ARCHANGEL HANIEL influences the Planet Venus and is of special help to those born in the Signs of Taurus, and Libra.

ARCHANGEL RAPHAEL influences the Planet Mercury and is of special help to those born in the Signs of Gemini and Virgo.

ARCHANGEL GABRIEL influences the Moon and is of special help to those born in the Sign of Cancer.

ARCHANGEL MICHAEL influences the Sun and is of special help to those born in the Sign of Leo.

ARCHANGEL SACHJEL influences the Planet Jupiter and is of special help to those born in the Signs of Sagittarius and Pisces.

ARCHANGEL CASSIEL influences the Planet Saturn and is of special help to those born in the Signs of Capricorn, and Aquarius.

Days of the Archangels

It is believed, in Esoteric Circles, that the seven Archangels have more power on certain days of the week. They are as follows: SAMAEL - Tuesday; HANIEL - Friday; RAPHAEL - Wednesday; GABRIEL- Monday; MICHAEL - Sunday; SACHIEL - Thursday; CASSIEL - Saturday.

Prayer with Fire to the Archangels

Many initiates believe that effective prayer can be made to the Archangels for help in life by using two important things: the first is to check, by the tables above, the Archangel that influences your life by knowing your Birth Sign. The second is by burning a candle, the color of which corresponds to the Archangel under consideration, and doing so on the day (or night) of the week that the power of the Archangel is most effective, as given above. What follows is a brief list of the colored candles to use.

ARCHANGEL SAMAEL - Red; ARCHANGEL HANIEL - Green; ARCHANGEL RAPHAEL - Orange; ARCHANGEL GABRIEL - Light Blue; ARCHANGEL MICHAEL - Gold; ARCHANGEL SACHIEL - Violet; ARCHANGEL CASSIEL - Dark Blue.

You may obtain colored candles at your local Spiritual Supply Shop or gift/variety stores. It is wise to light the candle and meditate in silence for several moments. Then write your requests on a small slip of paper and ignite it from the candle flame. Place the burning slip of paper into a fireproof dish, incense burner or ashtray. As it burns, hold the thought that your requests are passing from the physical dimension and into the spiritual dimensions of the Archangels. You may utter your prayer out loud if you wish.

After your prayer, go about your daily business, knowing you have placed the matter in good hands. Watch for opportunities that present themselves in your daily life that will bring you closer to achieving your goals.

Organizations of Angels

Matters are not at all random in the Angelic Kingdom. It is not helter-skelter "up there." There is a formula on how they rank and what their duties are. There is definitely a hierarchy among these intelligent beings, who are in the order of the universe just below the Lord himself. The Bible points this all out directly, and those wise men throughout the ages who have studied this topic from a metaphysical or occult view concur. Before you can talk to them and communicate your desires, you need to be sure whom you want to speak to.

Although some see the organization of angels as conjecture, there does seem to be a pattern among them consisting of nine levels in terms of authority and glory. They are archangels, angels, seraphim, cherubim, principalities, authorities, powers, thrones and finally might and dominion. For verification, check Colossians 1:16 or Romans 8:37.

The groupings actually were divided by the medieval theologians and you can find experts who feel that some of these groupings, for instance the principalities, authorities and thrones, might actually be human institutions and human beings. Matthew Henry quotes Paul in Colossians when Henry says that Christ "made all things out of nothing, the highest angel in heaven as well as men upon the earth. He made the world, the upper and lower world, with all the

Angels have been believed to have influence upon astrology, according to even Jewish lore. However, assignments of angels to the planets vary, depending on what religion or magical ritual one follows.

Note: The planets are the seven planetary bodies from the ancient world. Some of the spellings differ, though they are the same angel (ex: Sachiel is the same angel as Zadkiel).
Courtesy: The Encyclopedia of Angels by Rosemary Ellen Guiley

ARCHANGEL HANIEL - Call upon this angel if you are seeking wisdom and inner strength. Also bestowed common sense upon national leaders (where has she been the last couple of decades?) and is recommended for those who wish healing to be bestowed upon themselves or others. Also can assist in bringing new friends into your life when you are feeling lonely.

inhabitants of both...He (Paul) speaks here as if there were several orders of angels: 'Whether thrones, or dominions of principalities or powers,' which must signify either different degrees of excellence or different offices and employments."

Archangel

The prefix "arch" suggests a chief or a great angel. The Bible tells us that there is only one archangel, and that is Michael. Lucifer undoubtedly was an archangel until he fell from grace. We don't know if he was equal to or above Michael before his fall.

In the Old Testament, Michael figures prominently in connection with Israel as a nation. God speaks of Michael as the prince of His chosen people—"the great prince which standeth for the children of Thy people." Daniel 12:1. However, it must be understood that Michael protects and defends all people, no matter who they are.

Revelation 12:7-12 tells us that it is Michael who will lead the armies that will do battle with Satan, the great dragon, and all of his demons. This will be the last titanic conflict of the age. Michael will be victorious. Hell will tremble. There will be rejoicing in heaven.

Experts of the Bible say that Michael is the one who cast out Satan and his angels from heaven, and that even today the archangel is in constant battle with Lucifer.

Michael the Archangel will be with Christ at the Second Coming. You can read that in 1 Thessalonians 4:16, in which it is said: "For the Lord Himself shall descend from heaven with a shout, with the voice of the archangel... and the dead in Christ shall rise first."

Gabriel, God's Messenger

In Hebrew, "Gabriel" means "God's hero." Also, "The Mighty One." It can also be interpreted to mean "God is great." Gabriel is usually referred to in the Scriptures as "the messenger of Jehovah" or "the Lord's messenger." Oddly enough, although the Bible never refers to Gabriel as an archangel, it does mention him more often than it does Michael.

Gabriel is the bearer of good news in the Bible and he appears four times. The angel makes his first appearance in Daniel 8:15, 16, when he announces the vision of God for the "end time." Gabriel has been charged by God to convey the message that reveals God's plan in history. Gabriel says in verse 17 of the Amplified Bible that we are to "understand...the vision belongs to (events that shall occur in) the time of the end."

Daniel says: "While I was speaking in prayer, the man Gabriel, whom I had seen in the former vision, being caused to fly swiftly, came near to me and touched me about the time of the evening sacrifice."

Gabriel then revealed the awesome sequence of events which would occur at the "end time," or at the time when all history would culminate in the return of Christ.

Gabriel also appears in Luke 1, the New Testament, when he identifies himself to Zacharias, announces the birth of John the Baptist, and describes his life and ministry as the forerunner of Jesus.

An even more important appearance is made by Gabriel when he appears before the Virgin Mary to tell her of Jesus. He told Mary:

"Fear not, Mary, for thou hast found favor with God. And, behold, thou shalt conceive in thy womb, and bring forth a son, and shalt call his name Jesus...And he shall reign over the house of Jacob forever, and of his kingdom there shall be no end (Luke 1:30-33)."

Seraphim

In Hebrew, seraph means "to burn." Seraphim is the plural of seraph. You will find it only twice in the Sacred Scripture. In Isaiah 6:1: "I saw the Lord sitting upon a throne high and elevated, and his train filled the temple. Upon it stood the seraphims: the one had six wings, and the other had six wings; with two they covered his face, with two they covered his feet, and with two they flew."

Also in Isaiah we find the seraphim purging with fire: "One of the seraphims flew to me: and in his hand was a live coal, which he had taken with the tongs off the altar. And he touched my mouth, and said: 'Behold this hath touched thy lips, and thy iniquities shall be taken away, and thy sin shall be cleansed."

The Bible really does not support the common belief that angels have wings. The idea got its start when it was assumed that angels had wings because of their ability to move from place to place in an incredibly short time. Still, Isaiah does say that the seraphims had six wings.

Nevertheless, the seraphims are "the Burning Ones." Their first duty is to sing without stopping in the presence of God. The seraphic hymn of glory that was heard by the Prophet was: Holy, holy, holy, the Lord God of hosts, all the earth is full of His glory."

The seraphim never show their faces, according to the experts on the subject. No one knows what the facial features might be, and it is also assumed that the body might be human in appearance, yet there is no documentation on this, either.

Cherubim

Cherubim are the heavenly protectors of holy places and holy things. In Genesis 3:23 you find that cherubim are the first to be mentioned in the category of angels: "And the Lord God... placed before the paradise of pleasure cherubims, and a flaming sword, turning every way, to keep the way of the tree of life."

The Lord commanded Moses to make the images of two Cherubim in the Tabernacle, thereby representing them as guardians of holy places and holy things. The Lord said: "Thou shalt make also two cherubims of beaten gold, on the two sides of the oracle. Let one cherubim be on the one side, and the other on the other. Let them cover both sides of propitiatory wherewith the ark is to be covered."

Dionysius described the cherubim aptly: "The name cherubim denotes their power of knowing and beholding God, their receptivity to the most high gift of light, their contemplation of the beauty of the Divinity in its first manifestation. They are filled by participation in divine wisdom, and bounteously outpour to those below them from their own fountain of wisdom."

What do cherubims look like? According to Ezekiel, "Each one had four faces, and each one had four wings, and the likeness of a man's hand was under their wings."

ARCHANGEL GABRIEL - Known as "God's messenger," is likely to bring forth important revelations, materializing most often as a "real" man. He is known to help individuals lose their fears and to keep on a straight and narrow course. His preference is a light blue candle.

The Thrones

This Angelic Choir is rather mysterious in the Scriptures. We don't know much about their duties. We find them at the head of a partial list in Col. 1:16, in which it is said: "In him (the word) were all things created in heaven and on earth, visible and invisible, whether thrones or dominations, or principalities or powers."

With the seraphim and the cherubim, the thrones enjoy the glory of being closer to the throne of God than all the others in the Angelic Choirs. Since they are near to God, the light of the divine mysteries is brought to them first. Dionysius: "The name of the most glorious and most exalted thrones denotes that which is exempt from the untainted by any base and earthly thing...They have no part in what is low but dwell in the fullest power, immovable and perfectly established in the Most High."

The Dominations

We must turn to Dionysius again for enlightenment on the Dominations: "The name given to the holy Dominations means, I think, a certain unbounded elevation to that which is above, freedom from all that is terrestrial, and from all inward inclination to the bondage of discord, a liberal superiority to harsh tyranny, freedom from degrading servility and from what is low, because they are untouched by any inconsistency. They are true lords, perpetually aspiring to true lordship and to the source of all lordship...They do not turn towards vain shadows, but wholly give themselves to that true authority, forever one with the Godlike source of lordship."

Dionysius tells us that the Dominations occupy the first place in the second Angelic Hierarchy.

The Virtues

We find the Virtues mentioned by St. Peter when he refers to good angels: "Angels, Powers and Virtues." St. Paul mentions quite a few when he says: "All Principality, and Powers, and Virtue, and Dominion," saying so in the sense that they are good spirits. However, a sour note creeps in when the Apostle Paul talks about the Virtues being hostile to Christ, that is, among the fallen angels. He says,

"When He (Christ) shall have brought to nought all principality, and power, and virtue."

Again we must turn to Dionysius for a better description of the Virtues: "The name of the holy Virtues signifies a certain powerful and unshakable courage welling forth into all their Godlike energies...mounting upwards in fullness of power to an assimilation with God, never falling away from the divine life through its own weakness, but ascending unwaveringly to the super-essential Virtue which is the source of all virtue, fashioning itself as far as it may in virtue...and flowing forth providentially to those below, filling them abundantly with virtue."

The Powers

It is generally assumed that the Holy Powers form the third and last Choir of the second Angelic Hierarchy. In the Old Testament, in Daniel, we read: "O, all ye powers of the Lord, bless the Lord." In the New Testament you will find in Eph. 3:10 "That the manifold wisdom of God may be made known to the Principalities and the Powers in heavenly places through the church."

Again, Dionysius tells us: "The name of the Holy Powers, co-equal with the Domination and Virtues, signifies an orderly and unconfined order in the divine receptions, and the regulation of intellectual and supernatural power which never debases its authority by tyrannical force but is irresistibly urged on in due order to the divine. It beneficiently leads those below it, as far as possible to the Supreme Power which is the source of power."

The Angels

The angels are the real link with man. They are the lowest Choir of all of the Hierarchies and are the last of the heavenly beings possessing angelic nature. The word angel means messenger, and their Choir is more directly in contact with visible and earthly things.

How Angels Are Ranked

THE SUPREME HIERARCHY: Seraphim, Cherubim and Thrones.

MIDDLE HIERARCHY: Dominations, Virtues, Powers.

LOWER HIERARCHY: Principalities, Archangels, Angels.

The Language of Angels

We know beyond doubt that angels have their own language when they converse with each other. We don't know what that language is. What we do know is that when angels appear before men, human language is spoken.

St. Thomas feels that angels talk to each other by means of illumination, which is nothing more than the conveyance of thoughts and ideas by opening their minds. No speech is necessary.

St. John says: "They (the angels) need neither tongue nor ears but without the help of any spoken word they exchange with each other their thoughts and their counsels."

The language of the angels, therefore, is much clearer, stronger and more perfect than the spoken language of men. Understand, our spoken words are merely the symbols of our ideas and thoughts. Sometimes these symbols are inadequate for full expression. We don't often get the full meaning, nor are we often very clear to our listener.

How Angels Get About

An angel is spiritual and immaterial. He does not occupy space, not even a single point—which brings up the inanity about how many angels can dance on the head of a pin. The question is silly, to say the least.

Another thing—an angel can be engaged in only one place at a time. He can, however, make himself known by the application of his power. If you read John 5:4 you will see the well-known account of the miraculous cures that took place in the pond called Bethsaida by the Sheepgate of Jerusalem. "An Angel of the Lord descended at certain times into the pond and the water was moved. And he that went down first into the pond after the motion of the water was made whole, of whatsoever infirmity he lay under."

We don't know by this account that anyone saw the angel, but we do learn that an angel can affect material objects just the way a soul or demons can. An angel can pass from one place to another with the speed of thought, but he can't be in two places at once. He can do in reality what we can do only mentally. We can picture ourselves in some far-off land, but angels can actually be there simply by thinking he is there.

The Bible tells us that angels have transported material objects and people with the same rapidity they enjoy at all times. Though most angels are depicted with wings, in actuality they can often appear as strangers willing to assist in many of life's problems.

Remember Daniel in the lion's den? This is a good example of an angel transporting a human being over a great distance. The Prophet Daniel was in the lion's den for six days. The Lord sent an angel to fetch food for Daniel. Was the angel's task to get some real food for Daniel, who, incidentally, was not touched by the hungry felines?

Daniel was in Babylon. The angel went to Judea, which was 600 miles west of Babylon. In Daniel 14:32-38 we read: "There was in Judea a prophet called Habacuc, and he boiled pottage, and had broken bread in a bowl, and was going into the field, to carry it to the reapers. And the Angel of the Lord said to Habacuc: Carry the dinner which thou hast into Babylon to Daniel, who is in the lions' den. And Habacuc said: Lord, I never saw Babylon, nor do I know the den. And the angel of the Lord took him by the top of his head, and carried him by the hair of the head, and set him in Babylon over the den in the force of his spirit. And Habacuc cried saying: Daniel, thou servant of God, take the dinner that God hath sent thee...And Daniel rose and ate. And the Angel of the Lord presently set Habacuc again in his own place."

We can assume that all of this took place in a moment of time, so that Habacuc was able to prepare another meal for his reapers. An angel is a finite being. He cannot perform miracles. The miracle at Bethsaida was not the angel's doing, but God's. A miracle is something done by God, and only God, outside the order of all created nature. God performs all miracles. He may use angels or saints as instruments to cause the miracles.

ARCHANGEL CASSIEL - Cassiel is one of the princes of the order of Powers. He is one of the rulers of the planet, Saturn, and associated with Saturday. He is known as the angel of temperance, solitude and tears. A simple affirmation is: "In my solitude, I find joy and contentment."

REV. MARIA D' ANDREA TELLS YOU HOW TO SUMMON ANGELIC ASSISTANCE – AND WHAT YOU SHOULD EXPECT

1. Preparing For Contact –

THE vast majority of readers will have only begun to understand the intricate Enochian language of John Dee and Edward Kelley. We suggest using the Sigillum Dei Aemaeth as a ritualistic altar, a kind of "base camp" to enable you to summon and communicate with a variety of angels who can best assist you.

Copy onto card stock (or preferably virgin parchment) this symbol and place it in the middle of a large table so you have room to work. This then becomes your altar. Place a colored candle on each of the four corners of the table/altar. Make sure the table is far enough away from anything that could cause a fire. Cut out and copy one of Maria D' Andrea's Angel Symbols and place it face down on top of a black-face scrying mirror or black stone scrying bowl in the middle of the Sigillum Dei Aemaeth. Pick the symbol that best represents why you wish to summon an angel. If you do not have a scrying mirror or black stone bowl, simply put the symbol face down on top of the Sigillum. Note: See back of book for information on how to order your own black stone scrying bowl.

2. Cleanse The Area –

In order to make sure your angel representative is pure and spiritually passive to your command, you will want to cleanse the area. You can sprinkle some holy water over the table or put some rose petals into a bowl of water that you have said a simple prayer over (use the one below or chose one of your own liking or take one from our ***Miracle A Minute*** book). Try to relax and to meditate as you do so. If you do not meditate, at least do the following (you can also incorporate this with your meditation): Take deep breaths. Inhale. Hold It. Exhale. Repeat this exercise maybe 5 or 6 times.

One prayer that is often used is a PRAYER TO YOUR GUARDIAN ANGEL, which goes like this:

Angel of God,
My Guardian dear,
To Whom His Love,
Enters Me Here,
Ever This Day,
Be At My Side,
To Light and Guard,
To Rule and Guide.
Amen

BASIC RULE - Remember to ALWAYS use protection for yourself as well as your space. You may be moving around and, if you are out of the protected area, you need to be safe, as it is possible – though highly unlikely – that a negative entity could be passing by your location.

3. Concentrate On What You Need The Angel To Help You With –

Relax as best you can. Take a deep breath. Exhale. Do this over and over again (as described above) as you ask for guidance and assistance. Try to picture your desire in your mind's eye. Concentrate. Try to take your mind off everything else happening around you. If you find yourself thinking of other things, simply go back to your focus and do not dwell on getting off track. It takes time to be able to hold your focus. Some days are also easier then others, so keep positive. A dimly lit room is best. Turn off all noise, such as your phone, TV, radio or anything else that may distract you. You do not ever want to be interrupted in this situation. Remember, angels did not have television or Nintendo in their day.

A noted shaman and oracle, Maria D' Andrea has created a set of symbols which will make it possible to establish contact with a variety of angelic beings for your own needs.

4. Make Sure Your Intentions Are Crystal Clear –

Do not be passive in your request. Make your desire as crystal clear as possible. Let your assisting angel realize that you can control the situation, otherwise the guidance you seek may stray from the course you want it to progress on. The more vibrantly, colorfully and thoroughly you "see" or think about your intent, the better the outcome. Think about what you will be focused on ahead of time so you will be clear when communicating with the angel. Think of it from every angle – emotional, physical and spiritual. Also focus on how you will feel and what you will do when the outcome you wish for comes to pass.

5. Listen Intently With Your Inner Ear –

At times, you may "hear" a whisper or a sentence that is coming to you from the spiritual plane. At other times, you may receive a vision that tells you what you should do or what will be coming to you. Sometimes it may simply be that, all of a sudden, you get a great idea "out of nowhere." This is your angelic assistant helping you. When you are working with the angel, you have to pay attention on all levels so you do not miss the information coming to you. After all, YOU called on the angel for help, so you need to pay attention to receive the help you are looking for.

Angels want to help us. We simply have to decide to work with them and learn the correct techniques to achieve this. After all, God wants you to be happy and the angel is available to you to help you to have a better and happier life.

Remember, our timing on this earthly plane is different than in the heavenly spheres. Stay with your goal and "feel" the emotion of expectancy to achieve your intent. After all, if you are not excited and you do not care, why would the angel feel it should hurry or that this may be important to you?

You have to give the angel time to work on your goal. It may take only a short time or it may take longer, but stay with it. You sent the angel out to work with/for you. Let the angel do its job.

6. Giving Thanks –

When you are finished communicating with the angel, make sure you say thank you. Angels need to feel appreciated and acknowledged for all the help that

A black stone bowl can be used to place one of Maria's symbols in while you concentrate on summoning an angel. Or you can use it as a means of seeing spirits. Fill it half way with water and gaze into the bowl.

is going to be given to you. As you communicate, say thank you each time you are finished with your ritual or you move on to the next part.

Remember to also say thank you when your intent comes to pass. This is a very important part and should never be neglected. Otherwise, the next time you want assistance, you might have provoked this angel into doing very little to satisfy your demands and will have to start from scratch. In fact, ask the angel guiding you its name. Listen for the angel to whisper it in your inner ear or in a dream. They may appear to you in this form as well.

7. Go Forth –

Tell your angelic assistant "to now go forth to achieve my intent." You called the angel in and you have to release it to go do the work. If you forget to do this and remember at a later date, send the angel forth then.

8- Remember –

Prepare for contact. Cleanse your space. Do your protection. Focus with clear intent. Then go forth to communicate with your angel. Thank your angel. As the last step, send the angel home.

IMPORTANT – Always protect yourself at all cost. Remember, whatever you do, good or bad will come back. That's the Law of Justice and Karma.

ARCHANGEL RAPHAEL - Gives mental and physical boost to weary travelers and is known most often as the "healing angel," working to heal mind, body and spirit. Orange candles will help cement the contract.

REV. D' ANDREA'S ANGEL SPELLS

Rev. Maria D'Andrea, MsD, D.D., DRH

MANY of us have had experiences with angels or have heard of people who had contact with them. There have been incidents in my life that made it so I personally have no doubt about their existence, intervention and help.

It isn't always an earth-shattering experience as some people think. Sometimes it is information that helps you avoid a problem or crisis, such as a bad feeling warning you to not drive on a certain road, thus avoiding being in an accident. Sometimes it is just a feeling of a loving presence that serves as a guide, warning you to avoid negative situations or to go toward positive ones, among other manifestations.

Any time I have encountered them, I have always had a feeling of love and, at times, some curiosity.

One time, I was walking through my apartment and wondering if I would ever be able to afford living in a house. I had two young sons, Rick and Rob, to take care of, and just couldn't see how this dream could ever be fulfilled. All of a sudden, I saw a very tall being, filled with Light, but not so bright as to not be able to look at this being. I didn't see any wings, as I would have expected, but I simply "knew" this was an angel. I had an overwhelming feeling that this angel was sending love to me and was saying that someday I would own a house and to just keep on the Path I was on. Now, I did not hear anything verbally. It was an experience of clairaudience, or psychic / inner hearing on a telepathic level. I had a feeling of trust and being safe after the angel disappeared. I knew eventually I would have a house.

Since that time, I have owned two houses. I bought a ranch house and then later sold it to buy a much bigger one. Plus, I bought a house as an investment to rent to others for a time. I could not have imagined this all those years ago.

Another time, I was helping a spirit of a lady who passed on to move from this earthly plane to her next life. She was not ready and was afraid that, due to her being such a negative person in life, she would not be welcomed and would instead go to a negative place. As I was working with her, I felt the presence of a being and "knew" it was an angel connected to her. I don't know what happened between them. It seemed as though they were communicating. After the angel disappeared, the lady was at peace, joyous and excited to move on. As she left, I had a feeling of joy.

There are many such experiences in my life, too numerous to write about. However, they all helped me in some way to do better or simply to learn to trust that the future outcomes of some situations will be better.

You never know how, why or when an angel will come. Also, when we specifically call them in, they will help us.

Look to work with them, and they will come to you. At times, you may have an experience you cannot explain. You never know – it might have been an angel helping.

Protection For Safety

Before talking to the angels, *always* say a short prayer of protection. The prayer can even be as simple as:

Lord Protect Me From ALL Forms Of Harm Now.

Even though you are calling in positive angels, you do not want any hitchhikers that may be negative.

This is an often-used, ancient technique to protect yourself:

Get a bowl of water; add some salt to it and some rose petals. Keep this in the room you are working in at all times.

Another protection formula is for Home Protection:

Pick Beth roots when the moon is waning and dry them. When dry, cut them into small pieces and write or carve the word "GOD" into them. Take Beth root and place next to any incense used for protection, such as Frankincense or Tobacco Incense. Light the incense and wait for it to burn out. Then sprinkle some of the ashes around the room in your home. Next, string the roots on a white or red thread or cord. Wear this as a necklace or hang in a room.

One of the protection prayers I received through meditation years ago works on a very high vibration. It also contains power, so we have the control, since our free will overrides everything, and is as follows:

Prayer For Power

I am one with God
and let the power of God flow in me, through me, and around me,
for God is ALL.
I trust the Divine Power
and all is perfect,
Knowing I am always protected and guided Divinely.
Whatever I choose
to manifest in my life comes easily to me, joyfully and with perfect harmony.
I walk the path of White Light
In truth, peace. love,
harmony and health.
Thank you Father, for I am,
You are,
We are ONE.
Amen

ARCHANGEL SACHIEL - In Christian and Cabbalistic lore his name means "the covering of God" and is associated with wealth and charity. Sachiel can be invoked for matters pertaining to law, politics, religion and money.

Remember to **always** utilize some form of protection of your choice. I cannot stress this enough. Do so and move forward to a better life with the help of the angels.

Talismans as Power Tools

Talismans have been with us in all cultures since ancient times. Whatever the belief systems were, whatever the names they called the angels, the angels have always been there in the other realm, waiting to be of help.

To connect to them, we sometimes utilize a talisman to make the contact quick, direct and powerful.

The word talisman means to "consecrate." This is an inanimate object that has been consecrated with powerful psychic energy by one who has the ability and the knowledge to do so. The aim is to attract changes to a person's lifestyle or their environment to make it better.

Talismans come in many forms. They can be on parchment or other paper, on wood, metal, buildings and other devices. They can be bought already consecrated or made by hand by the individual owner.

These talismans are always for a specific intent/purpose. They may have specific sigils, hieroglyphs, runes, words of power to speak, ancient symbols, or whatever the practitioner deems appropriate to bring the results sought after.

The techniques vary according to the individual and what the intent is. One makes a choice regarding which of several methods goes into the talisman being activated and the psychic energy imparted into the object. Such as: going by water or using fire, earth, air, sun, stars, rain, rhythmic dance, chant, drumming, power words, holding between the palms, or sending energy through the eyes, to name a few forms.

Once the talisman is activated, it is carried or wrapped up in a cloth, usually white or black, and placed in a safe place until it is used, worn or employed by some other method of the individual's choosing.

It should not be left outside uncovered or in the elements of nature because the power through time will deplete and go back to its source.

There are numerous reasons to utilize the talisman, such as for the heightening of healing, protection, spirituality, as well as any intent you can imagine.

Talismanic magick is at times ritualistic. The method is up to the individual as to what he/she resonates with/prefers.

Once the object is "talisman-ized," the energy is stored within the talisman and usually is consecrated only for the individual who uses it.

Once you start working with the talisman, it becomes yours by connecting to your vibration.

Connecting these talismans to the angels gives them a Higher Vibration and keeps them positive and powerful.

Work with the angel spells to bring a better life of joy and abundance to you.

Remember to focus on your intent and faithfully expect the outcome you are working toward. So move ahead and do so being happy, knowing your life is on the rise with the angels help.

* * * *

ARCHANGEL URIEL - He is known as "the Light of God" and stands beside the Throne of God. Has command over the earth and the wind and is known to be a patron of the arts (writers, musicians, artists take note).

PRAYERS, SPELLS AND MENTAL PROJECTION WITH ASSOCIATED TALISMANS CREATED BY REV. D'ANDREA

It is suggested that readers may copy all twelve symbols/talismans created by Rev. D'Andrea onto a heavy card stock, or the symbols may be purchased along with the others reproduced in this book and printed on VIRGIN PARCHMENT from the publisher: Timothy G. Beckley, Box 753, New Brunswick, NJ - mrufo8@hotmail.com

Archangel Michael
PROTECTION

Angel Prince Sandalphon
POWER & GLORY

1— Archangel Michael/For Protection

This archangel can be called in to work with you for *protection against your enemies,* as well as to *banish any negativity* around you. It is also good to call him at the time of *childbirth.*

To work with the Archangel Michael, do the following:

1. First, set up an altar. This can be done temporarily on a table, dresser, outdoors, or any number of places of your choice. Make sure it is a flat surface.
2. Place a blue cloth on top of the altar. The size does not matter.
3. Then place 1 blue candle in the center and on the right of it place a white candle. Also place another white candle to the left of the blue one. The candle size does not matter as long as they are all the same size.
4. Next, place the herb called basil or burdock in a small bowl in front of the blue candle.
5. Copy the talisman symbol for Archangel Michael contained in this book. Place your Talisman in front of the herb.
6. Take some sage and wave it over the table and focus your intent on cleansing this space from all negativity.
7. Next, focus on what your intent is as you light the blue candle 1st, then the white candle on the right of it, next the candle on the left. 8- Mentally or preferably verbally say:
8. I now call in Archangel Michael to help me and protect me in this situation <u>(Fill in with your intent)</u>. I am NOW under His protection. I declare it and it is so.
9. Let the candles burn to the bottom. If you can't let them burn to the bottom, then put the candles out without blowing on them. (You can use whatever tool you prefer or even aluminum foil.) If you use your breath, you will cancel out your intent. Next, do the following: First extinguish the white candle on the left, then the right, then the blue candle in the middle. Pick up the talisman and carry it with you until the situation is resolved.
10. Take the herbs and throw them outside to the wind to let go of the negativity and activate your intent.

11. Take what is left of the candles and throw them away outside your home. It can be on your property, just not inside your home.

Know that the protection of Archangel Michael is with you any time you carry this Talisman.

2— Angel Prince Sandalphon/Power And Glory

1. This is the angel of *power* and *glory*. (Metetron's brother.) When you are in need or wish to heighten these attributes, call in this angel to work with you.
2. When working with this angel, it is best to face East.
3. First light some Frankincense and Myrrh incense.
4. Take the Talisman for the angel Sandalphone, this angel prince, and hold it between your palms. Take 3 breaths and, at each breath, blow it on the Talisman and focus on your intent for power and glory to come to you.
5. Hold the Talisman over the incense so the vibrations can connect.
6. As you are holding this Talisman, invoke from your heart:

I now invoke the Sandalphone, my angel. Through the Power of the Divine.

Angel Prince Sandalphon, NOW share the abilities that you possess with me.

I require the power that is within me to heighten. I call in the power and glory to help me to stay positive, connected and joyous.

Help me to use these, your abilities, to walk the Path of Light and improve my life through the Angel Prince Sandalphon.

As I speak, so shall it be.

7. Let this incense burn out on its own. Throw what remains of the incense outside to the wind to carry your message.
8. Take the Talisman and carry it with you whenever you choose to work with these abilities.

Angel Azbuga
JUDGMENT

Archangel Raphael
HEALING

3— Angel Azbuga/Judgment

Call this angel to you when you need *fairness* and *judgment* on your side. This angel swoops in to bring *righteousness to your aid.*

1. Take a white cloth (could be a handkerchief) and put a little of the herb called violet in it.
2. Place the Talisman for the angel Azbuga in the white cloth with the herb. Fold the cloth over the Talisman.
3. Hold the Talisman in your hand.
4. Focus on your intent and say:

Azbuga, the righteous one,

Come to me, I conjure thus.

By air and sea,

By earth and fire.

Rain judgment down,

Just like fire.

So Be It.

5. Then thank Azbuga for coming.
6. You can now take the Talisman out of the cloth and carry it with you. When you are not carrying it, you can keep it in this cloth to recharge.

4– Archangel Raphael/Healing

Angel of the *healing* arts, knowledge and science. In this case, we are focused on the healing energy.

1. Take a mirror and place your picture on it. Pick one that looks the way you are when in perfect health. It does not matter if you are younger in the picture because it is still your energy.
2. Next get a small green pouch or bag.
3. Place the Talisman for Archangel Raphael inside with the following ingredients:

    A. The gemstone called red jasper (the size does not count).

    B. The herb called juniper or thyme. Also add a little mint.

4. Tie it closed with 3 knots.
5. Hold the pouch between you and the mirror and incant:

Raphael, now hear me speak,

Strength and healing I now seek.

Give to me thy healing power,

Come now in my needed hour.

As I say so shall it be.

Thank you, Raphael.

6. Carry the pouch with you at all times so Raphael can speed up your healing energy.
7. Take your picture and place it behind the mirror facing the mirror, not the wall. Leave it there till your health feels better. Know in your heart Raphael is helping you.

Angel Unael
Ward Off Evil

Angel Merod
Love Magick

5—Angel Unael/Ward Off Evil

The angel Unael *wards off evil*. At times we need to make sure we are safe from being harmed. This angel will come to your aid and repel the evil.

1. In a pouch of white, place the following:

   The Talisman for angel Unael

   The gemstone called tiger eye

2. The following herbs:

   A bay leaf, caraway seeds, ivy, basil & a piece of grass

3. Tie it closed with 3 knots.
4. Say the following with intent:

I conjure thee, Unael, to bring me peace. Cast away the evil spirits surrounding me. Ward off the evil around me. Banish the negative and give me the peace and joy that was promised to me by the Power of the Divine. Call forth your armies to aid in my fight against my enemies. I invoke thy power to do this in His name and mine. Go forth until this is completed.

Thank you Lord. Thank you, Unael.

5. Carry the pouch with you and place it by your bed while you sleep.

6—Angel Merod/Love Magick

This angel, also connected to the Key of Solomon, is called upon to help in *magickal operations.*

There are many forms of love, including friends, family, platonic and much, much more. This spell is to grant us help with *romantic love.*

1. In a pink pouch, place the following:

   The powerful Talisman of the angel Merod.

   The pink stone called rhodochrosite.

   herbs as follows: Adam and Eve root, dill, senna.
2. Tie it closed with 5 knots.
3. Set up your altar. Any flat surface will do. Place a purple cloth on it of any size.
4. On it, place a pink candle in the middle. In front of it, place your pouch.
5. Light the candle as you focus on your intent.
6. Take 3 deep breaths and focus on respect and your intent in a serious manner.
7. Next, put your arms above your head toward the sky forming a "v" shape.
8. Invoke the angel Merod with sincerity in your heart.

I now invoke the angel Merod, the Master of magick, for the purpose of attraction (or working on improving) my love life. I know that thou will attract and bring to me my desires and more, (or help me to attain my goal, which is - fill it in).

I only want this in a positive way so it harms none and is best for us both. I invoke thus – that it is what I wish for or better, in a perfect way.

Thank you, Merod

9. Lower your arms.
10. Let the candle burn to the bottom and then throw it away outside.
11. Then carry the pouch with you.

Remember that you have free will and always use your will and intent for only positive results.

The Lightworker's Prayer
By Archangel Lord Michael

I am (your name) of the Light, together with my guides this morning.
I invite my guardian angels, the archangels and other legions of angels.
I invite my personal guides.
I invite my family and friends who have crossed over to Spirit.
I invite my spiritual teachers with interest in my development and soul growth.

I thank you for coming to be with me now.

I declare that I am of the Light.
Light permeates my aura.
My Light extends into the auras of other people in a loving way.
My heart is filled with love and joy and peace.

I extend my White Light out into the world,
First into my city then into my country,
Then into those countries beyond.
It goes across the ocean and it goes around the world.

With a loving heart, I extend White Light to all those who are working
For the peace that we enjoy on Earth.
With a loving heart, I extend Pink Light to all those who may be opposed
To peace, or misguided in their ways to achieve it.

At this time, I wish to sit in quiet meditation for just a short time,
In order to dwell upon one particular world situation that needs healing.
I extend Green Light, as well as the Violet Flame, to these areas,
The Green Light of healing in order to help heal the people
And in order to heal the Earth in those places.
I extend the Violet Flame for the instantaneous transformation
Of negativity into Love.

I will now take some time to do my Lightwork.

♥ ♥ ♥

I bathe myself in the Green Light of Healing and extend it to my friends and family.
The color now changes to violet and our transformation begins,
A transformation into the Love of the Heaven Worlds and
Our transformation into Light, pure Divine Light.

I am (your name) of the Light. My Light shines all day.
My Light continues to glow all evening.
All night long, while I sleep, my Light extends to the Universe in Divine ways.
Oneness is assured. Thanks be to God. And so it is.

Angel Phamuel
Hope

Angel Akatriel
Intensify Prayers

7—Angel Phamuel/Hope

This angel has been called the angel of *hope*. When you are in a situation where you feel like all else has failed you and you do not know where to turn, then turn to this powerful angel of hope.

We invoke this angel to uplift our lives and to create a better one.

1. Wear something that is white or has white in it.
2. Then place a glass of water on any flat surface.
3. Next, hold the Talisman for the angel Phamuel over it.
4. Repeat the following:

I conjure thee thus- Angel of hope, angel Phamuel, come to me now to aid me in this my time of need. I trust that thou come to me quickly and positively. I know that you hear my call and offer hope and compassion. Give me the insight to move forward, the intuitive sense and the knowledge that can help me. Clear the Path for me.

I am ready to walk through the doors that you open for me.

I command thee thus.

Now go forth. Thank you, angel Phamuel.

5. Next, sprinkle some of the water in your home and throw the rest of the water outside your residence.
6. Carry the Talisman for the angel of Hope.
7. Know that this angel does not fail.

8—Angel Akatriel/Intensify Prayers

The angel of *Prayer*, the angel Akatriel, is here to assist you. This angel helps to carry the prayers of the saints to God as well as to carry your prayers.

There are other angels who also convey messages, but this angel is direct and is connected to the work of shamans and ministers, among others.

You will find a feeling of release and relief in your heart when dealing with this angel.

1. Take white paper or parchment paper and write your prayer on it with black ink. White to keep it with God Light and black to give it Power. As you write down your prayer, remember to do so with reverence and focus on what you are praying for.
2. Take your angel Akatriel Talisman and wrap it in this paper, still focusing on your prayer.
3. Get a red or a gold candle. If you cannot find a gold one, you may paint it gold for the vibrational effect. Place this candle in a room you feel comfortable in, or, if needed, any room that is private. With a sharp instrument such as a pen tip (black ink), a knife, or other tool of your choice, draw a cross on top near the wick.
4. Place the wrapped angel Akatriel Talisman near it.
5. Remember you are connecting to the Divine and focus with expectation to receive what is the best result for you concerning your prayer.
6. Light the candle with purposeful intent and expectation and affirm:

Angel, Angel Akatriel,

I beseech thee to hear my prayer,

Be my messenger to the Lord above,

To hear my prayer and send His love.

7. Let the candle burn to the bottom with the wrapped Talisman near it.
8. When finished, throw the candle away outside your home.
9. Now remove the paper that is around the Talisman so you can carry the Talisman with you. Take the wrapping and place it in your Bible.

Prayer is a powerful force. This technique has been utilized throughout history in all cultures and all belief systems. Use it, as always, with positive intent only.

Angel Gabriel
Compound Joy

Archangel Metetron
Liberation

9— Angel Gabriel/Compound Joy

One of the duties of this angel is to bring *joy* to people, to humanity. You simply have to have joy in your life to have more energy, greater health, greater abundance, and to be motivated to have inner growth. God wants us to be happy and to enjoy life.

1. Do the following to invoke this angel:
2. Set a glass or goblet of water in the center of the floor.
3. Next to the goblet, on the right, place the Talisman for Gabriel.
4. On top of the Talisman, place the yellow gemstone called citrine.
5. Take 3 slow deep breaths.
6. Close your eyes and focus on "seeing" or just "knowing" that you are happy, joyous and carefree. After all, God can take care of everything, so why would you worry? He wants you to be happy.

Now, ask the angel Gabriel to come and help bring joy into your life every day. Let him know that every morning you will wake up and before you get out of bed you will ask him to bring you joy and that you will pay attention to what comes to you that day to make you happy. It may be something small like the sun shining or something big like getting married, a birth, improved health or a job promotion.

7. Now, open your eyes. Take another deep breath and take the gemstone off your Talisman. You can now carry the Talisman with you.
8. Take the citrine and place it under your mattress or you can place it in your bedroom but no farther than 3 feet from your bed.
9. Take the goblet and drink the water.

The joy you expect will come. Remember to talk to the angel Gabriel every morning. Utilizing the same spell, you can call in the angel Gabriel for *protection*.

10—Archangel Metetron/Liberation

Archangel Metetron is known for numerous abilities. However, you can call on him for the purpose of *liberation* in this case.

It can be for the liberation from a person, situation or any circumstance that you may find yourself in.

To call on the Archangel Metetron, do the following:

1. Use sage to cleanse the room you will be working in. Light the sage and let the smoke permeate the room for the time you are working on connecting to Archangel Metetron.
2. Stand in the middle of the room. Place your Talisman for Archangel Metetron next to you on the floor.
3. Face the *East* , the connection to air, and say:

I now consecrate this Talisman through the power of Archangel Metetron:

Great Archangel Metetron, of the East, I call on you to bring me wisdom. Impart ancient and hidden knowledge that I may improve upon my life.

4. Turn and face the *South* , the connection to fire, and say:

Archangel Metetron, also of the South, bring to me the energy I need to take the actions that improve my life.

5. Turn clockwise again to the *West*, the connection to water, and say:

Archangel Metetron, also of the West, I call on you to bring my emotions into balance.

6. Now, turn to the *North*, the connection to Earth, and say:

Archangel Metetron, also of the North, I call on you to bring to me abundance. I am now liberated in all areas from all limitations. So be it!

7. Take the Talisman and hold it between your palms. Thank Archangel Metetron for coming. You can now carry the Talisman.

At this point, you can stay in the middle of the room until you feel you no longer need to stay and you are finished. Pick up the talisman and carry it with you.

Angel Guziel
Help Against Enemy

Angel Seraphiel
Heighten Communication

11—Angel Guziel/Help Against Enemy

This angel gives you *help against your enemies.* We work from a spiritual outlook, but there are times when we have to stand our ground and say enough is enough. To gain help from this angel, do the following spell:

1. Go to a private spot and create an altar. Find a flat surface and place an orange cloth on it of any size.
2. Place a white candle in the middle of the cloth.
3. Place your Talisman for Guziel in front of it.
4. Place a cup of water on the left of the candle.
5. Place Frankincense in front of the Talisman.
6. Place a dish with a little salt behind the candle.
7. Place any feather to the right of the candle.
8. Light the candle with intent to gain help against all enemies.
9. Light the incense with the intent of gaining help against all enemies.
10. Now, stand for a few minutes communing with the angel Guziel. You do not have to know exactly who is causing the problems. Say with intent:

O great angel Guziel, connection to all and with God, power over the earth, air, fire and water, working with the Power of Light, I call on you to sweep my enemies from my Path in a positive way, to harm none, away with my enemies from me, and replace it with Right, Joy and Light.

As the candle flame flickers, watch it for a few minutes and focus on it burning away all negative energies coming toward you and being replaced by positive energies and Light from the flame.

11. Pick up your Talisman to carry it with you. Let the incense burn out and also let the candle burn out. When they are both done, take the water, candle, feather and incense and throw them away outside your home. You are sending them out to work for you vibrationally.

12—Angel Seraphiel/Heighten Communication

Among other abilities, the angel Seraphiel is connected to *communication* and *intellect*. You can call on this angel to help you communicate better on a job, as an employee or employer, with family, loved ones, and so the list goes on. Communication involves speaking, writing, singing, and inspiration, among other things.

This ability not only helps to elevate your ability to communicate better but also to better understand when others communicate.

Do the following spell to achieve this ability:

1. Take a Tablespoon of the herb lavender or the plant named parsley and place it on a yellow cloth.
2. Place the Talisman of the angel Seraphiel on top of the herb.
3. Take an orange or violet candle and place it to the right of the Talisman and light it, saying: I light this candle to Light my Way.
4. Stand in front of the Talisman and with focus and conviction, look at the talisman and say:

I now call on the angel Seraphiel of the North to come to me. I gain, through your help, wisdom in business and all areas of my life, the heightening of intellect, the ability of communication and inspiration. I declare that you send these to me now. Teach me to use these abilities.

5. Focus on what you said for a few minutes. Let the candle burn down to the bottom and throw it outside.
6. Take the Talisman to carry and throw the herb outside so that it also goes back to nature.

Reminder - Angels In Our Lives

Angels are everywhere. They are here to help us to grow, to do better, to avoid problems and to be truly happy.

Look back at your life. You may see situations that you cannot explain where it might have been an angel's intervention.

We do not always have to call on them just for urgent or important situations. They are here for us even in simple things.

Try this:

Use your Protection method first- *always*. Call on a Positive Parking Angel the next time you leave your home and "see" where you want to find a parking spot. Trust the angel to come and help. You will either get that spot or something close, in a positive way.

Once I was focused on such a spot and I ended up three blocks away, and it was windy and cold outside. I kept thinking why three blocks? Since I use this method frequently when I know I am going to a difficult parking area and it works for me. As I approached my destination, there was an elderly gentleman getting out of "my" spot. It seemed he had a very difficult time walking. I felt very good for him. He really needed that spot more than I did.

Remember the angels are loving beings and want to help you. Work with them and remember to thank them for helping you. Move forward in your life with these, your new friends.

Guardian Angel

SECRET CIPHER of the UFOnauts

Allen H. Greenfield

Purveyors of the Authentic Tradition:
[seated, from left to right: Meade Layne, Jacob Frank, Aleister Crowley, Mark Probert, Max Theon.]
[Allen Greenfield, standing.]
Detail from an art piece by Jonathan Sellers.

SECRET CIPHER
OF THE
UFOnauts

Allen H. Greenfield

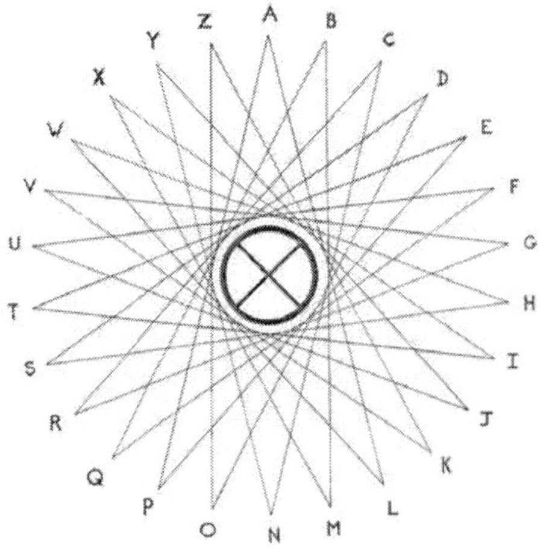

Library of Congress Cataloging in Publication Data

Greenfield, Allen H.
Secret Cipher of the UFOnauts / Allen H. Greenfield. – 2nd Expanded ed.
xiv + 94 p. 6 x 9 inches
Includes bibliographical references and index.
ISBN: 1-881532-04-6 ; $9.95
1. Unidentified flying objects.
2. Ciphers 1. Title
TL789.G74 1994
135'.4—dc20 94-31644

Second Expanded Edition: September, 2005.
Cover art from a painting by Debra Page, entitled *Nephilim Al-Kemy*.
Graphic Design by Jonathan Sellers / FACME_ORG.

Set in Adobe Garamond Pro and Futura Extra Black. Cover set in AI Regular.

10 9 8 7 6 5 4 3 2

Printed in the United States of America.

Acknowledgments

I would be remiss if I did not acknowledge with profound gratitude the role of my teachers in the occult: Patriarch Michael Bertiaux, Bishop Jack Hogg and the late W. W. Webb of QBLH. I should also like to acknowledge the profound contributions of Soror Ishtaria, Outer Head of QBLH and Jim Leas, Jake Stratton-Kent and Carol Smith . My teachers in the lore of UFOlogy have been very special: my good friend James W. Moseley, John A. Keel, the late Richard S. Shaver, and most especially the late Gray Barker have all profoundly influenced this work.

For early help with the manuscript, I wish to thank Bishop Oscar Samson Orion for his critical comments and constructive suggestions; H. Hilliard Gastfriend, Ph.D., for his work on the manuscript; and to the late Ron Bonds for encouraging me to write this book, and having the courage to publish this book's first edition. He died far too young as did Kerry Thornley, and Jim Keith, fellow IllumiNet Press authors.

I do so want to thank Ian Blake and James Borges, BSRA, for their invaluable help in advancing this work in the years since the first publication. The contribution of Jon Sellers I cannot begin to adequately acknowledge. For advancing the New Aeon English Qabala work against considerable resistence, John Crow and Gerald del Campo as well as Stratton-Kent need special mention.

Dedicated to the memories of C. S. Jones, Ron, Kerry and Jim.

"I am fairly familiar with all forms of secret writings, and am myself the author of a trifling monograph upon the subject, in which I analyze 160 ciphers, but I confess that this is entirely new to me. The object of those who invented the system has apparently been to conceal that these characters convey a message, and to give the idea that they are the mere random sketches of children."

Arthur Conan Doyle
The Adventure of the Dancing Men

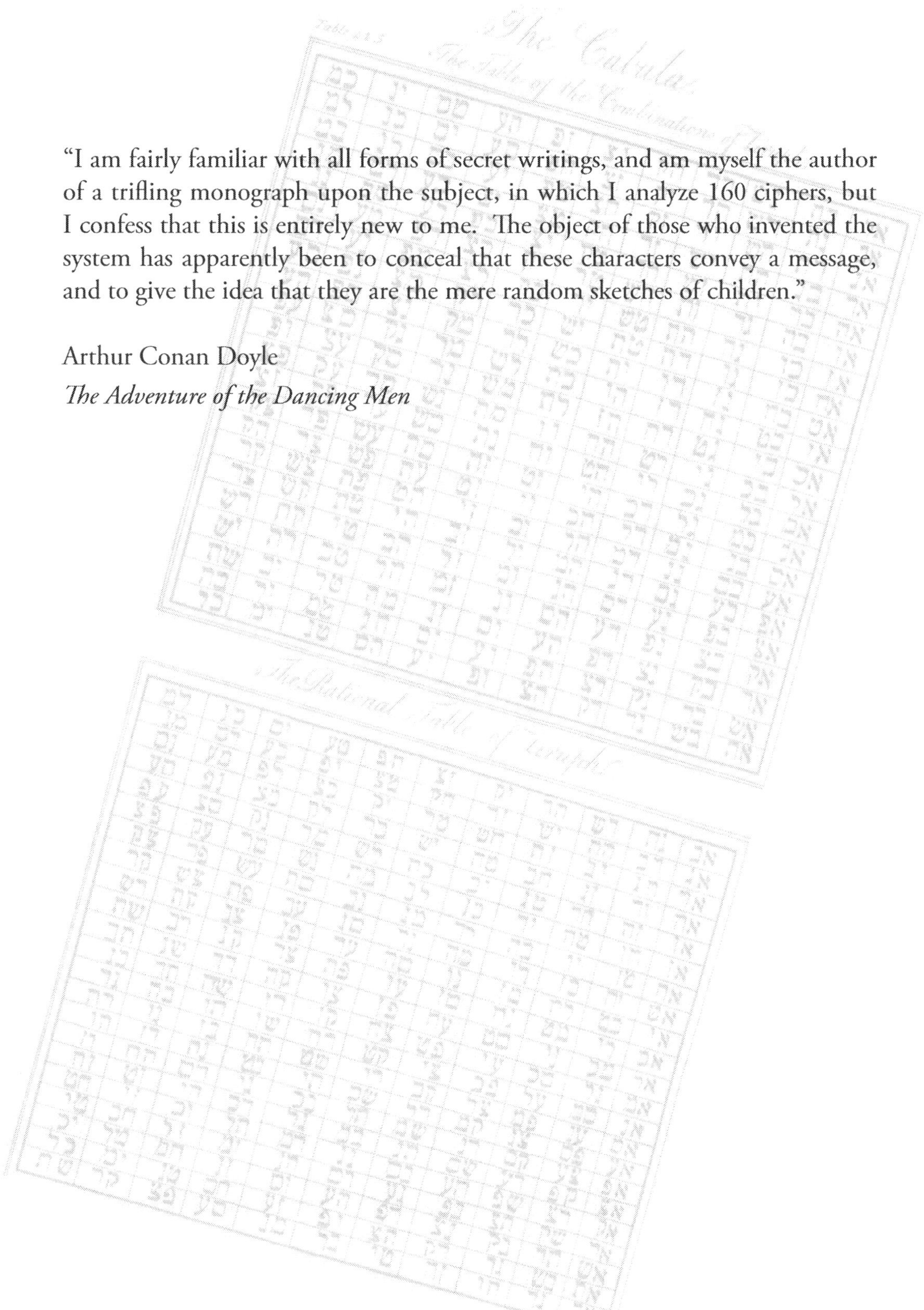

Introductory Remarks by Jonathan Sellers

I first encountered this interesting book in a catalog for Adventures Unlimited, ten years ago exactly, when I was receiving mail from conspiranoia mailing lists, under the monicker of "Harold K. Taylor" — we used to get some rather interesting junk.

I only wish I still had access to that old catalog, for I would have quoted the blurb written in it. That entire catalog was really written after the style of the famous Incunabula catalog, which first circulated in the early 1990s.

I had come to some conclusions of my own, as a result of study and practice of the body of works that have been written by and about Aleister Crowley, *The Book of the Law*, Thelema, and other related paradigms. These conclusions had a lot to do with the idea of contact — or — rather — communication: not only with the very same types of Entities encountered by Crowley and others, but Contact with what I came to regard as "The Authentic Tradition."

When I first started writing the material that became known as *The Brethren of the GIFT*, from 1996 to 1997, in its original hand-written manuscript form, I had no access to a computer, or the Internet. In fact, I had no access to the majority of my Library. Much later, I gained access to the Internet. I started publishing Antiquities of the Illuminati, and, one day, found Allen Greenfield's website.

From the first, I felt an affinity with Allen and with his words, which went beyond the standard familiarity with Crowley, Gnosticism, the Authentic Tradition. An examination of Chapter 2, "A Most Unusual Cast of Characters," will bring together many different strands of the Authentic Tradition, thus tying up some loose ends.

In fact, Allen and I share a lot of interests.

I first became aware of the New Aeon English Qabalah, by way of my involvement with T. O. P. Y.[1], in the late 1980s, when *The Equinox*, Volume VII was in production, and available to Members and Allies of T. O. P. Y. At least one of the names mentioned in *Cipher* was familiar to me: Jake Stratton-Kent. I briefly immersed myself in this New Method, for the New Aeon, of using the English Language, and applying numeric values to the English Alphabet. Some of us, in the Fullerton area, in Orange County, California, were involved in these studies. While I haven't done much with it in recent times, some of my earliest Ceremonial was performed using NAEQ values, including those which led to what became known as the Dur.An.Ki Working.

Ciphers and secret alphabets have played a significant role in the history of Religion; in the history of Secret Societies; in the history of Intelligence. These last two have often been intimately connected over the centuries.

The idea that there is an Authentic Tradition, whose Initiates (and Custodians)

1. T. O. P. Y., or ["thee"] Temple Ov Psychick Youth, which I was involved with from 1989 - 1992.

contact each other using these ancient tools, and whose Contact and Communication extends to those in the world of the Profanes is not an idea that is new or shocking, certainly, to those of us who have experienced such Contacts and/or researched and studied the histories of THOSE WHO HAVE.

Yet, there are those who find this sort of material to be disturbing to them. They find that even though they might fancy themselves to be followers of the Law of Thelema, proclaimed by its Prophet Aleister Crowley, who contacted "præterhuman intelligences"—such as "LAM," or Aiwass - an early prototype of the now familiar Grey Alien or E. T. — anybody who holds to the very well-founded idea that Contact is a Key ingredient in the recipe is regarded as some sort of mountebank or charlatan. People like that write about "Little Green Men" (why not "Little Green Women" too?) and are crazy. Really?

Then is it better to live in a "sane" form of hero-worship cults, doing what the dot-to-dot coloring book version of Magick tells the wanna-be practitioner to do? Perhaps for those who sell books like that.

It is for this reason that this book has not been very easy to come by over the eleven years since it was first issued. It may have gone out print, but the demand for this seminal work never diminished.

Now, I am pleased to be writing this short introductory memoir, announcing the second publication of *Secret Cipher of the UFOnauts*, not only in its first digital edition, but in hard-copy format, as well.

It is interesting to see what society regards as "real" research, "real" scholarship, and so forth: anything that further divorces us from our roots in the Authentic Tradition is considered a good thing. This is all just silly make-believe.

Sure.

But before settling in your new plot of New Jersey swamp-land, you might be glad you had the method(s) described in this book, should you need to summon the Jersey Devil!

Fall to!

Jonathan Sellers
Twin Cedars Lodge
12 August 2005 c. e.

Preface: UFOnauts, Ciphers, and the Cosmic War

"And there was war in heaven: Michael and his angels fought against the dragon; and the dragon fought ..."

Book of Revelation 12:7

As the secret ceremony of the Masonic Royal Arch nears its climax, the candidates are directed to bring before the King and High Priest a strange box with inexplicable writing on all four sides. The High Priest, in a ceremony at least hundreds of years old, looks at the box with surprise and exclaims, "Companion King, this is the Ark of the Covenant of God!" The officer playing the King agrees, saying, "It is undoubtedly the true Ark of the Covenant, Most Excellent." The High Priest opens the Ark and removes a book. On reading a few passages, the High Priest proclaims, "This is a book of the law — long lost, but now found. Holiness to the Lord!" The King and Scribe agree, and the High Priest tells the candidates for initiation, "You now see that the world is indebted to Masonry for the preservation of this sacred volume. Had it not been for the wisdom and precaution of our ancient brethren, this, the only remaining copy of the law, would have been destroyed at the destruction of Jerusalem." Other objects are removed: A pot of manna — a relic of the mysterious food that appeared out of nowhere to feed the Israelites fleeing Egypt; the Rod of Aaron, that which had turned to a serpent, which devoured those created from the wands of the Egyptian magicians. The High Priest then finds four pieces of paper that on inspection, prove to be the key to the Cipher of the Royal Arch Mason. With it, those present are able to decode the mysterious writing on the Ark, which includes the long-lost word of the Master Mason, the ancient names of three sky gods drawn together to form a single word. By such ciphers and codes have the initiates of all times communicated with each other — and with their ultraterrestrial masters, the Secret Chiefs of the Great White Brotherhood. Others have used the same or similar ciphers to communicate with their Opposition.

The simple English-based Cipher of 26 letters discussed in this book is directly traceable to the Qabala of Nine Chambers, a Hebrew-based cipher of unknown antiquity; used for centuries to decode messages and secrets communicated in mystical writings, names and holy books.

"*Symbolic Tree of the Great Work*" Conception and Drawing by Elmer E. Hartman

1
The Basic Premise

First, some people among us are in the know about UFO phenomena, which have manifested throughout history. Certain people have known the nature of this phenomena, and used its nature, for almost as long.

Second, those in the know are interactive with the phenomena and have long been so. Indeed, separating out the phenomena, the legend, the myth-makers and the Illuminati or Initiates of the True Nature of the phenomena is difficult.

Third, the phenomena themselves are inherently intangible, but are able to impinge upon our reality in a phenomenological way,. because they are archetypal. Through mythos, archetypes are quite capable of setting real events into motion.

Fourth, the Illuminati of the phenomena become intertwined with the legend or mythos itself, and thus take on the legend's Power to Impinge. The Fully Illuminated are in control of reality to the extent that the mythos itself is in control. They also, in a very real sense, acquire its intangibility.

Fifth, the Illuminati of the UFOnauts are scattered, informally organized on a worldwide basis. Until the modern Information Revolution, they communicated through Secret Societies, Allegorical Mystery Dramas and Ciphers. An outworn example is found in the mythos of Alchemy, its cipher language, etc.

Sixth, most ciphers have followed the decoding rules established in the various techniques of Qabalistic Number Analysis, including Gematria, Theosophical Addition, Notariqon, Temura, etc. The most recent past known cipher was that of Aiq Bakur, or "The Qabala of Nine Chambers" — a system laid out first in Hebrew (then a dead language of scholars) on a "number sign" or "tic tac toe" pattern, and adopted by Royal Arch Masons for English Language use. To some extent, this cipher is still in current use, but it has long been deciphered and is no longer utilized by Illuminati of the UFOnauts. *The ciphers are discontinued when they are cracked.*

Seventh, although in use for some time, an English Language Cipher, using the 26 letters of the standard alphabet and laid out on a grid or plotted out on a 26-pointed star, was unveiled to a select public by Aleister Crowley in 1904. He said he received it from the præterhuman intelligence AIWASS[1] Crowley was a high — and highly controversial — initiate of the Hermetic Order of the Golden Dawn, but he never decoded the cipher, which was built on the number 11. Publisher Ray Palmer told UFOlogists for years that he had a FACT which allowed him to decode cases. Palmer's "FACT" is actually the cipher itself; FACT = 56 in cipher, or 5 + 6 = 11, the

1. Aiwass was not Crowley's only contact. There is considerable discussion in UFOlogy of LAM, the being Crowley sketched that so closely resembled later UFO-related beings described in modern close encounter cases. His encounter, in 1896, with two "little men" in the Swiss Alps was mentioned in Jacques Vallee's *Passport to Magonia* catalogue of close encounter cases. Crowley's "magical mountain" — Mt. Mealfuorvonie near Loch Ness in Scotland — is said to be a UFOnaut base.

basis (i.e., the number 11) for deciphering the code.

Eighth, Crowley's "magical son" Frater Achad did partially decipher the code, but it remained for Carol Smith in 1974 to solve it, and for software programmer Frater Lamed to make it readily accessible to investigators in the 1980s.

Ninth, the UFOnauts themselves use the cipher when they five names to themselves, their home planets, etc. They know the case will be reported, and the key words will be communicated to the Illuminati.

Tenth, since I applied the cipher to such key words, the code is now completely accessible to UFOlogists and others. The cipher can help analyze cases, predict manifestations and trace the UFOnauts to their very doorsteps; and yes, they DO have doorsteps.

Eleventh, as soon as the UFOnauts and Illuminati know the knowledge of the cipher is widespread, the code will change again. Evidence shows it is already changing.

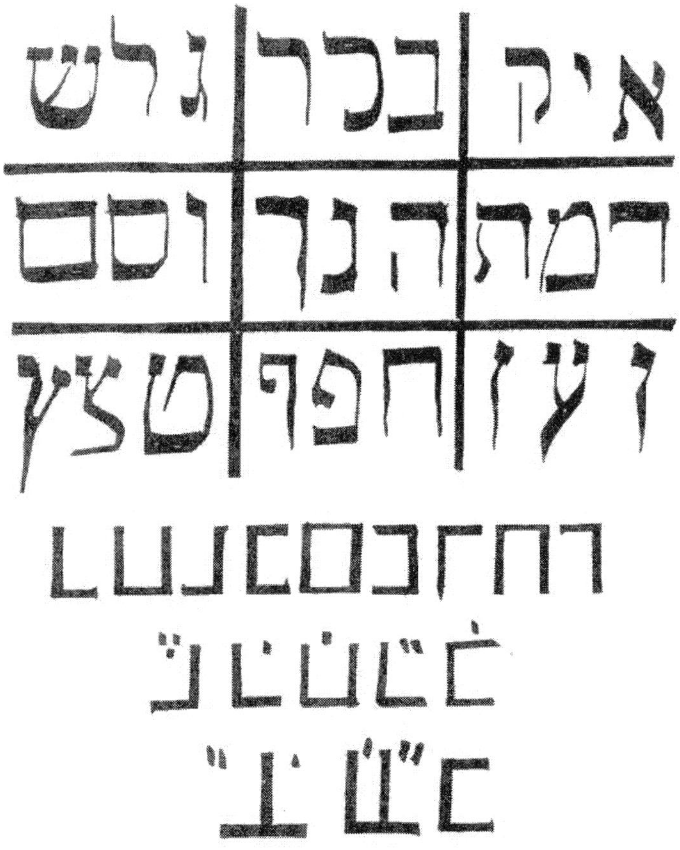

Old Qabalistic Cipher.

2
A Most Unusual Cast of Characters

In 1944, near the end of his life, Aleister Crowley wrote one of his students in California:

> "My observation of the Universe convinces me that there are beings of intelligence and power of a far higher quality than anything we can conceive of as human ... the one and only chance for mankind to advance as a whole is for individuals to make contact with such beings."

Scattered individuals throughout modern history and all over the globe have picked up on some aspect of this Ultraterrestrial mystery, but none, up until now, has pulled all of it together. However, this outstanding sampling of the best the human race has to offer have, in their own way, provided us with clues and building blocks. Some are geniuses, some saints; a few are absolute scoundrels. All are fascinating. What follows is a thumbnail sketch of some of these individuals, listed alphabetically.

Aaron, Rabbi Y. N. ibn, also known as Yonah Fortner.Rabbi ibn Aaron was a key figure in the 1950s and 1960s in the New York City area UFOlogy circle centered around the Saucers and Unexplained Celestial Events Research Society's (SAUCERS) Discussion and Lecture Committee. Rabbi ibn Aaron collaborated with the late Dr. John J. Robinson in the Consultants Committee on Semitic Philology. A satirist of some talent, ibn Aaron collaborated on the "I Go to See..." series, which took a wickedly mirthful look at various UFO personalities, cults and groups. Rabbi ibn Aaron's key contribution, however, was his "Extraterrestrialism" series published in *Saucer News*, which postulated that ancient documents, including the Old Testament, were really *specific accounts of extraterrestrial visitations*. A linguist of great talent, he postulated that many biblical passages had been mistranslated, especially when Aramaic texts were mistaken for Hebrew. For example, the phrase *Ruach Elohim* — usually translated "Spirit of God" or "Wind of God" — may actually refer to a specific form of energy used by a race of extraterrestrial beings. Rabbi ibn Aaron anticipated the "chariots of the gods" idea by many years, and was far more literate in his exposition than anyone in the field, up until the comparable scholarship of Robert Temple's *The Sirius Mystery*. Rabbi ibn Aaron was an early organizer of The National UFO Conference. He died in 2005.

Achad, Frater, also known as Frater Parzifal, real name Charles Robert John Stansfeld Jones, born 1886, died 1952. Frater Achad is a key figure in the magical revival of the 20th century. Recognized by Aleister Crowley as his magical son (and presumable heir), Achad quickly rose to the leadership and initiatory summits of both Crowley's Ordo A∴A∴ and the Ordo Templi Orientis (OTO). After World War One he and Crowley parted company. Achad produced a number of remarkable works on the occult, notable for their originality and logical consistency. His *Book Thirty One (Liber XXXI)* provided the first serious clue to the cipher of the UFOnauts.

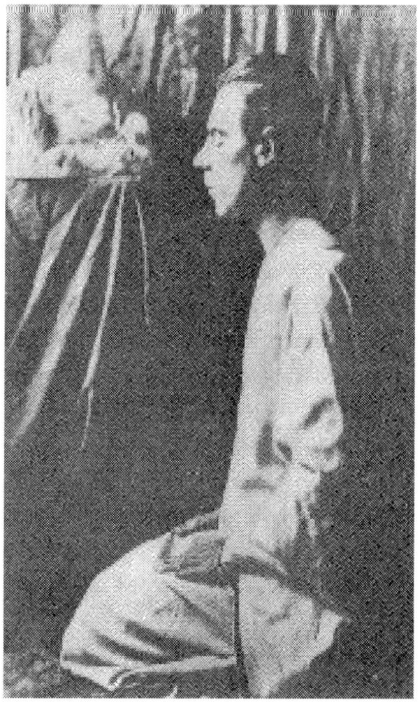

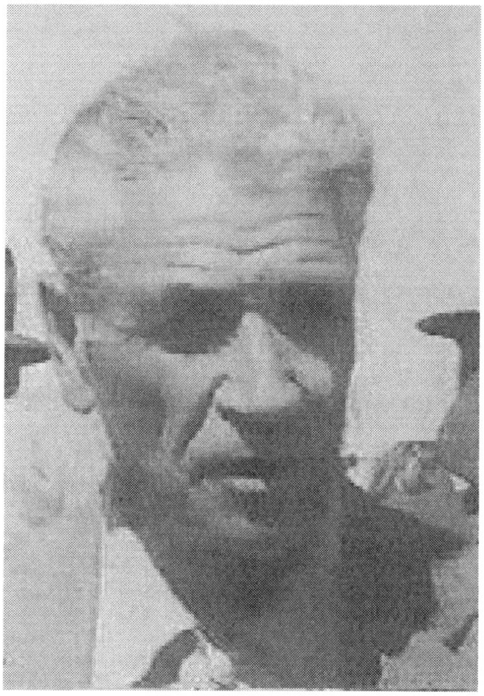

Adamski, George, the author of *Flying Saucers Have Landed* (with Desmond Leslie) and the first major claimant to UFO contact. Adamski's legendary contacts fell roughly into the category now called "the Blonds." The Polish-born American visionary was often derided for his humble vocation and high pretensions, as well as for his claims. But his story, first unsuccessfully submitted as a science fiction novel, has strong archetypal and mythic qualities that have repeatedly proven their psychological power. Said to have been seen immediately after his sudden death as a reborn space being with the name "Yamski." Adamski is buried at Arlington National Cemetary. His close early association with the initiate and New Age Guru George Hunt Williamson plays a key role in the saga of the cipher of the UFOnauts. He died April 22, 1965.

AIWASS, or Aiwaz, the "præter-human intelligence" who appeared to Aleister Crowley in Cairo in April 1904, dictating to him *The Book of the Law*, or *Liber AL vel Legis*. Although primarily associated with the Law of the New Aeon or Age of Aquarius, *The Book of the Law* predicts and contains the complete cipher of the UFOnauts. As far as is known, although not fully decoded until the 1970s even in the classical form, this cipher seems to have been in use both among the UFOnauts themselves for some time prior to the appearance of Aiwass. The physical description Crowley gives of Aiwass is virtually identical to those given in modern "men in black" cases.

Arnold, Kenneth. A pilot who made his way into history on June 24, 1947, when he reported sighting nine unidentified objects in the Cascade Mountains, which he described as "like saucers skipping over water" — the basis of the term "flying saucer," which has become part of the UFO story ever since. Arnold became closely associated with the late magazine publisher Raymond A. Palmer, for whom he investigated the first "men in black" incident.

Ballard, Guy Warren. Founder of the mystical I AM movement, Ballard was also associated with the fascist Silver Shirts prior to World War Two. George Hunt Williamson was associated with Ballard for a time.

Barker, Gray. Founder of Saucerian Publications and author of the first book on the "Three Men in Black" called *They Knew Too Much about the Flying Saucers*. Closely associated with Albert K. Bender, who founded the first UFO group (later suppressed by the Three Men in Black), Barker became a leader of the National UFO Conference. Never very far from the folklore of his native rural West Virginia, Barker's allegorical novel, *The Silver Bridge* ostensibly centers on the High Weirdness of the Mothman Scare and UFO sightings culminating in the Silver Bridge disaster of the mid-1960s. His work provides the closest clue to the solution of the UFO Mystery, up until the discovery of the Cipher of the UFOnauts. Barker, a close ally of James W. Moseley, died suddenly in the early 1980s.

Bell, Dr. Fred, contactee in communication with a female UFOnaut, one Semjase, a Pleiadean being, since 1971. Semjase has shown up in a number of other cases over the last twenty or so years.

Bethurum, Truman, became a contactee in 1952, with the female UFOnaut Aura Rhanes from the planet Clarion. A physical contactee of the Adamski type, Bethurum seemed a down-to-Earth person with an extraordinary story to tell.

Bimstein, Louis M., also known as Max Theon and Aia Aziz. The son of a Polish Rabbi, Bimstein traveled in nineteenth century Egypt and became a disciple of the Coptic Initiate Paolos Metamon, under whom he became the Grand Master of the Hermetic Brotherhood of Light. Bimstein later married the trance medium Mary Ware and became the conduit of "The Cosmic Philosophy." Virtually every modern occult movement, from the Theosophical Society to the followers of Sri Aurobindo in India, owe him a debt in their origins. Bimstein was a High Initiate, quite a mysterious person, and probably in constant contact with UFOnauts early on. He died in the early 1920s and has been largely forgotten until recently.

Blavatsky, Madame Helena P., affectionately known as "HPB" by her followers, co-founder and primary moving force of the Theosophical Society. A High Initiate, she was in communication with Exalted Adepts of the Great White Brotherhood through the main years of her career. She appears to be the first major historical personality to actively conceal the true names and origins of Initiates using the Cipher of the UFOnauts.

Crowley, Aleister, the scribe of *The Book of the Law* as dictated to him by the intelligence Aiwass. Crowley is the most significant figure of the occult revival of the 20th century. An initiate of the Hermetic Order of the Golden Dawn, and later leader of its successor Order, the A.·. A.·., Crowley was a magus, prophet, poet, mountaineer, author, lecturer and contactee. He wrestled all his adult life with the nature of the Higher Beings he contacted, such as Lam, Aiwass and Abuldiz. Reviled by many as a "black magician," he was a late Victorian English Gentleman to the end of his life. A man "intoxicated" with God, to borrow one of his biographers' terms, Crowley was neither a Satanist nor Black Magician. He died in poverty in 1947. Under his deathbed was found a considerable sum of money belonging to the Ordo Templi Orientis (OTO), which he had declined to spend, even on medicines that might have saved his life. His considerable contributions to the allied war effort in World War Two are little known. Little understood even by many of his (supposed) followers, his death in the same year that the UFO phenomenon came to public attention seems more than coincidental.

Damon, Frater, the Primate of the Qabalistic Alchemist Church. This organization, along with its sister group OAA in Britain, is most responsible for decoding and spreading the cipher of the UFOnauts. Damon studied the work of Frater Achad with the late Meade Layne in the 1950s, and co-founded the QAA/QBLH with Robert Dunlap in 1960.

Derenberger, Woodrow, a West Virginia contactee investigated by both author John Keel and, independently, by the late Gray Barker. His fateful encounter with a being "from a country weaker than your own" came during the heat of the Mothman Scare in West Virginia in 1966-67. An unassuming man, Derenberger, along with John Reeves, Joe Simonton and others, was a new breed of contactee with physical contact of the Adamski type, but without the philosophical content. These cases coincide roughly with the advent of the Betty and Barney Hill-type abduction cases.

Dick, Philip K., author from the 1950s until his death in the early 1980s of many allegorical novels dealing with alien civilizations and states of consciousness. He eventually revealed that his novels were built upon alien transmissions and a hidden cipher. In 1974 he received a spontaneous high initiation in cosmic consciousness. At his untimely death he was working on a series of novels based on his understanding of the aliens' intentions towards Earth. Notable works include *The Man in the High Castle, VALIS* and *The Divine Invasion.* The critically acclaimed science fiction film *Blade Runner* is loosely based on his novel *Do Androids Dream of Electric Sheep.*

Jung, Dr. Carl, the famed Swiss psychiatrist and creator of Analytic Psychology, a theory that relies on the importance of archetypes. Dr. Jung was a member of the National Investigations Committee on Aerial Phenomena (NICAP) and author of a book about UFOs considered from an archetypal and mythic base, *Flying Saucers: A Modern Myth of Things Seen in the Sky.*

Keel, John A., adventurer and author, his early pursuit of occult mysteries are chronicled in *JADOO*. His interest in UFOs led to the development of an Ultraterrestrial alternative to the Extraterrestrial Hypothesis. A prime investigator of the Mothman cases, his *UFOs: Operation Trojan Horse* and *The Mothman Prophecies* clearly show the linkage between things UFOlogical and things occult. A man of dry wit and a speaker with considerable personal charisma, Keel's hidden asset is his ability to tune one in to the high strangeness aspect of the UFO phenomenon in a way that can only result from direct field work.

King, George, one of the premiere "trance channel" contactees since 1955. King and his Aetherius Society form one of the direct links between occultism and UFOlogy, in that King claims to be a direct agent of The Great White Brotherhood working diligently with our extraterrestrial allies against the Black Lodge.

Lamed, Frater who, as the former Timothy Coutu, a chief of the QBLH and computer programming specialist, learned computer programming for an opportunity to do serious original work with the Cipher. Laying out the 1974 cipher solution on a 26-point star pattern, Frater Lamed was eventually able to generate thousands of "cipher star" variants, highly suggestive of a "starseed transmission" based on the cipher hidden in *The Book of the Law*.

Lightlines Group, organized in Kentucky by Carla Rueckert and the late Don Elkins. Lightlines is one of the few trance channel contactee bodies making no claims for the true nature of its channelings, and known for doing systematic research on the process of communication. Elkins was an Eastern Airline pilot but also an accomplished trance medium, best known for the work eventually published as *The Ra Material*.

Layne, Meade, founder of the venerable Borderland Sciences Research Foundation. Layne was for many years the editor of BSRF's *Round Robin* and other journals, and he worked closely with trance channeler Mark Probert. Layne was also a student of the work of Frater Achad. At one time, Layne had been a member of the Society of the Inner Light, a direct offspring of the Hermetic Order of the Golden Dawn. At the end of the 19th century, this Society developed its rituals from certain Rosicrucian cipher manuscripts based in the teachings of the Third Order, or Secret Chiefs, or Ascended Masters — which are identical with the Space People in contact lore. That so much cipher material shows up in and around Layne, who was said to be in frequent communication with the Great White Brotherhood, is highly suggestive that he was one of those who introduced the cipher into UFO trance-channeled contactee lore. Layne was also writing about flying discs before Kenneth Arnold's sightings. He also introduced the idea of channeled masters to UFOlogy.

Moseley, James W., the founder of the Saucers and Unexplained Celestial Events Research Society (SAUCERS). Since 1954 he has published some variation of *SAUCER News*. For many years Moseley was the primary mover and shaker in UFOlogy in the New York area. He was a fixture on early talk radio programs, and was an intimate collaborator with the late Gray Barker. The wealthy son of a U. S. Army General, Moseley has always approached the UFO mystery with a note of humor and common-sense skepticism, which has brought him more than a few critics. He has for many years served as Chairman of the National UFO Conference.

Newbrough, John, known mainly for his channeled communication of the mystical work *Oahspe* in the late nineteenth century.

Palmer, Raymond A., was a publisher of conventional science fiction magazines until 1943. Then he began publication of the writings of Richard Shaver, which purported to be accounts of real extra terrestrial visitations and an off-world origin for the human race. For this, Palmer was eventually drummed out of science fiction circles. After cofounding *Fate* magazine with Curtis Fuller in the 1950s, Palmer went on to publish *Flying Saucers* magazine and *Search* until his death in the 1970s. He republished the Shaver material in the early 1960s and was a fighter for unorthodox causes until the end of his life. He claimed for many years to be in possession of a mysterious "FACT" that explained the UFO mystery. This "FACT" appears to have been the cipher of the UFOnauts. Little known to his admirers and critics alike, Palmer was a victim of great physical handicaps, apparently the product of birth defects and a tragic accident in childhood. Living a retiring life in rural Wisconsin in his later years, Ray Palmer overcame great personal obstacles to be a literary figure of some note.

Prophet, Elizabeth, and the late **Mark Prophet**, (r), crossovers between classical mediumship and modern trance channeling. It is significant that some of the beings Ms. Prophet purports to channel are the very real and physical Adepts known a century earlier by Madame Blavatsky and others, under their assumed names.

Randolph, Dr. P. B., an American occultist who introduced some of the more profound secret hermetic doctrines to both American and European initiates.

Shaver, Richard Sharpe, an untutored, unlettered blue collar worker who began hearing voices and wound up developing an entire mythos peopled by cavern-dwelling survivors of ancient space-based races of beings who long ago settled and later abandoned the Earth. His wild, unstructured imagery was polished for publication by Ray Palmer, creating a major scandal and a now largely forgotten furor in science fiction circles in the 1940s. His Mantong Alphabet bears a startling resemblance to the Cipher of the UFOnauts. Shaver asserted that all languages were descended from Mantong, the ancient language of the universe, and could therefore be decoded by those not conversant in a specific language, such as English. In Shaver's view, English is a bastardized reinvention of Mantong.

Stranges, Rev. Frank, California clergyman and UFOlogist who met a man at the Pentagon claiming to be an alien being. A minister and the son of a minister, Stranges received much flack by talking about aliens in communication with the government a generation before other UFOlogists were even willing to consider the idea.

Tassel, George Van, early physical contactee and founder of the first UFO conclave, the long-defunct Giant Rock Conventions. Van Tassel also engaged in psychic communications and was closely associated with the earliest New Age groupings, which, to some extent, started at Giant Rock. Of particular interest is that, beginning in 1952, Van Tassel was in communication with a being calling itself "Ashtar" — the name of a medieval demon said, in the old magical texts, to have relocated to America. Ashtar has shown up in many subsequent cases.

Williamson, George Hunt ("Ric"), claimed a doctorate in anthropology and was a one-time follower of Guy Ballard's I AM movement, an organization with an unsavory reputation for overlap with the pro-Nazi Silver Shirts, an American subversive body broken up by the U. S. Government after America entered World War Two. Williamson, who was born in 1926, was one of Adamski's original contact witnesses, but speedily developed a vast following of his own for his channeled communications. Other communications were by radio. A mysterious and elusive figure, his best-known works include *The Saucers Speak* and *Other Tongues, Other Flesh*, but he was sometimes rumored dead long before his (presumed) actual demise in January 1986. Ric Williamson organized the mysterious Brotherhood of the Seven Rays, which he presided over as Brother Philip in a remote retreat high in the Andes Mountains of South America. He was certainly an Initiate, much given to ciphers and intrigue. One can only guess at his complex motives.

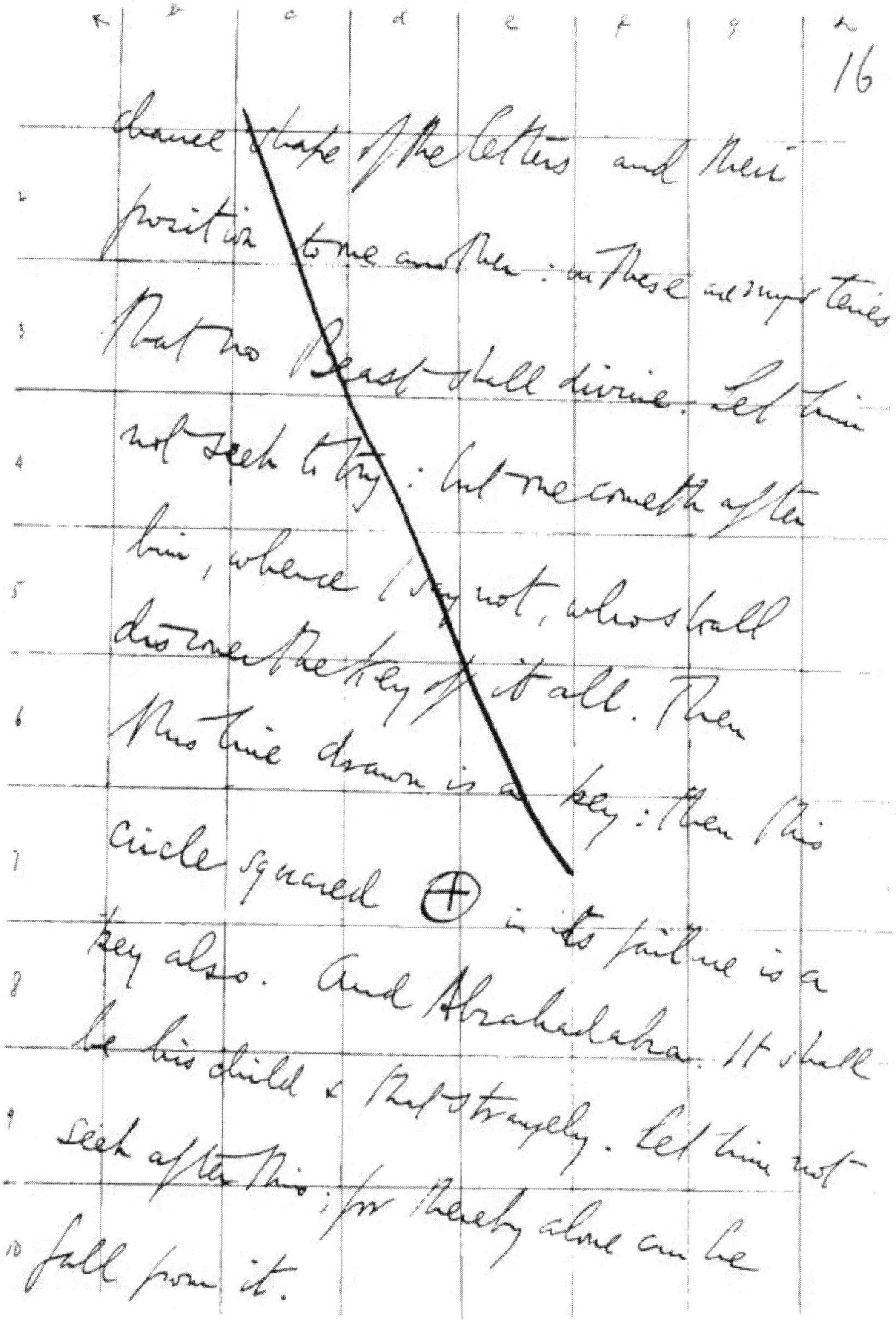
16

chance shape of the letters and their
position to one another: in these are mysteries
that no Beast shall divine. Let him
not seek to try: but one cometh after
him, whence I say not, who shall
discover the Key of it all. Then
this line drawn is a key: then this
circle squared ⊕ in its failure is a
key also. And Abrahadabra. It shall
be his child & that strangely. Let him not
seek after this; for thereby alone can he
fall from it.

The Grid Page from *Liber AL vel Legis.*

3
Secret Cipher of the UFOnauts Discovered

As those who have studied the prehistory of UFOlogy will tell you, UFOs and rumors of them have seemingly been around as long as human beings have looked up and wondered at the vast fantasia playing itself out every day and night in the sky. As the old song says, "At night the sky puts on a show for free." In the process of looking at the then-unpolluted skies, the Babylonian, Mayan, Chinese and Egyptian astronomers and magi developed both a vast and complex mythology of gods and heroes and a means of foretelling the future, or, as they would have it, the Will of Heaven. In time they would also learn that knowledge of the sky led to the ability to predict the seasons and impressive celestial events, such as lunar and solar eclipses. With this knowledge came power over humanity, and the magi were not mere philosophers and stargazers, but priest-kings favored by the gods with the foreknowledge of agricultural cycles, then fast becoming the basis of life and death for civilization.

That other, irregular events were noted as well can be defined as the beginning of UFOlogy. No doubt to some extent we can explain such events in terms of comets and supernovæ. However, these celestial occurrences leave unexplained such events as the mythos surrounding the Star Sirius and the knowledge of its dark star neighbor, or semi-aquatic beings called the "Oannes." (Oannes were considered visitors from the Sirius region who taught on Earth and left behind a divine mythos and a priesthood awaiting their return. They are known to the Sumerians and their Babylonian successors, and to the Egyptians, and held as legends to the present day by remote African tribal priesthoods.) Nor do comets and supernovæ explain the ascent of Elijah alive into heaven, nor the vision of Ezekiel the prophet, which in Hebrew is even eerier than in the English translation.

A priesthood protecting what it took to be the secrets of the divine visitors, whether an actuality or not, has existed since these remote times. In the early ages when the ability to build observatories overlapped with the ability to predict and therefore control civilization, the intermeshing of early Operative Masonic fraternities and the priest-kings or Magi or Magicians was to be expected. Because these guild secrets were of utmost importance in preserving both power and wisdom, a whole system of secret oaths, signs, ciphers and grips was developed to protect these secrets under the highest penalties for betrayal, along with a webwork of mystery plays or rituals to explain to the heirs of these secrets what it was they were preserving, and why. Here we have the beginning of a two-class system consisting of those who know and those who do not know.

While this was developing, millennia were passing, Aeons giving way to one another, and new observations of phenomena in the sky continued. New cults arose, only to intermesh with older ones through conquest or exchange of information. A rich and ever-developing mythology became more and more complex. The question arises, were there new contacts with the Divine Beings, or only new legends and variations of old legends? I suggest to you that present-day contact cases and sightings indicate ongoing communication. In fact, modern UFOlogy emerged from a narrow circle of survivors in possession of all or part of the "old knowledge" trying to look into the new sightings and contacts in the hope of renewing their communication with the Ancient Gods. Key figures included Meade Layne and Ric Williamson. Both Layne and Williamson show traditional knowledge of the lore of the Magi, trance mediumship — the 19th and early 20th century descendant of the ancient oracles and sybils — and an interest in developing trance channeling oriented upon the then-emerging modern flying saucer lore.

But I am getting ahead of myself. My subject here is the Cipher of the UFOnauts. I will document this cipher for you and show you how to decode the cipher, which has been in continuous use since the legendary visit by the gods of Sirius. In the early 18th century Craft Masonic bodies formally merged in a Grand Lodge that included Speculative Masons; these individuals — mostly aristocrats of wealth and power — were not skilled at the building arts and had no direct connection, in most cases, with the rich lore of Rosicrucian and Masonic legend. They settled on a system of three initiatory degrees, the Entered Apprentice, Fellow Craft and Master Mason. This tri-fold system does indeed correspond to the communication of the formal guild secrets of Operative, or practical Masonry, but has little of the metaphysical meaning and a distinct feel of incompleteness. Later a so-called "Royal Arch" degree, which attempted to deal with many questions unanswered in the Craft degrees, became popular with Masons. The Royal Arch came to include the communication of a Secret Cipher, cleverly built upon angles and dots and directly translatable into English. This would seem to suggest a late date for the cipher, but it corresponds to the Key to the much older Aiq Bakir, the Hebrew Qabala of the Nine Chambers, and is an obvious English adaptation of a much older cipher. In its present form it decodes easily and has been so often exposed in the last 150 years that its value as a cipher is actually now greatly diminished.

The Golden Dawn cipher documents are considerably more complex. They were probably drawn up in the 1860s or 1870s, and they seem to be notes rather than a complete system of occult work. Into this system Aleister Crowley was initiated. Born Edward Alexander Crowley, he changed his name to Aleister at about the same time he joined the Golden Dawn. He tells us the switch in names is from the Gælic form of Alexander, but, as he admits, this should be spelled properly "A-L-A-I-S-D-A-I-R" and not "A-L-E-I-S-T-E-R." This distinction becomes more important later.

Crowley was sometimes called "the wickedest man in the world" — an alleged Satanist, sexual pervert and perhaps murderer. By the time of his death in 1947, whatever one may have thought of Crowley, names like Hitler and Stalin made the charge almost humorous. In any case, most of what one hears about Crowley's wickedness is based upon false rumors and Crowley's experimentation with drugs and various forms of sexuality as methods for consciousness expansion, when such methods were decidedly out of favor. (Those who lived through the experimentation of the 1960s would actually find his activities relatively tame.) But Crowley developed his reputation in the late Victorian and Edwardian eras. (Oscar Wilde and D. H. Lawrence suffered similar fates.) That Crowley was a master occultist, though, is certainly true. Central to our premise is a single occult event in which Crowley, then on an extended honeymoon with his wife Rose in Cairo, acted as scribe in the transcription of what purports to be a Holy Book for the New Aeon, known as *Liber AL vel Legis*, or *The Book of the Law*. *Liber AL* in some ways follows the same pattern as Newborough's *Oahspe* or *The Book of Mormon*. It differs in its outlook, the richness of its poetry, and, for our purposes, in one other way. *It refers to an internal cipher or secret code which, it predicts, Crowley himself would never transcribe.* Predicted, however, is its deciphering by another, who turned out to be Crowley's magical child and one-time heir-apparent, Charles Stansfeld Jones, sometimes called Frater Achad. Achad, in his *Book 31*, does indeed find the key to the code, but 70 years passed before a full transcription of the code was made.

In the original handwritten manuscript of *The Book of the Law*, a single page is inexplicably overlaid with a grid, a line, and an enigmatic mark sometimes referred to as a "Rose Cross," although it looks much like one of the four keys to the Royal Arch Masonic Cipher. *Liber AL* was dictated in 1904, according to Crowley, by a præterhuman — some of his successors say extraterrestrial — intelligence calling itself Aiwass. Long after both Achad and Crowley were dead, one Carol Smith and a group in England calling itself the OAA fully deciphered the code. Another 10 years were to pass before a member of OAA's American counterpart, Frater Lamed of QBLH, was to apply computer technology to the cipher solution and produce Lexicon, a computer program that provides a vast, powerful tool for deciphering the code of *Liber AL*, as well as many variants.

I had been a UFOlogist for 30 years and a student of the western occult tradition for almost as long before I hit upon a discovery that could completely change forever the way any intelligent student thinks—or should think—about either UFOlogy or the occult. I had long noted, for example, that in the earlier contactee cases, when names were given by the purported aliens for themselves, their home world, etc., they often were very odd names. I looked many years ago for puns. I mused that perhaps, for example, Woodrow Derenberger's 1966 encounter in West Virginia with INDRID COLD from the planet LANULUS had something to do with myth and legend. Jacques Vallee and John Keel had both pointed out the connection with mythic names and legends, and I thought LANULUS might be a play on "LAND YOU LOST" or "LAND YOU LUST" — a reference to Atlantis lore, or legendary shadow lands such as Færie or Magonia. But such answers seemed, like the Masonic Third Degree, somehow incomplete.

I was aware, also, that similar names had shown up as discarnate beings and controls in 19th and early 20th century trance mediumship, UFO contactee trance channeling and, later, the trance channeling so trendy since the *Seth Material* of Jane Roberts in the 1970s. As a former elected member of the British Society for Psychical Research, I saw a connectedness but could not make out the actual connection.

When I started working with the 1974 cipher solution to *The Book of the Law*, however, as an idle experiment I began applying the cipher work to the "funny" names from mediumship, contacteeism and trance channeling, and what I found constitutes the solution to the UFO mystery.

I do not make such a claim idly. Others have made such claims, but verifiable proofs and methods of obtaining proofs have not been forthcoming. This volume presents for your illumination and, hopefully, edification, the cipher itself: its various decoding methods, its computer variants and some applications that will lead you directly to the truth about UFOs. I'm not suggesting that this is the only method by which one can solve the UFO mystery. I am suggesting that it is the easiest and most straightforward, and the most accessible to any intelligent lay person.

Although the Cipher Solution is embedded in *The Book of the Law*, it apparently does not originate there. While the Royal Arch Masonic cipher is communicated to initiates as an English Language cipher, it is actually, as noted above, rooted in the Hebrew Qabala, and is limited in function for English speaking adepts and initiates. It was soon exposed, but by the mid-19th century something new was afoot in the occult underground.

[I must return momentarily to the High Middle Ages, the Renaissance, and the period of the Protestant Reformation in Europe. The persecution of real or imagined witches, heretics, Jews, Moslems and occultists was then at a peak, and the heirs of the illuminated tradition—the Templars, Cathars, Albigensians and other Gnostics—were forced to resort to a roundabout code or cipher to carry on their ideas in relative safety. New ciphers were developed. The cryptic language of alchemy that so intrigued Carl Jung and others overlaps with the Rosicrucian tradition. A key work that dates to the 1600s, *The Alchymical Wedding of Christian Rosenkreutz*, contains a specifically Rosicrucian cipher.]

Beginning in the mid-19th century we suddenly see the occult tradition renew an ancient practice, speaking through oracular entranced prophets in voices other than their own. Trance mediumship to communicate with the dead was the first version, but this was soon followed by various kinds of channelings and contacts with higher beings manifesting in the so-called "Mahatmas" of the Theosophical Society. Examples include the Secret Chiefs of the Third Order in the Golden Dawn and related societies; the UFO-related channelings of Mark Probert and the Inner Circle, Dick Miller and many to follow; along with the alleged physical contacts of Adamski, Bethurum, George King and others; and finally the channeling of Jane Roberts' Seth, Jach Purcel's Lazaris, Don Elkins' Ra, and others down to the present time.

In short, the rules of the game seem to have changed. What happened? Did the exposé of Freemasonry by Morgan, who was murdered for his trouble, and others have something to do with it? The rules were reaching public knowledge just at the time the Fox sisters began to hear the spirit rappings that set in motion the Spiritualist phenomena. The result was routine and widespread trance channeling supposedly in a straightforward manner, without initiation, ciphers or symbols. If a control calls itself "Katie King," one tends to accept the name as just that: a name, not a cipher key. But, with the decoding of *Liber AL*'s cipher, this proved not to be the case. *The names are meant to convey a second, more important meaning, but only for those able to decode it.*

One premise I must suggest is that, after the 1974 cipher discovery, the rules began to change again. It took 10 years for the cipher to be exploited by adepts, and at least another 10 for you to read about it. But in the meantime, as if the phenomena responded to obscure events in human history, after 1973 the rules, for the most part, were different. The last classical UFO flap was in 1973, and this itself emphasized the growing "contact without communication" with impersonal nonhuman aliens very unlike ORTHON and AURA RHANES. "Grays" and "Blonds" were always present in UFO lore, although mostly in France and Latin America prior to the '73 flap. Indeed, the Betty and Barney Hill abduction case was, when it appeared in the 1960s, a total departure in American close encounter cases. But, after 1973, the "personal aliens with funny names" were nearly universally replaced with blonds and grays. Dr. Fred Bell's Semjase, also contacted by Billy Meier, began prior to 1973. Other repeat contacts of the Old School go on, but there are few new ones. The alien names have all but vanished from newer cases.

But now we can decode the older cases based on their key word or phrase, usually embedded in the name of the alleged alien, a planetary name or a strange turn of phrase. For example, George Adamski's long-haired visitor from the sky calling for peace on Earth and good will, one ORTHON, decodes readily to the name JESUS. The name Adamski means "Son of Adam"—he is said to have returned from the dead with a new name and renewed youth, apparently raised by Orthon and friends in a bizarre parallel to the New Testament's promise of redemption and resurrection. In the West Virginia flap of the mid-1960s, we can see now that the "beings with funny names" who appear dotted among the so-called "Mothman" accounts predict the latter, along with the very real and tragic Silver Bridge Disaster, for anyone who took the trouble to decode their names. But INDRID COLD and CARL ARDO appear in 1966 and 1967, and the classical solution to the Cipher in *The Book of the Law* wasn't discovered until 1974.

What goes on here? Like the old alchemical ciphers, the messages of the contactees are meant to be truly understood *only by deep initiates in possession of the code out of which the cipher was constructed.* Madame Blavatsky the Theosophist used the code in concealing the very real identities of her so-called "Mahatmas." She clearly knew the code, or her Mahatmas did, when she invented substitute names like Morya and

Koot Hoomi. But she was long dead when *The Book of the Law* appeared in 1904. As to UFOlogy, we have indicated that the cipher seems to have been introduced early on by such persons as Meade Layne and Ric Williamson. Williamson may have helped Adamski concoct or develop his Orthon story and the like. How great their individual knowledge was of what they were doing is unclear.

Layne seems an exemplary person, a student of Aleister Crowley's prodigal son Charles Stansfeld Jones (Frater Achad), and, from the 1940s, one of the saner, more decent sorts that occupied the more esoteric side of UFOlogy. Frater Damon, later to head one of the organizations following up on Frater Achad's work, recalls that it was Layne who introduced him to Achad's work in the mid-1950s. He also recalls how Layne would visit him in Arizona while on expeditions in search of UFO landing sights in the desert

These events become curiouser and curiouser. Damon's organization, the Quabalistic Alchemist Arcanum, and its British counterpart the Ordo Argentium Astrum or Order of the Silver Star, discovered and promulgated the very cipher we are discussing, and, indeed, does so to this day. I believe that through his occult sources, Layne knew the cipher and knew that the establishment of a "magical link with the Secret Chiefs," or contact with the UFOnauts in other words, could be effected by examining the available literature, and seeking the key words for clues to who and where the Secret Chiefs were to be found.

Both Aleister Crowley and Frater Achad were in contact with the Secret Chiefs. When Crowley engaged in a magical working, these præterhuman intelligences would consistently arrive on the scene. One of them, calling itself LAM, was sketched by Crowley and is the prototype of the current alien types seen in present-day abduction cases. In the cipher of *Liber AL,* which Crowley himself did not know, LAM is the equivalent of GOD. Crowley only associated the word with the Tibetan Lama, the living, consciously reincarnating Buddha. The peculiarity of LAM being the prototype of the current abduction type has been noted'by UFOlogists, but without the KEY they can only remark of the coincidence.

Does this mean that ORTHON is JESUS, or LAM is GOD?

Hardly. The cipher, as becomes apparent to the diligent researcher, only uses the name or key-word for those in the know to examine and find a curious correspondence, pointing the way to whatever the essence of the encounter is. The clues in the Adamski case would have yielded to the initiate of these runes, for example, that the Yamski reincarnation episode was bound to happen immediately upon Adamski's death. This leads to the well-known scientific prerequisite –the ability to predict the results of an experiment. For example, Truman Bethurum's contact, Aura Rhanes, a female and thus unusual in the history of contactee accounts, has the cipher meaning of female. One would then expect, in future funny-name cases with female entities, some cipher reference to the femaleness of the being hidden in the being's name. Thus, when Semjase arrives in Fred Bell's life, we are not surprised to find her name the equivalent of gynander, the female in a so-called male role. Further, when we find her to come from a planet she calls "Erra," the exact equivalent of Al Bender's contact word "Kazik," we can predict without knowing the details that first communication will be mental or telepathic, followed by more physical encounters. So it is.

But who plants such messages, and why? To answer this, one must apply the cipher knowledge to the world of deep occultism, of which UFOs are but a surface manifestation. The answers do not come from anything as simple as mental aberrations and hoaxes on the one hand, nor interstellar visitors and vast government conspiracies on the other. As historian Paul Johnson has shown, the Theosophical Mahatmas were neither the discarnate semi-deities of the believers nor Madame Blavatsky's fraudulent deceptions of the skeptics. Rather, they were real people—adepts or initiates of the Deep Wisdom perhaps, but people nonetheless—with radical political and spiritual agendas that made pseudonyms a necessity. The names such Mahatmas and Chiefs took were, in very truth, noms de guerre: the kind of names underground members adapt in wartime to protect themselves and their loved ones from arrest, murder or reprisal. Curiously, it was this term, nom de guerre, that Edward Alexander Crowley used to describe his adaptation of the name "Aleister," which carries the same cipher value as FRATER ACHAD, the magical name taken by his spiritual son and heir many years later. Such matters suggest varying levels of awareness of the cipher, and an agenda that can be learned, and indeed tapped into, by one in possession of the KEY. The word "Key" by the way, is equivalent to the word SOLVE in cipher.

Discovering and cracking the code is only a beginning. To use the code and trace the UFOnauts to their doorsteps requires understanding its specifics. I have avoided technicalities in this preliminary exposition so as not to detract from the momentous discovery itself. I will next go into the details of the nature of the cipher, the cipher itself, the Lexicon computer program (which, it needs to be emphasized, gives over 20,000 workable variations of the original cipher, a mere fraction of the number of potential ciphers), the mechanics of deciphering, what to look for to decipher, and what deciphering the secret code of the UFOnauts reveals of their origin and character.

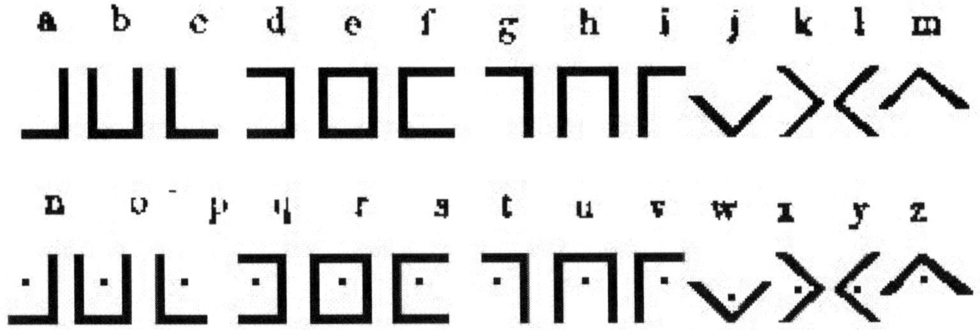

Masonic Cipher.

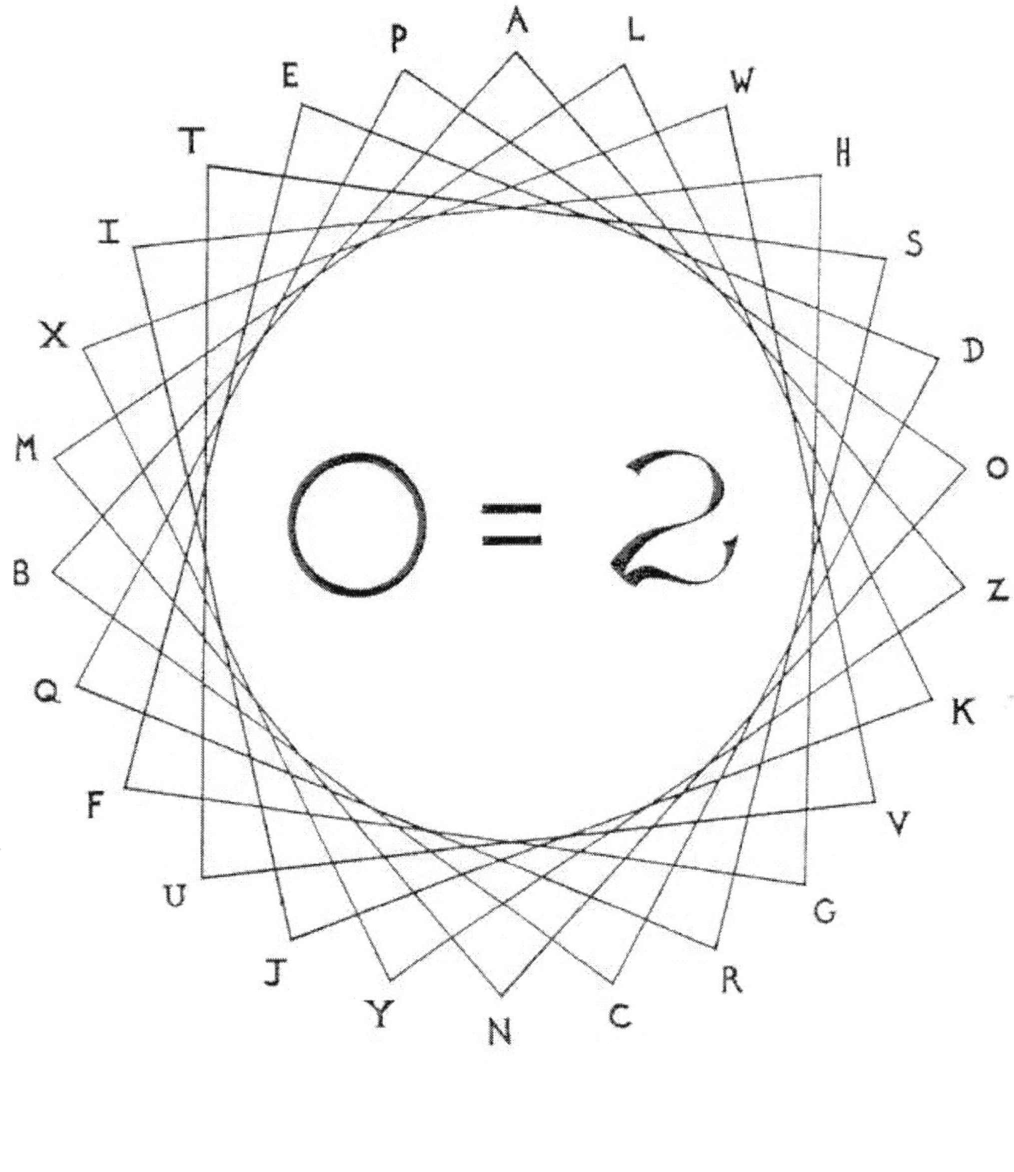

From The Equinox Volume VII, No. 1.

4

Secret Cipher of the UFOnauts Developed

It is impossible to understand the keys to the modern magical revival and its connection to UFOlogy and the Secret Cipher of the UFOnauts without understanding the context of the times in which modern ritual magical societies arose. Europe ruled the world in the late 19th century, and conspiracies proliferated. Literature abounded with stories of spies and revolutionists, real and imagined. A. Conan Doyle devoted the Sherlock Holmes story, "*The Adventure of the Dancing Men*," to explaining the rudiments of cipher analysis, a feature of many fictional works of the period.

The 1890s marked the beginning period, or revival, of many trends, organizations and tendencies that profoundly affected the New Age movement of the next 100 years. In Germany, Dr. Kellner and Dr. Reuss began organizing the Ordo Templi Orientis (OTO). In England, Victorian occultism reached its peak in the Hermetic Order of the Golden Dawn. In the Southeastern United States, the Hermetic Brotherhood of Light established its new headquarters. Shortly thereafter, strange airships began appearing across America. Their even stranger pilots would often tell witnesses that they were headed for the Southeastern U.S.

It should come as no surprise that various occult luminaries of the era were rumored to be secret agents (and perhaps revolutionary conspirators); Madame Blavatsky, Theodor Reuss and Aleister Crowley all were so suspected, and Blavatsky and Reuss certainly interacted with revolutionary conspirators on a regular basis.

The basic documents of the Hermetic Order of the Golden Dawn were written in a strange cipher that may have originated with such continental adepts. As noted earlier, all Royal Arch Masons were taught a special cipher on the occasion of their initiation. Thus, that a cipher was included in *The Book of the Law* —dictated to Aleister Crowley by the shadowy, mysterious Aiwass on April 8, 9, and 10, 1904 at Cairo—should come as no surprise. The cipher is repeatedly referred to in the text and is associated with the "grid page" in *Liber AL*. In *Liber XXXI* (*Book 31*), Frater Achad began the process of deciphering the code of AL, deducing the first three letters (A,L, W) but, as Crowley himself noted, little of value resulted.

Things could not rest there. "It is impossible to understand *The Book of the Law* without recourse to the English Qaballa, but those who possess the English Qaballa of AI will see by its numerical commentary the true meaning of existence and the mechanisms of the magick of the New Aeon," wrote Greatly Honored Brother P-Achad-O in *The British Journal of Ceremonial Magick*. He went on to say, "The law of Thelema is the green shoot of spring opening up amongst the death and decay of a defunct Aeon. It is hardly visible, yet it will grow to produce an as-yet unknown species of Mankind. A Mankind who will look back on these centuries as the truly dark ages of instinctual man: when men killed each other for illusory gain based upon the idea that it is possible to gain anything in a world in which we have no permanent home. It is as impossible to imagine Thelemic man as it would be impossible for an ape to imagine he could be us." ("Thelemic" being from the Greek word for Will, *thelema*—that is, a humanity governed by Pure Will rather than idle whim.)

So the matter, indeed, could not rest In 1974 a cipher solution consistent with all the clues in *The Book of the Law* was discovered. The solution produced immediate, specific results.

"A key has been left by Crowley, under the direction of Aiwass," wrote Carol Smith in 1980, "in order that 'Thou shalt obtain the Order and Value of the English Alphabet' (Ch.1 V.55) The instruction is in Ch.1lI V.47 'This shall be translated into all tongues but always with the originals in the writing of the beast; for in the chance shape of the letters and their position to one another; in these are mysteries no beast shall divine."' Aleister Crowley, in sardonic commentary on his fundamentalist Plymouth Brethren upbringing, called himself "the Great Beast."

In Crowley's original *Liber AL*, Sheet 16 of Chapter III is a page containing the balance of verse 47 written over a grid made with simple lines. An unexplained diagonal line crosses the page, and a circle with an X in it appears near the end of this line. Published versions of the text that do not reproduce the original omit this peculiarity, which the text itself cautions against.

Carol A. Smith continues:

> There are letters along the top of the page, and it would seem to be obvious to continue with the alphabet in the manner indicated, but the clue is in the numbers down the side. A is written instead of 1 which suggests that B is 2, C 3 and so on. Fill in all the squares on the grid in this manner, repeating the alphabet when one gets to Z. To proceed to the next step the instruction is written on the page, for those who have eyes to see. 'Then this line drawn is a key.' The line drawn is a diagonal line across the page. If one reads any diagonal across the square one gets the order of the English alphabet to be used in the English Qaballa. Whichever diagonal is read the order of the letters is obtained. There is only one order which can be obtained and all 26 letters appear in this order.

Crowley writes, "Then this line drawn is a key...and Abrahadabra." "Abrahadabra" is an 11-fold word, and counting down 11 spaces and numbering the letters thus obtained in sequence gives one the "Value of the English Alphabet." Thus we have both order and value, as mandated in *Liber AL*

"The line drawn and the rose cross symbol bear a striking resemblance to the area where the key is revealed, " notes Smith. But one cannot appreciate this without -he original handwritten text at hand. As I have discovered the "rose cross" (which looks like a circle with a simple cross superimposed, or a gun site, or register mark) may contain other secrets. By following the line drawn down from the top of the page to its end at the "rose cross" one can find a method for obtaining both order and value in a single operation, after moving the block of four letters suggested by the "rose cross" to the page top at the upper end of the diagonal line. Order and value then no longer fail—and repeat to infinity.

Jake Stratton-Kent puzzled over the strange string of letters and numbers in *Liber AL* 11:76:

> 4 6 3 8 A B K 2 4 A L G M O R 3 y X 24 89 R P S T O V A L "What meaneth this, o prophet? Thou knowest not; nor shalt thou know ever. There cometh one to follow thee: he shall expound it."

"When I first had my attention drawn to the existence of a purported English Qaballa, my first reaction as a quabalist was to use it on this meaningless string of digits and characters," Stratton-Kent tells us. "I converted all the letters into their numerical equivalents in the E.Q, and added them to the numbers in the series." In the original handwritten text, the string of letters and numbers is divided into two lines, the first ending with "Y" and the second beginning with "X." Stratton-Kent goes on: "There are seventeen numbers and letters in the first line and eleven in the second . . . but in the manuscript the 'X' at the beginning of line two looks like a multiplication symbol so I made this calculation; 17 x 11 = 187, the numerical value of the phrase 'ENGLISH ALPHABET.'"

There have been further developments. This cipher solution was uncovered in 1974, fully 70 years after the writing of *Liber AL* In 1979 Frater Lamed of the magical-qabalistic order known as the QBLH was introduced to the cipher solution, and soon began work on expanding the scope of knowledge in this area with computer technology. "My first attempt, " says Frater Lamed, "led me to producing a 26-pointed star" (After the 26 letters in the English alphabet). After various efforts over several years, "I began to re-examine the 26-pointed star that I had drawn years before. The Classical English Qabala contains a cycle of 11. That is, you start at A, count 11 letters and reach L, count another 11 letters and you reach W and so on until you get back to A again. It's clean and simple. So I wondered how many stars could be drawn." This eventually led to Frater Lamed's development of the computer program, Lexicon, which at this writing yields over 20,000 alternate cipher solutions, all mapped on a 26-pointed star pattern. Millions of failures were encountered in the process, and the surface has barely been scratched. Is this somehow embedded in the cipher of *Liber AL*? There are intriguing hints. For example, successful cipher 360 (as in 360 degrees in a circle) yields a circular pattern.

But to say that there are over 20,000 variants of the cipher embedded in *The Book of the Law* creates a certain intimidation factor. To say that these are only a small fraction of the actual number of successful ciphers hidden therein is, therefore, almost so intimidating as to scare away even the most dedicated reader.

To those who may find the whole process intimidating or confusing, let me make a few observations, and several clarifications.

The 1974 solution itself: when worked with by qabalistic researchers, produces profound, startling and immediate results. The technical nature of this work sometimes causes the uninitiated to pass it by, but the few who have examined it are generally convinced that magicians in the Thelemic Aeon, regardless of their degree, grade or level, are grossly at a disadvantage without proficiency in the tools of New Aeon English Qabala. *Liber AL* asserts this, but substantial research now backs up this claim. As the ciphers thus generated seem to be at work in UFO cases as well it should also be of vital importance to UFOlogists. Hidden grimoires—secret books of magick and knowledge of the inner secrets of the UFOnauts—are beginning to arise.

To begin with, there is probably more useful knowledge to be gained from the "original" cipher derived directly from the KEY in *The Book of the Law* than any person, even with computer assistance, could mine in a lifetime of creative effort. The number of cipher "Stars" is almost as large as the number of stars in the sky. Our inability to number, or name—let alone understand—them all should no more stand in our way than astronomers allow the great variety and number of stars, comets, planets and black holes in the heavens to prevent the investigation of an asteroid or, for that matter, the age of the universe.

If we confine ourselves to the single original cipher (see illustration), we discover that A=1, L=2, W=3, etc. Once you understand this, it becomes easy to see that the most basic function is to reduce a given interesting word or name or phrase to its numerical value. What constitutes an interesting word or phrase? The answer to that question depends upon one's line of research.

Using these three initial letters alone, A/L/W or 1/2/3, we can derive its numerical value by simply adding the value of each letter, or 1+2+3 which, of course, equals a value of 6. In this case, the letters themselves form an obvious anagram for the word LAW. This might be an interesting area for an occultist, as this initial finding is the key word in the name of the book in which the cipher is hidden, *The Book of the Law*. It becomes more interesting when we discover that the number value, 6, is the actual number of the successful cipher it is derived from in the computer program Lexicon. That is, it was the 6th successful cipher generated by computer. (An "unsuccessful cipher" would be one that duplicates a number value before giving a separate value for each of the 26 letters of the standard alphabet.) As noted earlier, Cipher 6 involves numbering the letters A-Z by counting down from the letter A 11 times, numbering the next letter (L) 2, counting down 11 spaces again, numbering W as 3, and so on around the 26-pointed star, each point of which is a standard letter in standard sequence.

For a UFOlogist, more interest, as has been the case with me, might lie in the conspicuous strange names given by purported aliens in the contactee lore. For example, by the late 1960s, I had noticed the Jesus-like qualities of George Adamski's ORTHON. He looked like the conventional European images of Jesus, came from the sky with a message of peace and love, etc. But I had no cipher key. Armed with Cipher Six, the classical AL W code, I was able quickly to discover that O-R-T-H-O-N equaled 7-12-24-4-7-14. Adding these letter values 7+12+24+4+7+14 gives a total of 68. Now, there might be a very large number of words or phrases with the number value of "68," but the cipher itself is derived from *The Book of the Law*. Therefore, using the number values ONLY of words contained in the code book itself: that is, in

Cypher 6

The Classical English Qabalah

A=1 B=20 C=13 D=6 E=25 F=18 G=11 H=4 I=23
J=16 K=9 L=2 M=21 N=14 O=7 P=26 Q=19 R=12
S=5 T=24 U=17 V=10 W=3 X=22 Y=15 Z=8

① ② ④ ⑥

	A	K	U	E	O	Y	I	S
	B	L	V	F	R	Z	J	T
	C	M	W	G	Q	A	K	U
	D	N	X	H	R	B	L	V
	E	O	Y	I	S	C	M	W
	F	P	Z	J	T	D	N	X
	G	Q	A	K	U	E	O	Y
⑤	H	R	B	L	V	F	P	Z
③	I	S	C	M	W	G	Q	A
	J	T	D	N	X	H	R	B

Using Cypher 6:

Add all of the letters of the English Alphabet:

A + B + C + D + E + F + G + H + I + J + K + L + M + N + O + P + Q + R + S + T + U + V + W + X + Y + Z = 351

Next add the following including the numerical values (from *Liber Al,* Chapter 2, line 76).

4 6 3 8 A B K 2 4 A L G M O R 3 Y X 24 89 R P S T O V A L = 351

Star 6
Cycle 11

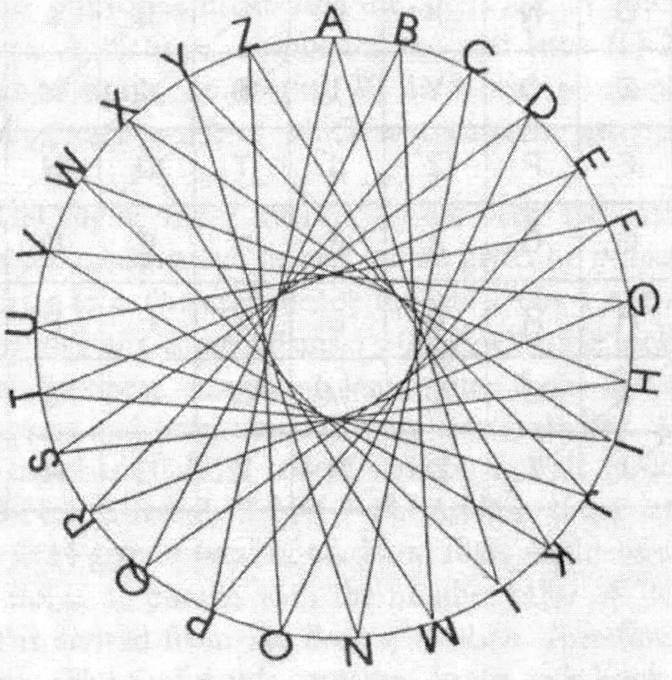

The Book of the Law, one quickly finds that the word JESUS, or J-E-S-U-S or 16-25-5-17-5 or 16+25+5+17+5, gives a total of 68 once again. Therefore ORTHON = 68 = JESUS, according to *The Book of the Law*.

Because there are an infinite number of numbers and many combinations of letters, words and phrases, obviously -and this is an old criticism of both simple numerology and Qabala—by stretching until one finds something that correlates to a preconceived notion, one can, if persistent, find just about anything. The difference here is that, by confining myself to the contents of the short book from which the cipher is derived, and limiting my search pattern to one or two attempts to find something significant with no preconceptions whatsoever, where UFOnaut personal and place names are concerned, there are virtually always case-specific correlations on the very first attempt.

As *The Book of the Law* was itself dictated by a Præterhuman Intelligence calling itself AIWASS who resembles modern descriptions of the Men in Black, and gives a cipher in what purports to be the LAW of the New Age, it seems reasonable to use this text as a reference for cipher values. Crowley, be it noted, tended to consider Aiwass an initiate of the Third Order early on, a physical person who he caught out of the corner of his eye more than once during the three dictation sessions and of whom he gave a fairly detailed physical description.

"He seemed to be a tall, dark man in his thirties, well-knit, active and strong, with the face of a savage king, and eyes veiled ...The dress was not Arab; it suggested Assyria or Persia, but very vaguely," Crowley tells us in 1936. In his later years, with the distance of time and variations of philosophy, more spiritualized interpretations of Aiwass came to be accepted.

Crowley justifies *The Book of the Law* itself by asserting that Aiwass "showed his KNOWLEDGE chiefly by the use of cipher or cryptogram in certain passages." However, other, related so-called Class A documents apparently inspired by Aleister Crowley can also be profitably employed in a similar way. Likewise, this cipher is apparently only the latest in a long series of codes spanning human history and employed by the UFOnauts and Illuminati of all ages and nations. Therefore, the earlier decoding techniques of the Qabalists, as well as certain reasonable analogies (as with Crowley's "Table of Correspondences" of a Qabalistic nature called *777*), and not a little detective work will put you quickly on the trail of the cipher of the UFOnauts. That will put you, very rapidly, on the trail of the UFOnauts themselves.

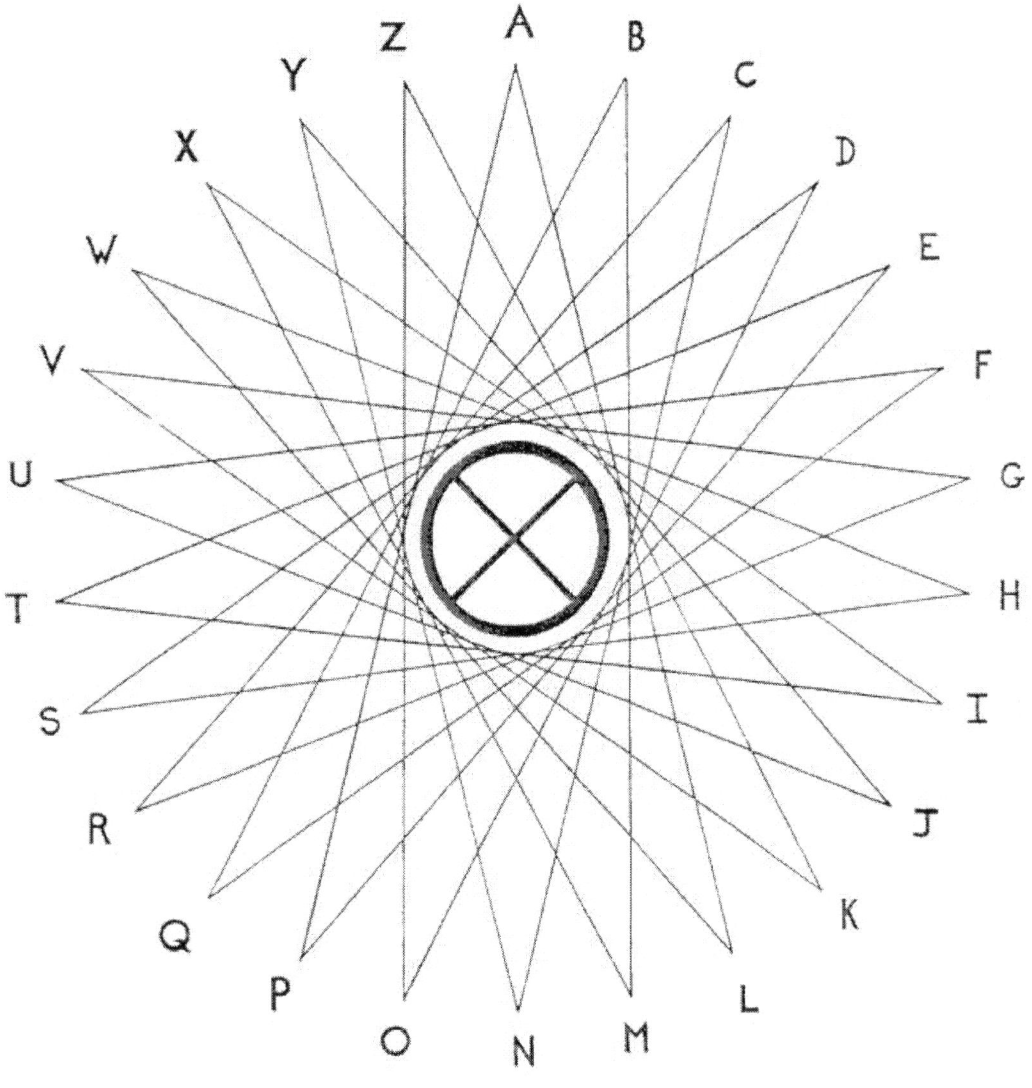

From The Equinox Volume VII, No. 1.

5
Secret Cipher of the UFOnauts Decoded

"Aleister Crowley ...was instrumental in merging the occult knowkdge of the orient with the western mystery tradition, and ... could be calkd one of the first contactees in particular [because of] a book transmitted by a 'trans-mundane' intelligence called Aiwass in Cairo in 1904. Several years later in America Crowley made contact with another extraterrestrial entity called Lam. and the reason I mention this is because a portrait drawn by Crowley of this entity bears a startling resemblance to the modern 'gray alien.'"
Borderlands. Second Quarter, 1993, page 21.

One thing I want this book to do is to demonstrate how, with a little effort and intuitive ability, YOU can decode the UFOnaut's secret cipher and find your way to the heart of the UFO mystery ...and hopefully back again in one piece.

The cipher, it turns out, is based in the English language, using the classical decoding techniques of the Qabala—the hidden wisdom of the ancient Hebrew civilization. Qabala was originally applied to Hebrew and Aramaic words. A classical scholar versed in these techniques, languages and texts could perhaps find the previous cipher of the UFOnauts or ancient astronauts by applying the principles of Extraterrestrialism to qabalistic studies. In the 1950s and 1960s Rabbi Yonah ibn Aaron came close to doing just that. Ibn Aaron brought qabalistic studies to the attention of the National UFO Conference as early as June 1965 in a speech given in Cleveland, Ohio. Most of us at that time were focused on the razzle-dazzle of Erich Von Daniken's ancient astronaut ideas and ignored ibn Aaron's basic point: *the secret is embedded in the language used.*

Qabalistic techniques involve reducing a word or name to its numerical value and working with that value. One need not even know the math or techniques involved, for example, to marvel at what the technique of applying the New Aeon English Qabala cipher does in decoding the "funny" names that show up throughout the history of UFOlogy.

Thus I should note UFO contactee Rev. Frank Stranges' contact, "Valiant Thor," has a name with the same cipher value as "Ramon Natalli," one of the original Inner Circle of contactee Mark Probert, and one of the first sources of UFO wisdom. The Inner Circle, which was promoted by Meade Layne and which was a key player in the crossover from occultism to contacteeism, itself has an odd secret or two hidden in its cipher value. There were 16 members of the Inner Circle, all said to be discarnate human beings in touch with aliens. The words INNER and CIRCLE each has a cipher value of 16—the number of members of the Inner Circle, or that together INNER CIRCLE has a value of 176, the same as INSTRUCTION or INITIATION, the precise function of the INNER CIRCLE. Deciphered, the name describes the Inner Circle itself as an instructional, initiatory body of 16 members. Another member of the INNER CIRCLE is called MAHARAJA NATCHA. Again, both words have the same cipher value—in this case 57. Added together, this gives us a value of 114, which equals THE NAME. But what name? 57 = KING. Thus, "Maharaja" means "great king." So THE NAME describes the function. We will return to the Inner Circle presently.

When we jump ahead to modern UFOlogy lore, we find contactee George King's MASTER AETHERIUS of the "Third Order" or, as it is otherwise known, "Great White Brotherhood," in cipher is closely akin to contactee Mark Probert's Ascended Master, known as the YADA DI SHI-ITE. Consider that MASTER AETHERIUS = 224 = ELIXIR OF GOD & LIFE, while YADA DI SHI-ITE = 156 = ELIXIR OF GOD. The connection is dearly there, but who made it, how, and why? And sometimes the values have a humorous touch, but who is the humorist?

The Cipher contained in *Liber AL* is indeed the secret code of the initiates of 19th century magick and occultism, and the Cipher of the UFOnauts themselves. Much is to be said for the revisionist historical notion, best expounded by Paul Johnson (*In Search of the Masters*), that Theosophical "Mahatmas" and magical "Secret Chiefs" are very human Adepts deeply enmeshed in the spiritual and political revolutions of the late 19th and early 20th centuries. Madame Blavatsky may indeed have been the first to change the names to protect the adept, but the fact that they can be decoded via the Ciphers of AL—revealed by Aiwass years after Blavatsky's death—indicates perhaps a secret code known to Blavatsky and later to Crowley and his heirs. As I have pointed out, the basic documents of the Hermetic Order of the Golden Dawn, for example, were written in a cipher, the originals still being readily available. I have also pointed out that all Royal Arch Masons were (and are) taught a cipher, since frequently reprinted.[1]

If there was a common occult cipher, it seems to have emerged in the world of mediumship. The cipher continues in the similar world of UFO contacteeism and trance channeling, which resembles mediumship as well as extraterrestrialism. The UFO contactees emerged as a distinct branch of mediums hip in the 1940s, first in Meade Layne's Borderland Sciences Research Associates (BSRA) and later all over the occult map. Officially, UFO lore begins in 1947 (the year of Crowley's death), but BSRA was developing contactee information a few years earlier. Strictly speaking, the crossover from cosmic communication, as with John Newbrough and his *Oahspe*, or

1. Louis Bimstein may have selected "Max Theon" as a pseudonym in part for the initials "M.T." In Rosicrucian circles, M.T. is the abbreviation for "Magister Templi" or "Master of the Temple"—the 2=8 degree. According to Kenneth Mackenzie, historian and initiate of that secret order, this Circle held assemblies at Camra in Poland every nine years. Bimstein was originally a Polish Jew. In his native Warsaw, the Adepts of the Philosophus Degree (6 = 4) assembled every five years. These degrees are closely paralleled in the A.A. system, and that of the Hermetic Order of the Golden Dawn. Note that Crowley regarded Blavatsky as a High Intitiate of the Great White Brotherhood, or A.A. He ranked her an 8 = 3 (Master of the Temple) in his class B commentary on *The Voice of the Silence*, in which he pointedly credits himself the lesser grade of 7 = 4.

Crowley and *Liber AL*, came in 1944, with Mark Probert and the Inner Circle UFO trance channelings, under the direction of Meade Layne's BSRA.[2]

Madame Blavatsky's first control in the parlance of 19th century mediumship was called 'John King"—a control name as common in 19th century mediumship as "Orthon" or " Ashtar" have been in UFO contacteeism, mediumship's 20th century counterpart. JOHN KING in the Cipher = 98. 98 = SCRIBE and also TONGUE, precisely the role 'John King" played in Madame Blavatsky's early career. In *Liber AL*, we also find that JOHN KING = 98 = IT IS I, a suggestion as to his nature, as well as both GOD SHALL DENY (or SHALL DENY GOD) and I ADORE GOD, suggestive of the spiritual eclecticism of Blavatsky's career.

One can play with this in a qabalistic manner, turning JOHN KING around to KING JOHN (same cipher value). KING JOHN equals 98, which equals I ADORE GOD and SHALL DENY GOD, a fair description of England's historical and much-hated King John, but also a description of a KEY occult mystery in classical (as distinguished from New Aeon) Qabala, pointed out by Frater Achad: the interplay of 31 and its reverse, 13, or GOD and NOT. Reference also Blavatsky's contemporary, medium Florence Cook's control, "Katie King" -the daughter of John King a/k/a Sir Henry Morgan, the famous pirate. KATIE KING = 139 = UNVEILING and THE BRIDE. "Katie King" appeared in spirit photographs as an unveiled bride. HPB's later "Mahatmas" KOOT HOOMI = 109 = ANDROGYNOUS, and, from *Liber AL*. THE LOVER; or HILARION SMERDIS = 183 = ASCENDED MASTER, which suggests conscious ciphering. When we take into consideration 'John King's" earlier role in Blavatsky's life, KOOT HOOMI = 109 = THOU KING seems of interest.

That Crowley's controls have similar associations many years later is also of interest; LAM = 24 = GOD, and also DAWN; ABULDIZ = 77 = 0 WARRIOR, another androgynous reference. The letter "0" used as a word has an occult meaning that, when used to refer to a male being, renders the phrase androgynous.

The cross references are complex. For example, KOOT HOOMI = 109 = ANDROGYNOUS, but also LORD HADIT NOW (from a qabalistic standpoint, identical with LORD HADIT WON). (Compare the 1970s New Age control Seth. SETH = 58 = HADIT. HADIT, NUIT and RA HOOR KHUIT are the Trinity of *The Book of the Law*.) Although the names are of ancient Egyptian deities, in *The Book of the Law* they are transformed into the Forces basic to the Present Aeon. The androgynous LAM = 24 = GOD but also NOW (or WON). Lam, as we note elsewhere in this book, is the prototype of the modern Gray Alien. Both beings carry the implication of "divine victory of the androgynous God." Interestingly, Aia Aziz (65,

2 Meade Layne is a major link between the worlds of magick and contacteeism, as we amply demonstrate in this volume. Through BSRF he developed in the 1940s the first major UFO trance contact group. He had been a member of the famous occult Society of the Inner Light, and in the late 1950s introduced future New Aeon English Qabalist Frater Damon to the work of Frater Achad, who made the first major analysis of the cipher of *The Book of the Law*.

one-time Grand Master of the Hermetic Brotherhood of Egypt) + Lam (24; Crowley's "extraterrestrial" control is also associated with the word "Lama" and "God") = 89 = GOLDEN DAWN.

Theosophical Mahatma Master Morya, on the other hand, was almost certainly the Maharaja of Kashmir, Ranbir Singh, much given to political intrigue with the Russians, including Blavatsky. Morya also had the strong Tibetan connections that Blavatsky in her less political and more spiritual mode desperately sought. MORYA = 56 = RULE and WISE in *Liber AL*. Ranbir Singh would indeed qualify as a wise ruler of considerable power and, historical impact Also see KOOT HOOMI = 109 = THE LOVER and MORYA = 56 = LOVER, a suggestive link.

As both John Keel and, in a way, the late Don Elkins have dem- onstrated, contactee control names show up in many cases and are often identical with ancient deity names. As a prime example, ASHTAR most likely derives from Astaroth, a "great duke in 'the infernal regions,'" according to the ancient magical text *The Lemegeton*. The mysterious *Grimorium Verum* (the "True Instruction") in that text informs us that Astaroth "has set up residence in America." Contactee George Van Tassel claimed to contact "Ashtar, commandant of station Schare" in 1952, and became the first organizer of contactee conventions, at Giant Rock, California. ASHTAR = 47 = STARS in *Liber AL* repeated many times, but also FLAP, a word which came to mean "UFO wave" in military and UFOlogy circles.

Recall that contactee George Adamski's contacts included the Jesus-like ORTHON. ORTHON = 68 = JESUS, but also CHOSEN and LIFE. Significantly, on April 24, 1965, a British subject named Arthur Bryant had a contact with a "newly made ascended master" called Yamski, only hours after George Adamski died suddenly. Bryant died June 24, 1967, the anniversary of the first "flying saucer" sighting, the same day as the death of UFOlogist Frank Edwards, and the day of the largest and most diverse convention of UFO investigators ever held, the 4th Annual National UFO Conference in New York City.

Dr. Gordon Melton has gone so far as to describe the contactees as "an emerging religious movement with an impetus and a life of their own." As with the Theosophical Masters and the Secret Chiefs of Magick, there is a political as well as spiritual undertone in contactee lore. Of particular note is the work of George Hunt "Ric" Williamson (a/k/a Brother Philip, d. January 1986), head of the Brotherhood of the Seven Rays with an Abbey near Lake Titicaca in South America. Williamson was a serious student of the "new bible" *Oahspe*, and, perhaps, *From India to the Planet Mars* (which influenced occultism in that period). Williamson acted as a bridge from 19th century occult mediumship to modern trance channeling. Veteran UFOlogist James W. Moseley tells us that "Williamson would go into mediumlike trances and receive space messages, which he would repeat to his listeners in a voice different from his own."

The mysterious disappearance of Karl Hunrath and Wilbur Wilkinsin is one of the more bizarre episodes in the early history of contacteeism. The story of Hunrath and

Wilkinsin is bound up with that of Ric Williamson, which, in turn, is inextricably bound up with the most famous of the early contactees, George Adamski. Williamson and his wife were key witnesses to Adamski's first contact with flying saucers, or so they would have us believe.

Williamson split with the anti-occult Adamski after he began to channel cryptic messages and occult markings in the early 1950s. This set major forces in UFOlogy in motion. Predictably, an occult circle grew up around Ric Williamson, including Karl Hunrath, an electrical engineer and inventor. They spent much time attempting to decipher the more cryptic channelings. In the middle 1950s—by now, joined in California by his friend Wilbur J. Wilkinsin, another electrical engineer from Racine, Wisconsin—Hunrath received from alleged communicators an offer to be flown to Mars. They took off in a private rented plane, allegedly headed to a meeting place in the desert with a spaceship, and were never seen again. A wall in Wilkinsin's home was found to be covered with strange symbols. One seems to be the Royal Arch Masonic glyph for "X" written three times, translated beneath as "Births give cataclysms."[3]

During Hunrath and Wilkinsin's channeling period, Ric Williamson took to calling himself by his space name, Mark III, and Hunrath and Wilkinsin became known as Firkon and Ramu. Later, after Firkon and Ramu mysteriously disappeared, Ric Williamson set up his Brotherhood of the Seven Rays in a remote South American location, to deliver messages from Ascended Master Araru-Muru and others, working with the Theosophically based light ray system under the Ancient Amethystine Order.

This information is all a treasure-trove from a New Aeon Qabalist's point of view, and points again to the continuity from the old mediumship and magical orders to the later contactees and trance channelers. It explains the funny control names and the reason for considering the New Aeon English Qabala to be the Cipher of the UFOnauts. ARARU-MURU, the secret ascended master of the Ancient Amethystine Order (yet another use of the significant "A. A.",[4]) = 110. in E.Q 110 = PURE WILL and NAME OF GOD and THE KING, but also LAPIS LAZULI. MARK

3 One of the cryptic markings on Wilkinsin's wall was: /.\ /.\ /.\ In the Royal Arch Masonic Cipher this marking is identical with three Xs. X = 22 in New Aeon Qabala. 22+22+22=66. In Lilltr AL. 66 = A GOD OF WAR and BABE

4 The initials "A.A." recur frequently in the literature. "A.A." itself is the Crowleyan name of The Great White Brotherhood, which Symonds and Grant attribute to "Argenteum Astrum" or Silver Star. (This hardly exhausts the symbolism—in New Aeon Occultism, the word AL [God] and LA [Not] have a great interplay, leading to the discovery of the "password of The Great White Brotherhood, " LAAL, the reverse of AL..-LA. The term is similar to the Buddhist concept of Nirvana. In *Book 31* Frater Achad discusses this mystery in detail.) The term A.A. is used by P.B. Randolph, MD., in his 1873 work on alchemy and magick, Eulis, as the secret name of a great magical order. Crowley encountered "the one eye" or "Achad Ayin" in Bou-Saada, near Max Theon's home, on December 4, 1909, while scrying the 13th Enochian Aethyr. We take note of Ric Williamson's Ancient Amythestine Order, and the (made up) name Aia Aziz. On the site where Arthur Bryant is said to have seen the reincarnated George Adamski in 1965, a glass phial of silver sand was found wrapped in a parchment, with the phrase Adelphos Adelpho ("Brother to Brother") written in Greek on the scroll.

III, Williamson's one-time space name = 112, which equals WE ARE ONE. This phase, as noted later by researcher John Keel, was a touchstone for a thousand New Age contact cults in the 1960s and 1970s.

The ill-fated Hunrath and Wilkinsin, or FIRKON and RAMU, are also of interest. FIRKON = 83 = MY STARS, MY FLAP and, interestingly, AMONG GODS. RAMU = 51 = SINK and SORROWS and A LIE. It is of interest that the space names given Hunrath and Wilkinsin suggest their apparently unhappy future; to create a UFO furor or flap by chasing flying saucers in a rented plane into the desert, perhaps abducted and coming to grief for having believed a lie. Perhaps they are among the gods indeed, but not via a spaceship headed for Mars. Perhaps, instead, they were food for the gods.

Another bizarre incident was the death of contactee-channeler Gloria Lee Byrd, who starved herself to death after a 66-day fast on the orders of her control, "J.W." (J.W. = 19 = SHOW and WAY.) Gloria Lee began her fast on September 23, 1962, collapsed and died several days later, on December 2nd, after being found unconscious in her hotel room. In yet another bizarre twist, the Mark-Age Metacenter in Miami soon began to receive channelings alleged to be from Gloria Lee shortly after her untimely death at age 37.

If there is a hidden cipher of mediumship showing up in the somewhat comic and sometimes tragic lore of contacteeism and trance channeling in modern times, what does it mean? The clue, I think, lies in the handful of common denominators in all the mythology that has emerged in the nearly 150 years since the Fox sisters heard rapping sounds in the walls, and the ship of spiritualism was launched.

In presenting certain ancient holy texts, Willis Barnstone notes that, "To use a secret language for purposes of exegesis is a common linguistic practice, and is actually a characteristic embedded in virtually all religious texts..." Thus, perhaps, ciphers embedded in Holy Books not only does not begin with *The Book of the Law* and the dawn of the New Aeon, but is as old as written language and is the basic premise which Qabalists have operated under for many centuries.

Our research for this book is dictated by necessity of illustration, not any attempt to create qabalistic connections. All the more reason to note, therefore, the frequency of the number 11, the number of magick, and ciphers.

AlA AZIZ = 65 = 6 + 5 = 11 (" Aziz" or "Max Theon" was a Secret Chief of the Hermetic Brothers of Egypt.)

AIWASS = 38 = 3 + 8 = 11

MORYA = 56 = 5 + 6 = 11

ASHTAR = 47 = 4 + 7 = 11

FIRKON = 83 = 8 + 3 = 11

AURA RHANES = 92 = 9 + 2 = 11

FACT = 56 = 5 + 6 = 11 (Remember that Ray Palmer always said his personal advantage regarding UFOs was to judge a case by his secret FACT.)

Aleister Crowley called 11 "the great magical number, as uniting the antithesis of 5 and 6 etc" (see Aia Aziz, Fact and Morya, above) and further, "the general number of magick, or energy tending to change." Rene Guenon calls 11 "the great number of the hieros gamos," or, as Annemarie Schimmel explains it, "the sacred marriage between macrocosm and microcosm"—which is the precise role of the medium and contactee as well.

I have mentioned the "Seth" material as indicating a continuity from the mediumship and UFO contacteeism of the past 100+ years to the so-called New Age trance channeling phenomenon. To be sure, a parallel exists with the Holy Books and the "Patience Worth" material channeled by Mrs. Curran from 1916. The alleged discarnate 17th century English girl who came through in correct period dialect shows the almost expected qabalistic qualities. PATIENCE WORTH = 201 = INTELLIGENCE and AIL MUST BE DONE WELL.

Actually, the Lightlines group in Kentucky, source of the RA Material, is the crossover point from UFOlogy to New Age religion. Jane Roberts' work—the Seth material—is of special interest, as it introduced the New Age community to trance channeling at a popular level. SETH = 58 = HADIT, indicating a New Aeon significance. We also note that the more current "LAZARIS," channeled by Jach Pursel beginning in 1974, has the connection. LAZARIS = 52 = AEONS 'and AS ONE. (Remember the phrase "we are one"—a catch-phrase updating the "I AM" of the early New Age lore.)

6

Classical Ufology Deciphered

In the last chapter we discussed the application of the cipher decoding technique to the mystery surrounding the disappearance of UFO contactees Karl Hunrath and Wilbur Wilkinsin.

Here we wish to apply the same technique to a more-or-less random classical UFO contact of the 1960s, that of Woodrow Derenberger. The contact with "Indrid Cold" and other space aliens in late 1966 was related to other West Virginia cases of the period, including the infamous "Mothman" cases surrounding the Silver Bridge disaster and the subject of books by John Keel and the late Gray Barker.

In their first encounter on a deserted interstate stretch, Cold had enigmatically told Derenberger, "I mean you no harm. I come from a country much less powerful than yours." Derenberger was driving a Ford Econovan. Cold, apparently, was driving an interstellar space ship, with his copilot, Carl Ardo.

According to Gray Barker, "They told him they came from the planet Lanulus, 30 light years away . . . Due to their skills at mental telepathy, they had no secrets between one another, and that was the reason for their peaceful existence . . . Cold had a wife, Kimi. ... During one contact Cold was accompanied by a man named Clinnel, from the planet Cerenabus."

As is usual with such cases, as ludicrous as they appear, and perhaps are, they arise amid a spate of strange phenomena reports. They inevitably have archetypal, mythic qualities.

I subjected many of the funny names and words of the 1966-67 case to the classical New Aeon English Qabala cipher. Remarkably, INDRID COLD reduces to a value of 112, the same value as the space name Ric Williamson took during the Hunrath and Wilkinsin period, MARK Ill. INDRID COLD = 112 = MARK Ill, but also, as noted in our last section, WE ARE ONE. I shall say more on this in a moment.

CARL ARDO, Cold's companion, has a cipher value of 54. LANULUS, their home planet, carries the value of 58. 54 + 58 = 112 again. CARL ARDO = 54 = SET and SNAKE. These terms have (very different) special meanings for demonologists, occultists and gnostics. Likewise, LANULUS = 58 = SETH, the name of the control in the first major modern trance channeling case, but also HADIT and HAWK'S HEAD, with similar occult meanings to those for CARL ARDO.

KIMI = 76 = NIGHT. CLINNEL = 93 (a special number for occultists, representing the Will -current of the New Aeon) = WRATH OF GOD, or simply TIME. Time, as a concept, is closely associated with the mythology of Set, Seth or Saturn.

CERENABUS, Clinnel's home world, carries the value 132 = PREY OF GODS but also ORTHON + MARKON, key names from contactee lore.

The occult connections, drawn without straining directly from contactee lore and magical mythos, are startling.

Examine, for example, Ric Williamson's MARK III. MARK = 43 = RA HOOR. III = 69 = CALIPH. Keep in mind that, as Williamson used it, the "III" was almost certainly a kind of title. But the use of "I"s has a special Thelemic use, as a delineation of a 22-year period. III in this mode is the year 66 of the New Aeon, that is corresponding to the year 1970 of the Vulgar Era. When Karl Germer died in 1962, he left the office of Outer Head of the OTO vacant. Major Grady McMurtry, acting upon his emergency authority, eventually took on the role of Acting OHO, taking the title "Caliph." His first public act was the publication, in 1970, of the Thoth Tarot Cards. III e.n. = 1970 e.v. (E.N. or Era Novis or New Aeon; E.V. or Era Vulgaris, or Common Era). III (considered as letters) in classical cipher mode = 69 = CALIPH, the word for the keeper of the prophet's flame; in this case Aleister Crowley, the Prophet of the New Aeon of Thelema, or True Will. We also see the same magical New Aeon mythos unfolded in the West Virginia case. INDRID COLD = 112 = WORD OF THE LAW and also WORDS AND SIGNS as well as the aforementioned WE ARE ONE. Connected to the MARK of MARK III (112) we get RA HOOR. Cold's wife, KIMI = NIGHT, another name for NUIT. Both are from LANULUS (= HADIT). They are accompanied by SET ("CARL ARDO") as the SNAKE. They sometime travel with CLINNEL, the 93 current All such terms, to New Aeon magicians, are of extreme importance.

At this juncture we need to say a word or two about the Lexicon computer program. Once the 1974 cipher solution was discovered, working with it was painstaking and abominably slow. A few years later a brilliant computer software development consultant and associate of the Qabalistic Alchemist Arcanum, Frater Lamed, began the development of a software program designed to research the cipher. The results were staggering. The 1974 cipher solution is perhaps best displayed as a 26-pointed star, with one point for each letter of the English alphabet. Using mainframe computer technology over a 10-year period, Lamed found that not only could one work easily and quickly with the original cipher, but literally thousands of alternative successful ciphers are embedded in the original star.

Such stars are rare; but people who have examined them geometrically as well as internally find them incredibly eerie—suggestive of a starseed transmission with an enormous store of information, a veritable library. It has been estimated that to find the 20,000-plus successful cipher solutions thus far discovered would, without computer technology, have involved every human being who has ever lived discovering eight successful solutions in their lifetime. Little wonder, then, that the name Aleister Crowley, adopted at a time when no computer technology existed, yields a value of 194, equal to COMPUTER KEY. Also, Achad's key of the rituals, IN MANIFESTATION = 237 = PERSONAL COMPUTER. Virtually none of the cipher work that has been done since 1974 could have been accomplished before the advent of computer technology and the widespread dispersal of the personal computer. Crowley died in 1947, Achad in 1950. They "could not" have known, but the Masters of the Great White Brotherhood embedded a key to the cipher of the UFOnauts in their very names.

Lexicon is available to any researcher with a personal computer.

7
Richard Shaver and the Mantong Cipher

UNTIL the Cipher of the UFOnauts was discovered and applied to the lore of UFOlogy, the rumors and reports of human-alien interaction, both past and present, were confined almost exclusively to literal descriptions of the cases, research into those literal descriptions, or, with more sophisticated researchers, comparisons with classical folklore and the symbolism of psychology.

The folklore and psychological investigations were the most rewarding, in that they disclosed a long series of repeated motifs, patterns and themes spanning the history of humanity and our interaction with alien beings. We long puzzled, for example, that a name such as ASHTAR seemed to show up in contact case after case in the modern lore of UFOlogy, but this name also has shown up throughout human history as the name of a fearsome alien being, sometimes referred to as a demon. When the Cipher of the UFOnauts came along, the name ASHTAR suddenly became less mysterious and more revealing.

Prior to the discovery of the Cipher, however, one public stab was made at developing a decoding formula, and it came very early in the development of UFOlogy .

The source was Richard S. Shaver, a blue-collar worker who, beginning in the 1940s, authored a vivid, evocative and extravagantly wild form of High Weirdness known as 'The Shaver Mystery." In the early years his editor and literary champion was Ray Palmer, an eccentric science fiction publisher who possessed a hidden FACT that we've already discussed. (Keep in mind, too, that it was Ray Palmer and Ken Arnold who investigated and publicized the first Men in Black case, at the end of the Shaver Mystery era.) Palmer converted Shaver's untutored erratic manuscripts into haunting and unforgettable stories of ancient space-faring races who first settled the Earth aeons ago, turning the entire planet inside and out into a technological marvel. Pal- mer brought out the great potential of Shaver's intense and striking imagery—the stuff that makes True Mythology.

The Shaverian mythos had it that our Sun developed a form of detrimental radiation which horrified the elder races, as this type of radiation is the source of mutation, aging and death in this otherwise ageless and deathless race. Abandoning the Earth to mutants long ago, these beings, called Atlans and Titans and remembered now only as legends, rejoined the Nortans, a race of beings who live only in Deep Space, avoiding nearness to all stars that have, like our own, a tendency to turn malignant. The surface of the Earth was left to our comparatively short-lived species, existing in abject ignorance of our origins, while the highly mechanized interior caverns of the Earth were inhabited by TERO and DERO, relatively intact and sometimes extremely degenerate beings with some knowledge of the use of ancient technologies. The perverse, degenerate DERO apparently uses this technology for the most bizarre and depraved purposes, giving rise to the surface people's legends of Hell. Surface people are, according to Shaver, frequently abducted and enslaved in the world below.

This brief synopsis of the Shaver Mystery doesn't even attempt to do the scope of it justice; the major point here is that Shaver and Palmer scandalized the science fiction Establishment by asserting that all of this was, essentially, real and not fiction.

The material began appearing in Palmer's *Amazing Stories* magazine in 1943. The circulation increased by 50,000 almost immediately, but by the end of the decade the scandal overwhelmed the publishing house, and the Shaver material ceased appearing. Palmer attempted to revive interest in the early 1960s, during which time I became involved with both Shaver and Palmer.

They were quite different types; Shaver, like Adamski a pragmatic visionary, considered these entities to be physical beings and a literally true reality. Palmer was inclined to see it more in metaphysical astral terms, leaving a few individuals like myself sort of on the fence. Palmer presented the material with a mystery that seemed to have physical, psychological and paranormal components.

Shaver first encountered Palmer when the former sent Palmer something he called the "Mantong Alphabet"—a sort of cipher that he claimed was the root-language of beings throughout the universe, and which bore a close relationship to English. Shaver maintained that English was a late, degenerated form of Mantong, relating rather like Spanish does to Classical Latin. Palmer took one serious look at the "alphabet" and recognized he was on to something.

Either Richard Shaver, or whoever (or whatever) his Source was, appears to have been attempting to introduce the Cipher of the UFOnauts to certain scattered Initiates through *Amazing Stories* and related publications. The base readership certainly overlapped with that of *Weird Tales* and other followers of the fantastic occultism of the Lovecraft circle. The new readership, which came and went with the Shaver material were prime candidates for introduction. Mantong is not the Cipher of the UFOnauts in its current form, but many key names and words used in the Shaver material, sometimes capitalized for emphasis, yield startling results for the UFOlogist and occultist when reduced to cipher and decoded, using the methods outlined in this book.

Example: According to Shaver, the Dero used advanced telepathy—augmentation machines, which serve as a kind of virtual reality projector throughout the caves *and* on surface people. The machine used is called a TELAUG, or 80 in the Cipher, identical to ALL CAVERN and RECORDS. MANTONG itself equals 92, the number of READING. As we have established, 92 can also be thought of as 9 + 2, which equals 11, the KEY to the Cipher of the UFOnauts. One could easily interpret this as, "READING MANTONG means using the cipher based in the number 11." At one point Shaver tells us we have allies in the caves, capitalizing for emphasis, ALL CAVERN PEOPLE ARE NOT DEROS which equals 329, the exact numerical equivalent of RESISTANCE IS NOT FUTILE, a phrase now showing up in the more contemporary science "fiction" of the Star Trek mythos. someone is, obviously, trying to tell us something.

"MUTAN MION," the central protagonist of Shaver's seminal "*I Remember Lemuria!*" has a value of 142, identical to MEN IN BLACK. Such capitalization is standard practice among modern cipher initiates as a means of pointing out phrases to be reduced to cipher for decoding. The overall cipher picture reflects certain qualities about the mythos itself, which predicted the flying discs, the Blonds and other features known in modern UFOlogy.

The Mantong Alphabet

A	—	Animal	(Use *AN* for short.)
B	—	Be	To exist. (Often used as a command.)
C	—	Con	To See. (*C*-on; to understand.)
D	—	De	Detrimental, disintegrant energy. (The second important symbol in the alphabet.)
E	—	Energy	(An all-pervading concept including the idea of motion.)
F	—	Fecund	(Used "fe," as in fe-male—fecund man.)
G	—	Generate	(Used "gen.")
H	—	Human	(A very metaphysical concept here, not fully under stood but used in the sense "*H*-you-man"; a human is an *H*-man.)
I	—	Self, Ego	(Same as our English I.)
J	—	Generate	(A duplication of *G*, but with a delicate difference in shade of meaning. Actually *Ja*, in contrast to *Ge*, is a very important distinction. *G* is the generating energy, while *J* is animal generation per se.)
K	—	Kinetic	(The force of motion.)
L	—	Life	
M	—	Man	
N	—	Seed	Spore (Child, as "ninny.")
O	—	Orifice	(A source concept.)
P	—	Power	
Q	—	Quest	(As "quest-ion.")
R	—	Horror	Danger (Used *AR*, symbol of a dangerous quantity of disintegrant force in an object.)
S	—	Sun	(Used "sis"; an important symbol, always referring to a "sun" whose energy is given off through atomic disintegration.)
T	—	Integration, Growth	(Used *TE*; the most important symbol of the alphabet; the true origin of the cross symbol. It signifies the integrative force of growth; as, all matter is growing—the intake of gravity is the cause. The force is *T*. *TIC* means the science of growth. Integration-*I*-Con [understand].)
U	—	You	
V	—	Vital	(Use *VI*; the stuff Mesmer called "animal magnetism.")
W	—	Will	
X	—	Conflict	(Force lines crossing each other.)
Y	—	Why	
Z	—	Zero	Nothing. Neutralization. (A quantity of energy of *T* neutralized by an equal quantity of *D*. Futility.)

E YADA DI SHI' ITE

This personality was born in the city of Kaoti (City of Temples) in a civilization called Yuga (Vast Body), or Yu. This civilization consisted of 180 million people and existed a half million years ago. It was located in the Himalayan Mountains. He was taken from his mother as a baby and raised in the temples, to become a Kata (Priest) and later High Priest or Yada. The word really means "Spirit Life": He was therefore one of the heads of a mystical order called "Shi Ite".

The "Yu" civilization had been founded by a man named Na Sep Ni Ha, meaning the seventh son of a family named "Ha". E Yada was killed in a violent quake that completely destroyed the civilization along with eighty million of its inhabitants. E Yada was about thirty-four when he died and the "Yu" civilization one thousand and twenty-four when it died.

LAO-TSE or LAO-TZU

This personality lived between 550-600 B. C. (b. 604 B. C. encyc.), in a town called K'uhsien. He belonged to a wealthy and educated family, and had no need to work for the Imperial Library, yet spent much time there poring over the books. He later became a roaming sage. Actually he did no writing at all, but his sayings were compiled by his disciples. Had a wife and seven children, and according to custom, several concubines. At about fifty years of age he abandoned his family and followers and was taken into the mystical school of the White Brotherhood. He died smiling happily at the age of eighty-two.

He had an extraordinary intellect and was a truly great philosopher; a central figure in Taoism.

PROFESSOR ALFRED LUNTZ

This personality was born in 1812 and died in 1893. He was a clergyman for the High Episcopal Chuhch of England. He was of English and German parentage and was born in North London. Graduated from the Eton School for Boys at the age of seventeen. He worked in his father's law firm in Hanover, Germany, until he was twenty. Attended Heidelberg where he took a course in philosophy and comparative religion, then on to Oxford where he received his Ph. D. in the Episcopal Theological Seminary and later served a donship. He was a devotee of Queen Victoria. He was not surprised when he died to discover that he had survived the grave, but stunned when he realized there was no heaven or hell as he had so eloquently taught and believed.

RAMOND NATALLI

This personality was born in 1598 and died in 1652. He was an astronomer and belonged to the Royal House of Astronomy in Rome, Italy. He was also a student of law. He was a close friend of the famous Galileo and secretly fought the bloody hand of the Inquisition. Ramond Natalli was an agnostic.

He continued to pursue the field of astronomy after passing into the astral. He was pleasantly surprised to discover he had survived the death of his physical body. He discovered two things of great interest after being in the astral world about two years - the first was that sun spots were atomic storms and the other was that atoms consist of photons of varied frequency levels moving in a series of quantum arcs.

Some Inner Circle Controls that operated through Mark Probert.

All this and more at:

www.borderlands.com

8
Recap: Meade Layne, Mark Probert and the Inner Circle

"All questions pose more questions and all answers are personal opinions -and the only sound rule and reply to lift's problems is to question nothing but to faa all situations with detachment."

Maharaja Natcha of the Inner Circle

Meade Layne, to review our premise, was best known among UFOlogists as the founder of Borderland Sciences Research Founda-tion (BSRF). He had an impressive metaphysical library and was a member of the Society of the Inner Light, one of several organizations that arose from the fragments of the seminal turn-of-the-20th-century ritual occult body called The Hermetic Order of the Golden Dawn. layne's successor, Riley Crabb, recently passed away, but Borderland Sciences continues as a foundation, publishing *The Journal of Borderland Research* (P. O. Box 6250, Eureka, CA 95502), with some emphasis on the link between the occult and UFOlogy.

The Golden Dawn attracted a diverse membership: Gothic writers including Bram Stoker, Arthur Machen and Algernon Blackwood were members, as were the famous occultists Aleister Crowley, S. L. Mathers and A. E. Waite, and poet W. B. Yeats. Founded upon certain cipher documents probably drafted by Kenneth Mackenzie and based on his earlier initiatory experiences with Continental Rosicrucian groups, the Golden Dawn in its wake spawned generations of occultists and, indeed, now has a number of (highly dubious) claimants to its mantle.

Meade Layne was ahead of his time writing about the UFO phenomenon in the early 1940s, before the Kenneth Arnold case, as well as focusing on the more metaphysical aspect of the mystery with his patronage of trance channel Mark Probert.

Probert himself merits some comment. In many ways his story resembles that of Richard S. Shaver, though Shaver always insisted that there was no metaphysical aspect to his stories of Dero, Tero and a hidden world beneath the surface of the Earth. Probert, even with Layne's patronage, never made the extraordinary splash that Shaver did. Yet Shaver, through Ray Palmer, impacted on the highly skeptical world of science fiction fandom -then smaller and, I speak from personal knowledge, meaner-spirited than today. These fans ultimately rejected and forgot both Shaver and his sponsor, while Probert operated from a very early date in the metaphysical world on that thin line between occultism and contacteeism. The enduring impact of trance channeling on UFOlogy and, indeed, on all New Age consciousness is considerable.

Like Shaver, Probert's channelings became conspicuous when, shortly after he married, his wife Irene began noticing that Mark spoke in what seemed a variety of languages in his sleep. This may, in fact, have been a form of speaking in tongues. Presumably, prior to his marriage, if he spoke in his sleep there was nobody around to hear. In any case, one is reminded of Palmer's eerie account of hearing Shaver do something very similar on an early visit with the welder- turned-author .

At an early point the channelings turned more specific, and reflect the kind of occultist thinking with which Layne, if not Probert, was certainly well acquainted: the world of Ascended Masters, Tibetan Brotherhoods and, of course, Masters with funny names. When I encounter the funny names I begin to look for something amenable to deciphering using the New Aeon English Qabala (NAEQ). Did Probert know such a code? Almost certainly not. Bryant and Helen Reeve give us an account of their 1955 visit to the Probert home in San Diego, and Mark and Irene come across as rather ordinary people in an extraordinary situation.

Layne's early work was with Probert and the Inner Circle. We've noted earlier that the Inner Circle was a group of 16 intelligences who were Ascended Human Masters, including the ancient YADA DI SHI-ITE, RAMON NATALLI and one MAHARAJA NATCHA.

MAHARAJA (= 57) NATCHA (= 57) is one of the silliest of the silly names. It not only rhymes, but repeats the same cipher value in NAEQ6.[1] 57 + 57 = 114 = THE NAME (i.e., the name is the key). "Maharaja" means "great king" and 57 = KING, or KING KING, i.e., Great King. The name, "Great King," means great king in NAEQ6. The Inner Circle names are filled with this kind of stuff The senior member of the Circle is the YADA DI SHI-ITE = ELIXIR OF GOD, linking it to the (apparently) unrelated MASTER AETHERIUS of George King's Aetherius Society in England. The latter claims to be part of the Great White Brotherhood at war with the Black Lodge. MASTER AETHERIUS = ELIXIR OF GOD & LIFE. RAMON NATALLI = 122 = VALIANT THOR, the name of Rev. Frank Stranges' *Stranger From the Pentagon.* I discovered the link while work- ing on a speech to be delivered in Cleveland, Ohio, in September 1994, sharing the podium with, you guessed it, Frank Stranges. The last time Stranges and I were on the same program was in June 1967 at the same convention, held that year in New York.

1. New Aeon English Qabala Cipher Six.

N. Meade Layne

AT LEFT is a copy of a portrait photo of the late founder and former director of BSRA, N. Meade Layne. He began his public borderland work with the publication of the "Round Robin", a mimeographed journal, in 1945. His sincere and liberal-minded effort to review and report on the Borderland Sciences: Psychic Research, Radionics, Radiesthesia, Fortean falls, Occultism, Flying Saucers, Dowsing, etc., slowly gained a following and in 1946 he decided upon the title, Borderland Sciences Research Associates. It was in this year also that the unusual trance mediumship of Mark Probert was brought to his attention, and through Mark the contact with the members of the Inner Circle, including the Yada di Shi'ite. Mr. Layne continued as director of BSRA until June 1, 1959. He passed away at a rest home in San Diego at the age of 78, May 12, 1961.

AT RIGHT is the present (1961) director of BSRA, Riley Crabb. For reasons of ill health, Mr. Layne asked Mr. Crabb to take over directorship in May 1959. He had been a member since 1951. Mr. Crabb's background qualifications for such work include 25 years of metaphysical study in the Theosophical and Rosicrucian schools, editor and publisher of magazines and industrial journals, industrial work with Minneapolis-Honeywell and the Naval Missile Center, Pt. Mugu, California and personnel work and counseling in U.S. Civil Service. His primary responsibility to borderland researchers is to give them recognition, attention and encouragement, through the Round Robin Journal of Borderland Research and through personal contact.

Riley Crabb

From THE FLYING ROLL (Alpha-Beta Issue, originally published March and June 1946, re-published May of 1971).

Frater Achad (Charles Stansfeld Jones).

9
Frater Achad

Frater Achad, as much as Crowley and later Frater Lamed, is responsible for cracking the cipher. His gnostic view of reality has been summarized by his followers thusly:

> "The Qabalists tell us that the Sephiroth were emanated by means of the Flaming Sword, or Lightning Flash, which descended from Kether to Malkuth. They also say that this was followed by the ASCENT of the SERPENT OF WISDOM who thus formed the PATHS. They showed his head at the top of the Tree, in the path leading from Kether to Chokma, which is the first path of the FLAMING SWORD.
>
> "All the known authorities have then continued to number the remaining 22 of the 32 Paths of Wisdom from Path 11 (joining Kether to Chokma) to Path 32 (Joining Yesod to Malkuth).
>
> "One may now question how it was that the SERPENT who formed the Paths by ASCENDING the Tree could possibly have started at the top, and why previous commentators have never taken this vital idea into consideration."
>
> -*The Sword and the Serpent [Official QBLH text]*

Charles Stansfeld Jones is an enigmatic historical figure for orthodox Thelemic Magicians. Proclaimed by Aleister Crowley to be his magical child, a ranking member of the A:.A:. and a National Grand Master of the Ordo Templi Orientis (OTO), he is inherently a force to be dealt with seriously. Crowley tells us in his autobiography, "What I had really done was therefore to beget a Magical Son [in a magical operation]. So, precisely nine months afterwards, that is, at the summer solstice of 1916, Frater O.I.V. (the name of C. Stansfeld Jones as a probationer) entirely without my knowledge became a Babe of the Abyss." Crowley goes on to cite a number of proofs, relying upon the expected child in *The Book of the Law*. "It is further predicted," Crowley goes on, "that his 'Child' shall discover the Key of the interpretation of the Book itself, and this I was unable to do ... in actual fact he did so discover that Key."

Of the Key in question there can be no doubt that it is the building block of all New Aeon Cabalistic interpretation. The present OTO Grand Master, Hymenaeus Beta, for example, acknowledges that "... his *Liber XXXI* held the key to *The Book of the Law* ... While his Qabalistic teachings are sometimes 'unorthodox' ... they are unfailingly self-consistent." Indeed, in recent years, there has been some effort by orthodox Thelemites to posthumously rehabilitate Achad whose decidedly unorthodox views led to a permanent break with Crowley in 1919 ev.

In 1948 e.v. Achad further alienated conservative Thelemites—and endeared himself to radicals—by proclaiming the Aeon of Ma, which superseded the Aeon of Horus proclaimed by Crowley in 1904. Achad's proclamation, be it noted, was a quiet one, made to a few individual friends and initiates. Some of these quietly formed a Fellowship of Ma-Ion including high-level A:.A:. initiates following upon

Achad's work.

The Ma-Ion Fellowship should not be confused with the later would-be rehabilitators of Achad, notably Kenneth Grant, who have no direct connection with Achad and have been much noisier about the "Aeon of Maat." Achad himself, in his private correspondence of the period, shows no dogmatism, and none of the emotional instability later attributed to him, in much the same way that Crowley's critics tended to dismiss his last years as a vegetative period of feeblemindedness.

The Ma-Ion Fellowship continued a largely clandestine existence, gradually focusing upon the whole of Achad's contribution to Thelema and his approach to the A:.A:. system, with much less emphasis upon the "Aeon of Maat" concept that he eventually questioned himself as perhaps premature. Achad claimed the 10 = 1 Grade in the A:.A:. in 1919, and is conceded by even the most conservative to have held 8 = 3 status. One student of Rosicrucian Occultism was Frater Robertus, a High Degree Freemason and Martinist who would eventually claim the 9 = 2 Grade, though, almost certainly, not until well after Achad's death in 1950. Robertus and his associates, as if following upon Achad's suggestions and warrants, organized an order structure in line with Achad's Qabalistic attributions, under the initials Q:.A:.A:. (Quabalistic Alchemist Arcanum).

In 1960 the QAA organized as a Church, and shortly thereafter the A:.A:. style titles were dropped from public consideration along with the tell-tale "AA" in the initials "QAA" in favor of QBLH, the Qabalistic Alchemist Church. The QBLH continued, however, to teach something closely akin to Achad's vision of the A:.A:. curriculum revised, based upon the New Aeon Qabalistic interpretation of *The Book of the Law*, and the restored Tree of Life following Achad's point of departure from the arcane tradition.

What kind of ideas are we talking about? The following quotations are gleaned from Achad's very late private writings. If they are hard for the more orthodox to take, consider the rank and relative position in the A:.A:. structure of Charles Stansfeld Jones, or Frater Achad.

> "... in 1903 Aleister Crowley wrote his essay 'Berashith' in which he affirmed: I ASSERT THE ABSOLUTENESS OF THE QABALISTIC ZERO and concluded that all things happened by CHANCE...
>
> "Against the assertion of the absoluteness of the Qabalistic Zero, and Crowley's 'chance' we affirm THE INFINITE PLENUM OF ALL PERFECTION which fills the Qabalistic Void ... there is the fact that I am just as much A.C.'s magical child, in fulfillment in a very real sense of Liber Legis, as ever I was. I can't get away from that, any more than he could, whether either of us liked it or not. The proofs are overwhelming.
>
> "... we are dealing with a full-size world-mystery and a real fight between the Black and White Brotherhoods.
>
> "The Scientific Illuminism of the A:.A:. must continue. The System of initiation came to an end with the Aeon of Horus, but must be revised and continue according to New Aeon lines ...
>
> "I may well have been over optimistic in thinking that the Aeon of Truth and justice

is very near at hand."

-Frater Achad, various letters, 1948 e.v.

Using New Aeon English Qabala classic cipher (NAEQ6), we find an impressive "cipher trail" involving the work of Frater Achad. ALEISTER = 117 = FRATER ACHAD. ALEISTER CROWLEY = 194 = ONE TO FOLLOW THEE, which is generally held to refer to, and predict Frater Achad. When Crowley mentions that Stansfeld Jones had, without his knowledge, become a Babe of the Abyss (an A:.A:. title), there is a double meaning; BABE OF THE ABYSS = 190 = I STANSFELD JONES.

After Achad proclaimed the Aeon of MA, a semi-clandestine fellowship arose to continue the A:.A:. work as interpreted by Achad, under the name Fellowship of MA ION. Leadership of the alchemical aspect of this work fell to FRATER ROBERTUS = 214 = QUABALISTIC MA ION. Although Robertus was not directly a student of Achad's, the cipher trail strongly suggests connections. The unusual spelling of "quabalistic" is integral to Robertus' organization QAA. Frater Robertus is actually Robert DUNLAP. DUNLAP = 66 = MA ION.

The secrets of the vampirism of the gray aliens (and how to resist it) in their physical examinations -- which are obviously of a sexual nature -- are concealed in the names of the organizations inspired by Frater Achad's work. QUABALISTIC ALCHEMIST ARCANUM = 345 = LESBIANS + LESBIANISM + SAPPHISM while FELLOWSHIP OF MA ION = 206 = THE SECRETIONS and also the alchemical cipher term VERY SHARP VINEGAR. The name FRATER ROBERTUS = 214 = SODOMY SECRETIONS. These terms are consistent with the inner secret teachings of the Great White Brotherhood. The terms also provide a clue, as noted, as to how to do battle with the UFOnauts. As others have remarked, UFOnauts frequently use bizarre forms of sexuality in their physical examinations or probes on humans, in order to obtain certain secretions of a physical, emotional and even spiritual nature.

Be sure and check out "The UFO Silencers"!

10
The Men in Black and their Magical Origins

"...we are dealing with a full-size world-mystery and a real fight between the Black and White Brotherhoods." - Frater Achad, 1948

"Throughout medieval times, a major current of thought distinct from official religion existed, culminating in the works of the alchemists and hermetics. Among such groups were to be found some of the early modern scientists and men remarkable for the strength of their independent thinking and their adventurous life, such as Paracelsus. The nature of the beings who mysteriously appeared, dressed in shiny garments or covered with dark hair, and with whom communication was so hard to establish intrigued these men intensely."
- Jacques Vallee, *Passport to Magonia.*

In 1947 the CIA was organized and the first UFO cases burst upon the American media landscape as "flying saucers." In that year, also, the first modern visitation by the infamous Men in Black took place in which a witness, one Harold Dahl, was silenced. From that point on, a pattern began to emerge.

The Men In Black legend is perennial; that it shows up in connection with the UFO lore should come as no surprise. UFOlogy bizarro chronicler John Keel (*Disneyland of the Gods, Jadoo*, etc.) observed in his *UFOs: Operation Trojan Horse*: " The records of demonology are filled with striking parallels ... the general descriptions of the vampires themselves are identical to the 'men in black.' The dark skin and angular, Oriental-like faces were commonly reported ..."

The Autobiography of Malcolm X described Malcolm's encounter with an MIB in prison: "He had on a dark suit I remember. I could see him as plainly as I see anyone I look at. He wasn't black, and he wasn't white. He was light-brown skinned, an Asiatic cast of countenance, and he had oily black hair..." It is interesting that the celebrated film Malcolm X chooses to imply that this figure was Nation of Islam leader Elijah Mohammed. While Elijah Mohammed and his mysterious teacher Wallace Fard (who vanished without a trace) had come out of High Degree Prince Hall Freemasonry, and certainly knew some of the esoteric secrets, the being Malcolm X described is more in accord with Aleister Crowley's description of the Præterhuman intelligence Aiwass than of Elijah Mohammed.

> "In the shadows, the Men in Black had long lurked, biding their time, waiting. Here and there, now and then, some people thought they had seen them, but they weren't quite certain; perhaps they more sense than actually regarded them...
>
> "Fourteen years earlier, the shadowy visitors had shown themselves openly. Then they had descended upon flying saucer buffs, threatening and terrorizing them, hushing them up...
>
> "Al K. Bender, a UFO researcher, had been the first known victim ...he performed a

> certain experiment and the lurking horror came. It began with glowing blue lights. Then came the stranger with the luminous eyes in the darkened theatre, and later on a dusky street. It culminated when the Men in Black, three of them, paid him a visit ...."
>
> - Gray Barker, *The Silver Bridge.*

UFOlogist Gray Barker got his one and only best-selling book in detailing the Albert K. Bender story and the world-wide wave of silencings. *They Knew Too Much about the Flying Saucers* was an international success. It was widely assumed that the Men in Black were either government agents or extraterrestrials, but as researchers Wilgus and Keel have shown, the eye in the triangle was sometimes their only insignia, while my own research showed startling parallels to certain black magick rituals in medieval times which provoked visitations by what was often called "the Man in Black" -- widely understood to be *the* Devil himself. Even Barker noted that Albert K. Bender's experiments were more like a magical conjuration than an attempt at extraterrestrial communication. Any initiated magician reading Bender's accounts would recognize the elements of magical conjuration immediately.

Maybe, I mused, we were dealing more with magick than with Martians.

The Black Lodge

> *"Mathers, of course, carried on; but he had fallen. The Secret Chiefs cast him off; he fell into deplorable abjection, even his scholarship deserted him. He published nothing new and lived in sodden intoxication till death put an end to his long misery. He was a great man in his way..."* - Aleister Crowley

> *"What I am out to complain of is what I seriously believe to be an organized conspiracy of the Black Lodges to prevent people from thinking..."*
> - Aleister Crowley, *Magick Without Tears.*

Often when a person or institution allied with the historical Great White Brotherhood approaches success (variously defined) or comes into possession of certain aspects of transcendent wisdom, Something Intervenes. That 'something' has been defined as the Man in Black, the Men In Black, the black lodges, or The Black Lodge. The latter term most nearly accommodates my own view. That they need to do this, and that they often fail in their efforts, is itself an indication that (A) the Black Lodge is opposed by Something Else, equally as strong, and (B) they are afraid of something we might find out -- about them, about their opposition, about ourselves or all three.

The story of our interaction with the UFOnauts begins with the Qabalistic Tree of Life, and the Chakra system of the body.

According to the primal occult and frequently secret and subversive view, the manifest universe emerges from an Ultimate NOT-Thing, a Consciousness or Beingness beyond words or expressions sometimes referred to as the Unmanifest or The

Limitless Light. This Unmanifest cannot be understood in the external sense, but can be Known in the Gnostic sense by the initiate or perfected sentient being, the Ubermensch. It can be plugged into.

For reasons equally inexpressible, this uniqueness unfolds itself in manifestation. Thus, the limitless light becomes a series of emanations or expressions or Intelligences that devolve increasingly toward our material form of existence and thus towards accessibility in the conventional sense. But the manifestations also increasingly become subject to subdivision into arbitrary concepts such as "good" and "evil" as these are commonly understood. And they also become closer and closer in form and content to our own mundane reality, though in the relativity of things, these Higher Intelligences may seem unspeakably powerful, mythic and divine.

The Gnostic view has tended to be that what the external world of the conventional person understands as god, devil demon, angel or, more recently, extraterrestrial beings are, in fact, such emanations of the unspeakable ultimate. Indeed, the ancient Gnostics saw the 'god' and 'devil' of conventional theology as an ego-maddened entity under the delusion that it, indeed, IS the Ultimate Being! The late Phil Dick, in his last Gnostic allegorical fiction, eventually settled on the name "V.A.L.I.S." or "Vast Active Living intelligence System" for this being or Demiurge. He wrestled through his literary career and secret life as a Christian Gnostic philosopher with whether VALIS was a benevolent, if machine-like deity of a sort, or an insane extraterrestrial supercomputer.

Throughout recorded history, and, from the evidence of primitive objects and works of art, for aeons before, certain humans have had the capacity to tune into or channel various of these Higher Intelligences with varying degrees of accuracy. These humans have been our Seers, Oracles and Prophets. It appears, in fact, that much of the source-material of all religions comes from such channelings, including, arguably, The Book of Revelation, *The Book of Mormon*, and *The Book of the Law*.

Concurrently, and not coincidentally, the two great initiatory bodies, or orders have been generated and regenerated throughout history. The so-called Great White Brotherhood, when undistorted, appears (according to legend) guided by Intelligences associated with the dual star system Sirius or Sothis in some manner.[1] This brotherhood also seems to have the purpose of uplifting human character and initiating biological and social evolution designed to move towards identification with Ultimate Being. What is sometimes called "the Black Lodge," which we may associate with the Gnostic Demiurge or Phil Dick's VALIS, is generated to keep humanity in a state of materialist trance and evolutionary stagnation.

Mystics generally consider that understanding the motivations of either of these Sources may be beyond our knowledge or even our capabilities. Existentially, however, it may be stated with confidence that one is dedicated to keep us in subjugation, misery and stagnation; the other to our betterment and enrichment though both at

1. See *The Sirius Mystery* by Robert Temple for a discussion of the Sirius connection—also Kenneth Grant's *Outside the Circles of Time* discusses the matter from a magical perspective.

times have made claims to being our saviors.

There are keys for decoding which is which—for example, rituals that have been generated or handed down to the magical lodges of modern times which refer to a star or the stars directly or indirectly tend to be transformative and thus of the Great White Brotherhood. Ciphers for decoding messages between the black lodges and their alien sponsors have always existed. But confusions of a deliberate nature exist; the ancient Gnostics uncovered a cipher which clearly indicates that the story of the Garden of Eden in its conventional form is turned on its head. The Serpent is clearly the symbol of Knowledge, Wisdom, the Kundalini Yogic force, the Will-current—that is, it is the symbol of Liberation and Self-Mastery. The jealous "gods," as read in the original manuscripts, are clearly the forces of blockage, self-denial and repression—which is to say, the Intelligences governing the Black Lodge. This Knowledge of Good and Evil and Life and Death has been the Terrible Secret of Initiates throughout history, recorded in ciphers and myths, and passed on through ritual.

The Black Lodge may be defined as the *organized* institution guided by VALIS for the purpose of holding back human evolution and keeping a slave mentality in place. Its human leaders are the "black brothers" who are not to be mistaken for mere black magicians. Indeed, Aleister Crowley observed that "the 'Black Magician' or Sorcerer is hardly even a distant cousin of the 'Black Brother.' The difference between a sneak-thief and a Hitler is not too bad an analogy..." The Black Brothers are highly advanced adepts of the Art who have simply, as the popular phrase goes, "been seduced by the dark side of the Force." At certain times and places in history -- for example, medieval Tibet or, in more modern times, Nazi Germany—the Black Lodge has operated more or less openly with characteristic occult symbols of human skulls, lightning bolts, etc. out in the open. But like the Great White Brotherhood that it actively seeks to subvert and overthrow (as it did in the time of the Knights Templar), the Black Lodge has generally communicated by cipher and myth, in silence and secrecy, often within religious, fraternal and political institutions dedicated to the status quo.

In the West since at least the early 18th century, the Black Lodge has tended to operate along crypto-Masonic lines, and its development has tended to coincide with and mirror that of the Great White Brotherhood. This development may, in fact, be attributed to a cosmic principle of "equal generation of forces." Thus, the birth of the modern form, as the fraternity of the knights militant of the New Aeon in the cultural and political turbulence of Germany in the 1890s, may fairly (along with the coincident peak in the development of the Hermetic Order of the Golden Dawn and the Universal Gnostic Church) be characterized as the resurgence of the Great White Brotherhood and its rejuvenation out of the degeneration of classical speculative freemasonry. This coincides closely with the "Great Airship Scare" of 1897.

At almost the same moment, and in the same unhappy land, the Black Lodge reasserted itself in the form of such fraternities as the Vril Society and the Thule Group. The full story of the Vril Society, the Thule Group, the Ahnenerbe, the Schwartze Orden (The Black Order) and other manifestations of the Black Lodge in the pre-Nazi and Nazi era has yet to be told, though Pauwels and Bergier take an informal stab at it in *The Morning of the Magicians*. Rudolph Hess, the last known member of the Thule Group, told Jack Fishman (*The Seven Men of Spandau*) that Thule leader and occult initiate General Karl Haushofer (1869-1946) "was the magician, the secret Master..." of Nazi Germany. Hess believed in the cause to the end of his life. The last prisoner at Spandau, Hess died at the significant age of 93, proclaiming his loyalty to the Thule ideal to the very end. The period, in the middle 1930s, in which these groups attained their greatest, ruinous power over the German state coincides closely with the reports of "ghost rockets" over Northern Europe.

The British Raj in India, and the European Christian colonization of the East in general, had all but destroyed the classical Tantrism and Illuminism of the Great White Brotherhood in the East, finding such institutions as Temple Prostitution, chakra-puji, Shiva devotion, etc. to be sexual obscenity.

On the other hand, fearing the power of the Black Lodge as a political entity and eroding its hold on esoteric Eastern Religion as a practical necessity had provoked the British to effectively dismantle the classical Eastern manifestation of the Black Lodge, and Western occultists visiting the East in the 19th and early 20th century already could only find watered-down remnants and secret adepts carrying on the hidden wisdom in either form. The Great White Brotherhood survived in Tibet along with the Dark Lodges, and, since the Chinese occupation, many of its chiefs have found their way to India and around the world.

As far as is known, the last classical chakra-puj to be observed by a Westerner was in the 1930s, while the last ancient intact body of adepts of the Eastern Black Lodge, ironically dedicated to foisting upon sleeping humanity a rank and demoralizing materialism, was discovered and destroyed in accordance with the insipid Marxism which guided the Chinese "People's" Liberation Army into Tibet in the late 1950s. Among various Tantric Buddhist and Bon religious institutions, the P.L.A. liquidated the cavern retreats of Schamballah and Agarthi, the former being possibly the oldest surviving branch of the Black Lodge on the planet. (See Ossendovski's *Men, Beasts and Gods*, circa 1925, for an account of Schamballah and Agarthi.) As survivors of the Marxist massacre from the Tibetan Great White Brotherhood are known to have come to the West in subsequent years, it may be assumed that survivors of the Black Lodge have set up operations in our own society as well. We can see the marks of their presence in so-called right-handed Eastern circles that have gained a certain currency among Westerners, and which peddle a useless baggage of New Age platitudes.

The traditions do survive here and there in the East; a friend of mine—for 10 years a high high official of the International Society for Krishna Consciousness in India—was seduced by a Black Tantric Magician, and wound up leaving a life of celibacy as a Hari Krishna for the lurid existence of a Madame in an upscale American house of prostitution. I leave it to my readers to decide whether she was seduced from the Great Brotherhood to the Black Lodge, or vice versa.

Certainly, prior to the destruction of the Tibetan black lodges, the German SS—

under Thule and Vril influence and directed by the infamous Ahnenerbe Group—imported a number of Black Brothers and Adepts from Tibet during and prior to the Second World War. The Tibetan colony in Berlin in fact predates the Nazi rise to power, having been established in 1926. One Tibetan Monk, termed "the man with the green gloves" and a reputed psychic, was frequently visited by Hitler and was rumored to hold the keys to the Kingdom of Agarthi. Such keys are best understood in terms of ciphers.

Western mystics including Karl Kellner, P.B. Randolph and G.I. Gurdjieff received instruction from surviving institutions of the Great White Brotherhood and carried their influence back with them to Europe, just as the Templars had done centuries before, and incorporated their teachings into the Western Esoteric System.

It is known that the Black Lodge—which, as it opposes evolution, inherently fights a rear-guard action—has made unceasing war on the Great White Brotherhood in the West from the beginnings of the magical revival. Indeed, fallen and failed adepts of the Great White Brotherhood have become the tools and pawns of the Black Lodge, from Mathers to Hubbard and beyond. It would seem that the immediate goal of the Black Brothers is to delay the Manifestation of the New Aeon, the birth of the magical child and the realization of the ubermensch through diversion of the Will-current into less than useless power plays, demoralizing materialist and superstitious delusions, New Age jargon, etc. The classic example in the Twentieth Century was the Nazi appropriation, under Black Lodge influence, of the very concept of the ubermensch, and sidetracking it into a pathetic racialist caricature of Nietzsche's super being.

"We should found society upon a caste of 'men of earth,' sons of the soil ..." said Crowley, "The worst thing they can do is what is done in America, to disenchant the man of earth with his destiny; to fill him with the facts and fancies that enthrall etiolated and degenerated idealists and unfit him for his evident purpose, that of supplying society with supermen." The Black Lodge in the Nazi era totally discredited the concept of the evolved human supermen by grafting it onto German nationalist and racialist conceits, while suppressing the Gnostic Church, the OTO, the Anthroposophical Society and even lost-word freemasonry -- in short, anyone who might have an actual understanding of the coming Being. The leading figure of the OTO in Germany, the future Grand Master Karl Germer, was placed in a concentration camp. His official crime was that he knew and maintained relations with Aleister Crowley. The Chief Bishop of the Universal Gnostic Church in France was executed by the Nazis. Crowley, for his part, "on the outbreak of the War ...was invited to see the Director of British Naval Intelligence." According to Gerald Suster, "Crowley claimed that he advocated the use of two magical signs which were to boost British morale and frequently used by Winston Churchill: the 'V' sign, which, in magical terms, is the counter of the Swastika; and the ' Thumbs Up,' the Sign of the Phallus and Victory, which was published in a pamphlet of Crowley poetry during the most desperate days of 1940 and whose use spread throughout the nation." War of the magicians, indeed!

I believe the New Age distortion of the New Aeon concept is a direct attempt by the Black Lodge and its Inner Planes Rulers (which we call, for convenience VALIS) to delay manifestation of the Aeon by creating confusion among the receptive. Much of the "White Light Channeling" clearly bears the stamp of the Black Lodge and VALIS, an empty metaphysical blind of insipid psychic trivia. Many self-improvement groups have their origins in the ideas of failed magicians like L. Ron Hubbard. We have new age centers that teach nothing useful, UFO message-oriented cults waving flashlights on mountains, and, as I have shown end-of-the-world doomsayers touting this or that grand cosmic alignment, harmonic convergence or polar shift.

The UFO cults have clearly influenced even Kenneth Grant's so-called "Typhonian OTO," which appears to use valid magical currents to pursue the hideous old ones of H.P. Lovecraft's fictional Cthulhu Mythos. Phil Dick's last efforts were marred by insipid trivial UFO cult channelings -- the kind of stuff that was old hat to hardened UFOlogists by the late 1950s. Compare Phil Dick's musings in *The Last Testament* with, for example, the Mark Probert or Dick Miller or Gloria Lee Bird materials of UFO contactee lore.

The magick of the Black Lodge can be defined and thus identified in only one way and by one set standard: the subversion of the True Will. *This is the essence of Black Magick*, and is its only true definition. Aleister Crowley explained it this way:

> "The Magical Will is in its essence twofold, for it presupposes a beginning and an end, to will to be a thing is to admit you are not that thing.
>
> "Hence to will anything but the supreme thing is to wander still further from it—*any will but that to give up the self to the beloved is black magick*—yet the surrender is so simple an act that to our complex minds it is the most difficult of all acts; and hence training is necessary ...
>
> "The majority of the people in this world are ataxic; they cannot coordinate their mental muscles to make a purposed movement. They have no real will, only a set of wishes, many of which contradict others ...and at the end of life the movements cancel out each other..."

Crowley's references to his wars with the Black Lodge are scattered throughout his writings and bear further study. From these writings, one can come to understand that the form of the attack upon the magician can range from political repression to seduction.

The great magicians, Theosophists and other Western sources have devoted even more testimony to the other side of the coin—the "Great White Brotherhood" or "The Secret Chiefs" or "The Masters." In the early days of the magical revival, the existence of an inner order was taken for granted. This was followed by a long epoch of expose, disillusionment and world weariness. But now, revisionist historians are finding evidence that these groups, usually described in mythic terms, are as material as they are archetypal. They are, in very Truth, the "Inner Order"—in communication with and overlapping with Ultraterrestrial Sources.

The Reality of the Secret Chiefs

The mythology of the secret masters or chiefs and the myth of the black lodge form an archetypal substratum of modern magical lore which is almost a necessity if magick is not to drift into a kind of bland parapsychological secular humanism or offbeat psychology on the one hand, or a religious fundamentalism grounded in a new faith substituted for Christianity. But one should at least allow that the legend of secret chiefs may have some rather literal basis in fact; that there are high masters of the art scattered around the world, that they are in communication with one another, and that how they use their illumination depends upon their character and predisposition. This is all that one must grant to consider the great brotherhood, or secret chiefs, as well as their opposition plausible.

In medieval Tibet, this was known as the "whispered succession." It is an open part of the literature of Tantric Yoga, and the often-invoked Tibetan connection of adepts and publicists comes quickly to mind. It was the Hidden Church of Karl von Eckartshausen that brought Aleister Crowley to the path, and small wonder; von Eckartshausen wrote in the 18th century of

> "...the society of the Elect, which has continued from the first day of creation to the present time; its members, it is true, are scattered all over the world, but they have always been united in the spirit and in one truth ...
>
> "It is from her that all truths penetrate into the world, she is the School of the Prophets, and of all who search for wisdom, and it is in this community alone that truth and the explanation of all mystery is to be found. It is the most hidden of communities yet possesses members from many circles; of such is this School ...From all time, therefore, there has been a hidden assembly, a society of the Elect, of those who sought for and had capacity for light, and this interior society was called the interior Sanctuary or Church."

In medieval European graal mythology, we find a strain of accomplished Graal Templars going out in secret to govern and protect far-flung populations, but (as in von Eschenbach's *Parzival*), "...writing was seen on the Gral to the effect that any Templar whom God should bestow on a distant people for their lord must forbid them to ask his name or lineage, but must help them gain their rights ...members of the Gral Company are now forever averse to questioning, they do not wish to be asked about themselves..."

As magical mythologist Aleister Crowley has a wonderful time with both friend and foe in the fictional *Moonchild*, but his nonfictional recounting of the same period comes uncomfortably close to the metaphor of the war between the Great White Brotherhood and the Black Lodge. Then we find the matter of fact (if remarkable) essay on sexual magick, "*Energized Enthusiasm*," interrupted, as it were, in midcourse by an anecdotal accounting worthy of *Moonchild*.

> "Thus far had I written when the distinguished poet, whose conversation with me upon the Mysteries had incited me to jot down these few rough notes, knocked at my door ...'If you come with me now, we will finish your essay.' Glad enough of any excuse to stop working, the more plausible the better, I hastened to take down my coat and hat. 'By the way,' he remarked in the automobile, 'I take it that you do not mind giving me

the Word of Rose Croix.' I exchanged the secrets of I.N.R.I. with him..."

What followed was an account of a close encounter of a Most Peculiar Kind, best read in the original.

Crowley, ever both rationalist and mystic, was aware of the superficial difficulties in the idea of secret chiefs. Yet he tended to be rather unambiguous on this matter.

> "Yes; this involves a theory of the powers of the Secret Chiefs so romantic and unreasonable that it seems hardly worth a smile of contempt...I propose to quote it here in order to show that the most ordinary events, apparently disconnected, are in fact only intelligible by postulating some such people as the Secret Chiefs..."

He remarks in this manner in his autobiography, but is still quite convinced 20 or so years later when he notes, in *Magick Without Tears*:

> "They can induce a girl to embroider a tapestry, or initiate a political movement to culminate in a world-war; all in pursuit of some plan wholly beyond the purview or the comprehension of the deepest and subtlest thinkers...But are They men, in the usual sense of the word? They may be incarnate or discarnate: it is a matter of Their convenience..."

We should take note of Paul Johnson's recent trailblazing study of the theosophical masters. The essence may be boiled down to this: secret chiefs or hidden masters may have good reason to mythologize themselves, and encourage those in direct contact with them to follow suit on the border where magical philosophy meets with its political implications, the need for secrecy assumes a more practical rationale. The Secret Chiefs may be secret not because they are myths or immortals, but because they are neither.

Do the Gods Leave Footprints?

The recent revisionist histories, especially Paul Johnson's *The Masters*, Joscelyn Godwin's "hidden hand" articles, and our own work with the "ciphers of the Secret Chiefs" (identical with that of the UFOnauts) have begun to restore the political component to historical understandings of the magical revival of the late 19th century.

For Westerners, especially in America, the separation of Church and State has been sufficient to make it difficult even to *think* in terms of spirituality and political philosophy as a continuous sphere. Even hardcore Bible-belters are unable to truly imagine an established religion in the European sense, let alone in the Asiatic. I believe most of us have virtually *no idea* of what makes Islamic Republicanism tick, and we stand appalled not only at the atrocities of Islamic Government, but at its sheer zeal. The idea of Pat Robertson driving a truck filled with explosives into an enemy military compound shouting "Jesus is Lord!" is ludicrous in our imaginations. Put Billy Graham behind the wheel ... but you get the point.

Yet, it has been shown that the founders of speculative freemasonry in the 18th century, especially in its continental version, were upholders of a radical spiritual, sometimes republican political vision that captured the imagination of many, including early socialists on the one hand and occultists on the other. These tendencies meet and overlap, and explain much about the nature of Masonic and occult secrecy, the cell structure common to political radicals and occultists, and the hostility of the established State and Church to both.

The Secret Chiefs of Theosophy, the Golden Dawn and the OTO may be able to, as Crowley said, "initiate a political movement to culminate in a world-war" (or prevent one), but if Paul Johnson's thesis is correct, one should not conclude from this that they are immune to arrest, torture and execution. Alessandro di Cagliostro, almost certainly a (rather more public than would seem judicious) Secret Chief, was arrested and condemned by the Inquisition, dying in a Roman prison.

Johnson observes of some of his successors: "They were all committed to an international effort to combat religious dogmatism, extend the range of democratic government, and direct public attention to the values of liberty, equality and fraternity ...Sotheran's acquaintance with HPB began in Europe among the disciples of Mazzini. Sotheran's account of Cagliostro makes it clear that he regarded the work of Mazzini and the Carbonari to be direct continuation of Cagliostro's mission..."

Johnson's cast of characters in early Theosophical history overlaps with occultist-magical history considerably. The great Magi Papus, P.B. Randolph and John Yarker all come under consideration by Johnson.

But before we inaugurate Karl Marx or Anarchist Emma Goldman as "Secret Chiefs," we do need to avoid losing sight of the fact that those who professedly encountered these hidden beings were apt to describe them in terms of, at the least, superbeings in human form.

Consider Henry Steel Olcott's account of an encounter at Lahore with the legendary "K.H.":

> "I was sleeping in my tent, the night of the 19th, when I rushed back towards external consciousness on feeling a hand laid on me. The camp being on the open plain, and beyond the protection of the Lahore police, my first animal instinct was to protect myself ...'Do you not know me? Do you not remember me?' It was the voice of the Master K.H. A swift revulsion of feeling came over me, I relaxed my hold on his arms, joined my palms in reverential salutation, and wanted to jump out of bed to show him respect. But his hand and voice stayed me, and after a few sentences had been exchanged, he took my left hand in his, gathered the fingers of his right into the palm, and stood quiet beside my cot, from which I could see his divinely benignant face by the light of the lamp ...Presently, I could feel some soft substance forming in my hand, and the next minute the Master laid his kind hand on my forehead, uttered a blessing, and left ...I found myself holding in my left hand a folded paper enwrapped in a silken cloth..."

The letter, as it turned out, predicted the death of two enemies of the Theosophical Society, which swiftly came to pass. The actual identity of "Master K.H." seems to be one Thakar Singh, an enlightened radical Sikh leader, in contact with the worldwide network of radicals of the 19th century.

Contrast Olcott's encounter with S.L. MacGregor Mathers' account of his relations with the Secret Chiefs:

"It was found absolutely and imperatively necessary that there should be some eminent Member especially chosen to act as the link between the Secret Chiefs and the more external forms of the Order. It was requisite that such a member should be me who, while having the necessary and peculiar educational basis of critical and profound Occult Archaeological Knowledge, should at the same time not only be ready and willing to devote himself in every sense to a blind and unreasoning obedience to those Secret Chiefs..."

Israel Regardie described Mathers' fateful encounter in this way:

"While walking in the Bois de Bologne one day, meditating ... Mathers claimed triumphantly that he was approached by three men. He asserted that these were Adepts belonging to the hidden or Secret Third Order, and therefore belonged to that category of men described in The Cloud Upon the Sanctuary. Apparently, so he claims, they had materialized themselves, and in that tense emotional and spiritual atmosphere of Psychical phenomena, confirmed him in the sole rulership of the Order."

Mathers observed that, for his part, "I believe they are human beings living on this Earth, but possessed of terrible and super-human powers."

As outre as these tales are, they coincide remarkably with close encounter accounts from as early as St. Paul's fateful experience on the road to Damascus, to Albert K. Bender's three Men in Black.

The most intelligent discussion of what is delusion, dishonesty and deception in all this, and what is not, is in Crowley's *Magick Without Tears*. That it is scattered through the work and written under an implicit assumption that the proofs of a residue of concrete reality, however bizarre, are readily obvious to the reader is unfortunate, in today's (properly) more wary magical and UFOlogical circles. All that we attempt to demonstrate here is that a plausible case can be made for historical revision at this time. Johnson's tentative identification of Theosophical Masters both demythologizes them and adds to the credibility of their existence. If Johnson is correct, the Secret Chiefs are not only real but they probably have phone numbers -- doubtless unlisted.

Crowley observed dryly in a postscript: "A visitor's story has just reminded me of the possibility that I am a Secret Chief myself without knowing it: for I have sometimes been recognized by other people as having acted as such, though I was not aware of the fact at the time."

Brad Steiger observed in 1988, that, apparently, "...Space Beings have placed themselves in the role of messengers of God, or that we, in our desperation for cosmic messiahs who can remove us from the foul situation we have made on this planet, hope that there are such messengers who can extricate us from the plight we have brought on ourselves." Only with the coming of cipher knowledge can we decode the Pretended Saviors from Authentic Benefactors or, better Allies. Taking into consideration that UFO contactee George King and his Aetherius Society are earnestly engaged in the war being waged by the (Great White) Brotherhood against the Black Magicians, a group they feel seeks to enslave the human race," as Steiger puts it, the UFOlogy mythos and the magical mythos are shown clearly to be cut from the same cloth. The nature of that cloth, in the hands of Crowley or King, is now no longer obscure.

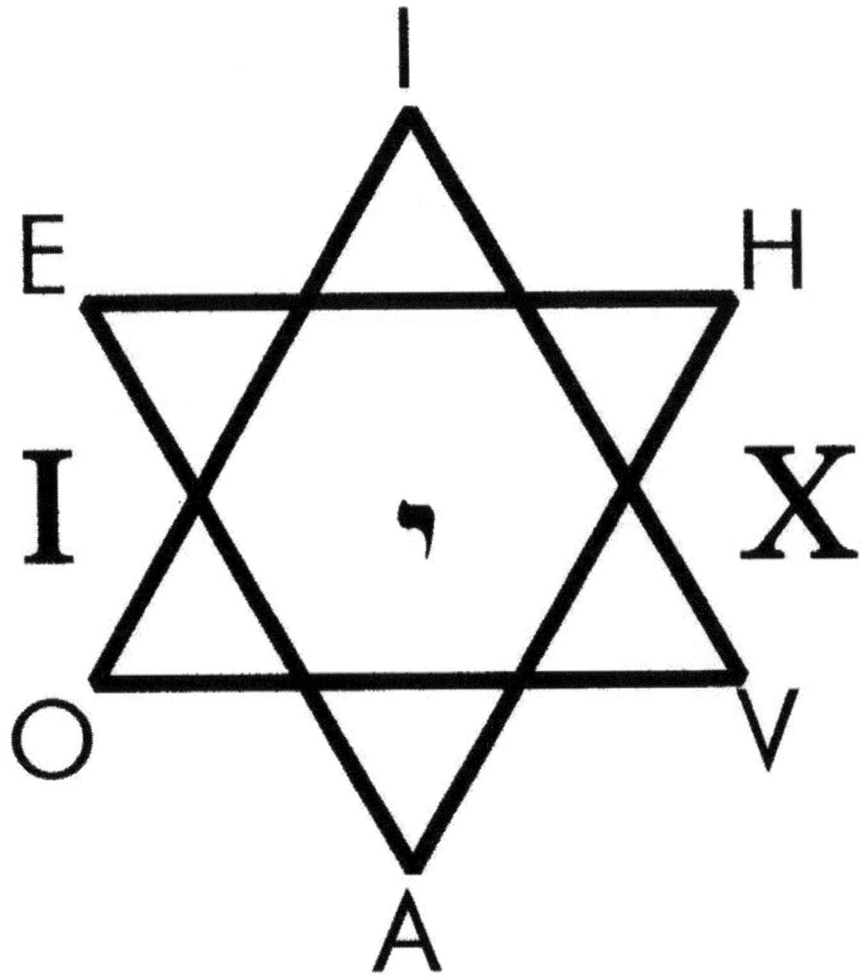

Ancient Gnostic Symbol.

11
How to Defeat the UFOnaut Body Snatchers: Law of the Battle of Conquest

"The purpose of this series of ceremonies performed by Parsons and Hubbard was to unseal an inter-dimensional gateway that had been sealed in deep antiquity, thereby allowing other-dimensional entities known as 'the Old Ones' access to our space/time continuum..."

George C. Andrews, *Extra-Terrestrial Friends and Foes*

"Enochian is the lingua franka of the space races, much as Swahili was the lingua franka of the many African !dnguages. Enochian is the correct time-tested traditional way for Earthlings to communicate with extra-terrestrials. "

George C. Andrews, *ibid.*

THE Inner Order tells us clearly, through the New Aeon cipher, how to resist Alien Abduction and Alien Conquest The Earth has been invaded by various claimants throughout its history. Invaders have always attempted to present themselves as invincible, veritable gods. For a time many have gained control over whole civilizations. Aliens controlled Babylon for a time. They exercised, through the Black Order, considerable control over Nazi Germany. They made war, at various levels and dimensions, on the Adepts of Ancient India and the High Lamas of Tibet, with fire and blood, seduction and dark magick. They did not lose, but they did not win. They made spiritual war on Gotama the Buddha, and some of them were converted. Then they knew the terror of the Ubermensch -the "super man" human- ity is even now evolving into. They were afraid of us, as well as of our Allies. Though they had conquered planets, planes and whole Orders of Reality, the gods of outer space for whom men were but pawns on the spiral arm of a minor galaxy were no match for The New Man. "I have seen him," their pawn of pawns Hider once said, "he was intrepid and cruel. I was afraid of him."

Unable to control a Buddha or a Christ with their Powers, the Aliens resorted to poisons and executions. The Buddha laughed at them as he lay dying, the Christ would not stay dead at all.

"You are so far outstripped in terms of physical weaponry that you must find a source of strength that transcends the physical," Khyla of Procyon tells us, "such as techniques of centering conscious- ness on powerfully motivating energy, which would be different from one individual to another." KHYLA OF PROCYON = 150 = MEDICINE but it is also DEATH and MYSTIC ROSE, the ultimate Holy Graal of Magick as well. In elevated mystical states, the very secretions, psychic and otherwise, which humans emit and which desperate vampire-aliens consume like the soul-famished pathetic creatures they are, become poison to them in the Transformed

Human. Cosmic Consciousness is literally poison to them. MEN IN BLACK = 142 = THEY PASS AS SHADOWS. If such powers are' physical, they cer- tainly manifest in the occult form.

RESISTANCE IS FUTILE, the Borg of the Star Trek mythos tell us. RESISTANCE IS NOT FUTILE, the answer, carries the cipher value of 329, that of QABALISTIC ALCHEMIST CHURCH and 11, I SEE TO LEARN THIS WRITING, i.e., to decode the Cipher of the Ufonauts. Also THAT LIE THAT THOU MUST DIE and, our having not forgotten that Mohammed and Alexander were Higher Men as well, LAW OF THE BATTLE OF CONQUEST. Carry to the Alien Nest the Law of the Adepti and the Knowledge of the Portal and, as Andrews puts it, " ...in the Golden Dawn Enochian system, the Great King of Air is the appropriate intermediary to be called upon as a benign go-between in negotiations between Earthlings and extra-terrestrials." The Great King of Air, in the Enochian Language, is called "BATAIVAH" and is invoked by the 2 = 9 Grade Opening in the System of the A.A. All Adepti know this. But a 9mm pistol in your pocket wouldn't hurt either. Aleister Crowley used to say that the correct magical operation for leaving a room is turning the door knob and pushing the door. RESISTANCE IS NOT FUTILE = 329 = ABROGATE ARE ALL RITUALS, ALL ORDEALS, ALL WORDS.

In the seminal and quintessential Chapter 36 of *The Book of Lies*, Aleister Crowley informs us, "Let the Adept be armed with his Magick Rood [and provided with his Mystic Rose]." The Magick Rood, or wand, is the supreme male symbol; the Mystic Rose the female complement. The ritual, called "The Star Sapphire," is the revelation to the initiated of the key Secret of the magick of the conquest of the universe.

Thus, we find THE WAND: THE DOUBLE WAND OF POWER = 329 = RESISTANCE IS NOT FUTILE. The blond alien KHYIA OF PROCYON, our alleged informant from the stars = 150 = MYSTIC ROSE. Combined, by Theosophic Addition, the Wand and Rose together are 3+2+9 = 14 = 1+4 = 5 and 150 or 1+5+0 = 6, or 5+6 or 56. 56 = ISIS (5+6 = 11, of course, the number of magick, of transformation by will, of decoding). At the end of "The Star Sapphire" in Crowley's commentary we find, "it is not he (the Adept) that shall arise in the Sign of Isis Rejoicing." The transformed Adept, greater than the most advanced aliens, is the ultimate victor in the Battle of Conquest Not merely Earth, but the Omniverse is his domain.

12
Interview with Terry R. Wriste
June 24, 1994

["The Law of the Battle of Conquest" section presented previously is, essentially, the work of our friend and sometimes comrade-in-arms, who goes by the name "Terry R. Wriste." This interview was recorded during our most recent encounter.]

Allen H. Greenfield: Terry, when we first met I certainly knew that "Terry R. Wriste" was a nom de guerre, because you were then writing rather inflammatory stuff about guerrilla warfare and revolution, and what-not. It never occurred to me to apply the cipher to your name, because I've known you so long, but Frater 99 of QBLH broke it down, not knowing you, and TERRY R WRISTE, he points out, has a cipher value of 192, as in SECRET MASTER.

Terry R. Wriste: Um? So?

AHG: So, have I been dealing with a Secret Chief all these years?

TRW: C'mon. You know how I got into this stuff. It was the Shaver thing and -

AHG: O.K. So, let's take this from there. You met Dick Shaver in?

TRW: That'd be 1961 or '62. Anyhow, Ray Palmer was then reprinting a lot of the Shaver stuff from the 1940s, about the hidden world, which Shaver claimed was the survival of an antediluvian civili- zation that had moved inside the Earth, while Palmer and others thought this was more esoteric, something fourth dimensional or whatever.

AHG: I thought it was charming mythology, kind of the "demons" of the Shadow Mind vs. the Self in Jungian terms. NICAP told me it was all bunk, so, naturally, I wrote the guy.

TRW: Well I read the stuff Palmer was publishing, plugged into you, and you were by then corresponding with Dick. You also had a collection, as I recall, of old *Amazing Stories* with Shaver stuf£

AHG: No, the collection was later, late sixties.

TRW: Anyhow, Dick got into trouble with the law, skipped Wisconsin and went into hiding. Oddly, it was during that lost period when you were the only one publishing new stuff by him, that I got his address and got involved with the little group of dedicated guerrillas who had decided, in a most unmetaphysical way, to take the best weaponry they could "into the caves" as Shaver would have it, and blow the mind-controlling bastards up. Dick had given several previous groups directions, and they had gone. Mostly [they] didn't come back, but a few did, and I met a few, including one World War Two vet who had been with a team that entered a so-called "cave" located, and get this, near Dulce, New Mexico, under the Archuleta Mesa.

AHG: Isn't that now said to be a joint Gray Alien-Human base?

TRW: You bet. I doubt there was anything there of the sort in 1948, though, and this guy and his team went through a door, and down what seemed to be an old -VERY old -elevator shaft, into a city beneath the Earth, found the Dero -this is what I was told - blew up some machinery, got Rayed and mostly zombied, killed a few DERO-types, and retreated back the way they came in. It was surprise that probably saved their asses, the few that came back.

AHG: Did you believe the story?

TRW: 'Course not. But, I figured, this could be an artifact of something real, and Shaver gave us a couple of locations right here in the South that, he said, were entrances to the caves.

AHG: Right. I investigated both. One was Brown Mountain, North Carolina, and I found plenty of UFO witnesses there, including this guy, Ralph something, that claimed he had been inside the mountain, and whisked off from there to outer space. Quite a yarn. I went there with Gene and Geneva Steinberg once, and with Jim Moseley and his daughter Betty and Tim Beckley, on Christmas Eve, in 1968 as I recall. The other entrance dates back into Cherokee Indian legend of the entrance to Fairyland, Magonia, or whatever-you-call-it. It was the home of the Yum-Wee-Chum-Dee, the Little Men, and was near Tallulah Falls in North Georgia. I searched for years for that entrance. Up where *Deliverance* was filmed.

TRW: You can see it

AHG: Excuse me?

TRW: The entrance. You can see it clearly in the background in one of the rafting scenes in *Deliverance*.

AHG: Coincidence?

TRW: Who knows? Shaver told you the general idea. He also sent you a map.

AHG: What map?

TRW: Thought you had all this figured, didn't you? Remember those rocks he sent you with the pictures in them?

AHG: Sure. They did contain interesting images; they seemed, as I said at the time, like holograms, especially when sectioned and made into 35mm slides. Shaver claimed they were the Record of the antediluvian civilization on Earth, literally preserved in stone. I gave them to you, I recall.

TRW: When I got ahold of them, I resectioned the rocks, used an overhead projector and came up, in one of them, with a map of that little area of North Georgia where Tallulah Falls, Toccoa Falls, Brasstown Bald—you know, the Chattahoochee National Forest. The cave entrance is clearly marked.

AHG: So, this 'map' includes southern North Carolina, and White County, Georgia?

TRW: Yep. With the entrance marked with a red circle.

AHG: That's where Peter Davidson, the Frontal Chief of the Her- metic Brotherhood of Light, set up his utopian colony a hundred years ago.

TRW: You bet, and no coincidence. Where was the previous headquarters? In Scotland, right where the Findhorn Colony was later set up, another haven for the little people.

AHG: So, you and a groap of paramilitary types sought out the marked entrance and found it Then what?

TRW: A door opened, we went in. We were a lot better armed than the guys in the '40s. An odd lot. Recent 'Nam vets, fugitives from R. Y.M. One ...

AHG: For benefit of younger people, that, more or less, [was an] armed militant wing of the anti-Viet Nam War movement

TRW: Exactly. And one guy, the only black guy with us, who was then in the Black Panther Party.

AHG: Quite an odd lot. How many people, all told?

TRW: Ten, in all, plus a photographer who chickened out at that point. He saw the entrance and left.

AHG: So you go in. Then what?

TRW: Practically a replay from the WWII thing. No elevator shaft, but a long downward slope. It got real cold. I still figured that Shaver had been there, that this was some old mining deal right up until I heard the hum.

AHG: Machines? "Mechs," as Shaver called them?

TRW: Exactly, and, I gather, we were expected. By then we were in a kind of cavern, only, I'd say, artificially hollowed out and illuminated by a greenish glow, defuse; not from a single, identifiable source. Anyhow, the whole area resembled Shaver's less exotic subterranean story descriptions, and, in more recent terms, some of the modern alien base stories. We were confronted by these small, grayish beings—humanoid only in the technical sense—and one of our guys said "Dero!" and started shooting. He had an M-1 rifle, if I recall. One shot, and [the little gray being] was illuminated in blue, and just gone. Then there was a sound, and I felt my own gun, an M-16, get unbearably hot I dropped it, turned to run, and was confronted by two of these little gray-skinned guys with a net. Whatever had convinced me my rifle was hot had apparently not focused on my pistol, a vintage Luger, and one of the little net-holders received the last surprise of its life. It kind of exploded, and the other one dropped the net and ran, up the slope, with me suddenly in pursuit. When we got beyond the lighted area, though, it was just gone. I heard gun fire and explosions behind me, and that god-awful hum, and I continued, pistol in hand, looking around wildly, to go back the way I came. Only three of us ever made it back to the surface. One of them died a year or so later, of leukemia, I think. He was only about 24-25, so maybe there's a connection.

AHG: What about the other guy?

TRW: Still alive, as far as I know. He has been back twice since; once alone at another entrance not given by Shaver, but traced from legend. The other with a group similar to my own, all of which returned alive, and is now linked with several Cavern guerrilla groups.

AHG: Why haven't you gone back since?

TRW: For the next year, I was really pretty messed up emotionally. I tried to dissuade you, you'll recall, from one of your expeditions in search of that same entrance. I kept the "Map Stone" for years, but by then had gotten completely deflected into radical political activity, both here and abroad. I thought I was satisfied for a long time that this was a physical cave, that Shaver had been correct—and the metaphysical stuff had nothing to do with it. And we were, I thought, hopelessly outclassed technologically. I've realized that Faerie is neither physical nor metaphysical because I've—in the last five years, I've seen too many experiments of an occult nature where the same beings have been conjured up and dealt with in a variety of ways. So, this stuff seems on the border of the physical and metaphysical realms, and I'm not sure, to borrow a phrase, that a truly advanced technology could be distinguished from magick.

AHG: So after our political association, you dropped out of sight, and were, what, studying magick?

TRW: Until you came up with this cipher stuff: I was mainly concentrating on the abduction cases, to see if I could actively intercept and intervene. When you turned me on to the cipher stuff: I applied it to the West Virginia cases, and went out and met Indrid Cold.

AHG: That's the being that Woodrow Derenberger encountered in '66 in West Virginia.

TRW: Right You correctly pointed out that the cases rich in funny names, as you call them, contain messages that are meant to be conveyed through media unconsciously, by simply reporting the case. The whole Mothman flap of that period was full of predictive information, and even working on it in the late '80s I was able to predict and intervene in several abductions. But the fact that the name "Indrid Cold" that the being gave has a cipher value of 112 in classical New Aeon cipher told me that this was important, because 112 shows up, as you know, over and over in important cases. I was intrigued by Cold's statement to Woody that he "comes from a country weaker than yours" which is not so much cipher as simple metaphor for being a native of one of the worlds already conquered by the Grays and their allies. I figured he was a fugitive, and probably looking for contact with others in the know, so he probably lived fairly near the contact point, as a fugitive from the Grays. I looked at 112 in that light, and some of the other cipher values involved.

AHG: So, what did you find?

TRW: His home address, virtually.

AHG: Embedded in the number 112?

TRW: In part; I am going to protect him as much as I can; although he is neither blond nor androgynous, he is what the current UFOlogy jargon calls a "Blond" and he does indeed come from the Procyon System. Like me, he's been an outlaw all his life. In any case, just from the number 112, a number he gave an unknowing Woodrow Derenberger on a stretch of interstate, taking the context and using *The Book of the Law* for the deciphering purposes Aiwass and the Third Order intended, I discovered clues in the very fragmentary phrases you regard as "noise" rather than "signal."

112 = WE ARE ONE, the code phrase that tells you you're in important territory, but also THY WIFE and LETTER and WORDS AND SIGNS and INK AND BLACK and ALL HOUSE OF GOD and THE WHEEL and I AM 49 PLACE and, as you noted CROSS 52 I FLAP.

AHG: Good stuff What does it mean?

TRW: Like I said, I am leaving other values out I used in order to protect Mr. Cold, but from this I began looking near the Ohio- West Virginia line, the Mothman area, for a church (112 also yields ALL HOUSE OF GOD), with a graveyard adjacent (AND THE DEAD) near the Kentucky-Ohio-West Virginia border along U.S. Highway 52. Near a location where Mothman had literally been sighted flapping across Highway 52, I found such a Church next to a restaurant called The Wagon Wheel (THE WHEEL) with a church- yard on the other side and an address related to I AM 49 PLACE; I won't be more specific. There was one little ramshackle house with words and signs allover it about colds and stars and the like.

AHG: So you just walked up to the door?

TRW: A guy, with one big difference from the descriptions, walks up, like he had been waiting; I didn't knock, and I said, "Mr. Cold, I presume?" He smiled and said, "My friends call me Indrid."

AHG: Let me guess, he was a black guy. The Blonds can be black.

TRW: The Blonds is a conceit started by Adamski and Ric williamson. They have the same racial features and range we do, and can project features at will, as Cold did for Derenberger, in the interest of security. Ric Williamson, I guess, believed all that Nordic-Aryan race crap from the Nazis. How'd you guess?

AHG: 112 equals INK AND BlACK, so it was just a guess.

TRW: Very good. We had a long talk, and he and his little group are really isolated fugitives. Their messages were primarily a distress signal, but to this date none of their own have shown up, and they continue to lay low. The story Cold told me is the basic one you hear, how much I believe I don't know, but they speak of being over run by the Grays and other more serious Deep Aliens working for the Negatives. The most unusual point was his claim that they had been invited to take refuge on Earth by the Third Order—humans and posthumans who are advanced enough to qualify as Earth's representatives in space-based governments. But Indrid Cold, or whoever he is, hasn't heard from the Third Order, either. I think he may have moved on, but I will continue to conceal some details until I know he is safe, as I promised.

AHG: I respect that, but let me make one guess, just to see if I get the pattern. 112 = THY WIFE. Does that refer to Cold's wife, called KIMI by Derenberger? And does the cipher value of Kimi provide additional clues?

TRW: Right. This was a distress beacon, disguised as a contact episode. The whole Mothman thing was a distress beacon that failed.

AHG: So the whole mystery can be decoded in this way?

TRW: Probably.

AHG: So are you a Secret Chief? ..

TRW: That would be telling.

Painting by Richard S. Shaver

APPENDIX ONE

Select control names from mediumship, adepts hip and contacteeism

ASHTAR, MAAT, THOR, OSOMO all = 47 (4+7=11)
AURA RHANES = 92 (9+2=11)
MORYA, VOLTRA, MANCO all = 56 (5+6=11)
VAL THOR = 60 = RA DISC .
MASTER AETHERIUS = 224 = ELIXIR OF LIFE & GOD
But, curiously, also INDRID COLD+CARL ARDO+LANULUS. (The complete myth cycle.)
AURA RHANES = 92 = FEMALE and LET HER.
She is one of the few contacts who is named and female.
ORLON = 42 = SANANDA and ZAGO+ZO
ORTHON = JESUS and LOMEC
HAA TON = 64 = MARKON
J.W. = 19 = RO (see Shaver Mystery)
LAZARIS = 52 = MONKA
COSMOS = 58 = LANULUS and MADACANA and SETH RAMTHA = 63 = ORION
KIMI = 76 = SOLTEC
SUTTKU = 96 = LRAETON

APPENDIX TWO: The Sirius Mystery and V. A. L. I. S.

" ...The teachings of the Order of the Silver Star derive from the Star of Set (i.e. Sirius). "

Kenneth Grant

PEOPLE speculate about extraterrestrialism and its relationship to the "Secret Chiefs of the Order." Although many consider this poetic metaphor (at best), magical writers Kenneth Grant and Michael Bertiaux, along with a few perceptive UFOlogists, have made serious speculations in this direction.

Certainly, the Aiwass, Lam and other experiences of Aleister Crowley relate to certain types of contactee material. An example is *The Ra Material* generated by the late Don Elkins, Carla Rueckert and others. The stellar references in magick are numerous, and specula- tions along the lines of Philip K. Dick's gnostic VALIS trilogy, along with the more creditable visitation literature (as in Robert Temple's *The Sirius Mystery*) seem worthy of examination in the light of New Aeon English Qabalah.

Indeed, New Aeon Cipher work with Lexicon and the Star 26 program have some resemblance to the kind of communication we have proposed for transmission via radio telescope.

Phil Dick's V.A.L.I.S. ("Vast Active Living Intelligence System") seemed a suitable point of departure. The phrase value of the complete term VAST ACTIVE LIVING INTELLIGENCE SYSTEM = 515 = I AM LIFE AND THE GIVER OF LIFE OF EVERY STAR, a most suggestive phrase considering that VALIS is supposed to be a kind of god-computer capable of transmitting meaningful transformative messages to Earth. The acronym VALIS = 41 = HER (repeated many times), but also = WHOLE. In the VALIS story, a magical child is created as a messiah. The child is female. Phil Dick died at age 54 during the filming of *Blade Runner* based (very loosely) on his antima- chine novel *Do Androids Dream of Electric Sheep?* In his last year he became a follower of British contactee Benjamin Creme and maintained that his earlier works of fiction—allegory, really—contained a sort of cipher. The last of his novels published in his lifetime, *The Divine Invasion*, dealt with this theme from a Gnostic religious vantage point He maintained that the phrase "King Felix" was a cipher for the coming of a New Being, who would deliver humanity from the "black iron prison." KING FELIX = 147 = RESISTANCE.

Much of the starseed speculation centers on Sirius or Sothis, the Dog Star so important as a calendar yardstick in ancient Egypt, and the object of *The Sirius Mystery* speculations on ancient visitations from the stars. SIRIUS = 85 = OF OUR LADY (see VALIS = 41 = HER), a phrase'from Crowley's *Liber Cheth*. From *Liber AL*. SIR-

IUS = 85 = AM ABOVE and VISIT and FOLLOW ME. The Sirius tradition has apparently been perpetuated by many generations of priests, so it is interesting that SIRIUS = 85 = BISHOP.

The cycle quoted here does seem to lend weight to the starseed transmission concept as it applies to the Crowley Class A documents, including the deciphering of *Liber AI vel Legis, The Book of the Law*.

APPENDIX THREE:
Working with the Secret Cipher

WHAT follows are several "raw" bulletins that appeared on computer networks with the intent of rapidly spreading cipher knowledge to researchers around the world.

Although in rough draft form, they should explain themselves.

QBL UPDATE V1 Nl
MAY BE REPRINTED
REPLY VIA THIS BOARD

[QBL UPDATE is an ongoing communications link displaying recent discoveries using the New Aeon Qabala of *Liber AL* vel Legis. All cipher values given, unless otherwise specified, utilize the classic 1974 cipher, also known to Lexicon users as Cipher 6. Comments and contributions are welcome. All information is more-or-less raw and subject to further evaluation and revision.]

CIPHER SIX ON Liber LXVI—a new table: *Liber LXVI*, or *Book 66*, the "*Book of the Bloody Star*" may be thought of as the Inner Order instruction in a kind of sexual magick designed to make the Adept superior to any 'mind control' available to the Gray Aliens or any such beings who use psychosexual and implant techniques during Abductions to control humans. The number recurs in and out of the Cipher context:

11) EARTH = 66
12) MEANS = 66
13) GATES = 66
14) ARISE = 66
15) HEART 66
16) MIX = 66
17) COME = 66
18) BABE = 66
19) The Book of the Bloody Star is itself numbered "66."
10) Gloria Lee Byrd was told to fast by enemy Aliens posing as benevolent beings. She collapsed and fell into a coma on the 66th day, and died shortly thereafter.
11) After Hunrath and Wilkinsin disappeared -apparently Abducted—the number "66" was found written on Wilkinsin's wall at home in the old Royal Arch Masonic Cipher.
12) The Ordo Templi Orientis began its revival in the 66th year after the writing of *The Book of the Law*, which was predicted by MARK III, also known as George Hunt Williamson.

The name ALEISTER Crowley qualifies as a magical name, as it is a chosen name. It is significant, therefore, that the chosen name ALEISTER = 117 = FRATER

ACHAD. ALEISTER CROWLEY = 194 = HANGS UFON THE CROSS and BLACK TO THE BLIND and LUST & POWER OF LUST. Also BRING THE GLORY and SING HER LOVE CHANT. But also ONE TO FOLLOW THEE and, not from *Liber AL*, but interestingly, COMPUTER KEY.

On the subject of the KEY, KEY = 49 = SOLVE and CROWN. KEY OF IT ALL = 126 = ROSE CROIX and SHALL TURN NOT as well as NOT TALK NOT. All of these are references specific to the "key" interpretation of the text on the grid page of *Liber AL*. Also NOTHING IS A, an obvious reference to 'The Fool' and a seeming reference to the lack of a number in the upper left square of that page, itself a key to the discovery of cipher 6. See Achad's *Liber 31* on the words "Not" and "Crown."

Reference List for QBL students—Achad's *LIBER XXXI*; Damon's *LIBER XIII*; booklet Quabalistic Alchemist Arcanum V1, N1; "*The Key to the English Qaballa*" by Carol A. Smith; "*The English Qaballa*" by Jake Stratton-Kent, "*Liber Trigrammaton*" by Althotash; "*Qaballa for the Querulous*" by Asharat, *The ParaUFOlogist* V2 N1 and V2 N2; Controls.txt by 171.

QBL ONLINE UPDATE
V1 N2
REPLY VIA THIS BULLETIN BOARD
MAY BE FREELY REPRINTED

QBL ONLINE UPDATE is an ongoing informational project for disseminating relatively raw data on New Aeon English Qabala research.

Do what thou wilt shall be the whole of the Law.

The following research work requires a little explanation. In general, I have been resistant to facile "conversions" from traditional Hebrew qabala to New Aeon work, because English is a very different language from Hebrew—number of letters, cultural context, etc. are vastly different. On reflection, though, once something is reduced to pure number, it should be subject to analysis, particularly if Frater Achad's point about the Holy Books is correct: "Holy Book: *Liber AL* vel Legis; with recognition of former Scriptures." One need not accept—and I do not—Achad's proclamation of an "Aeon of Maat" to consider his qabalistic work of great importance, and his other claims to be either valid or not amenable to the critique of others.

Thought of the month: "New Aeon English Qabala" was a term I introduced to distinguish our work from English numerology and earlier attempts at developing an English Qabala without the complete KEY of *Liber AL*. From this point, I will encourage abbreviating this work NAEQ6 or classical cipher (six in Lexicon) of the New Aeon English Qabala for convenience.

In any case, the work that follows resulted from a lengthy conversation between a classical student of Talmudic studies and his son Tau Samson, a Gnostic Bishop. The work centers on the Hebrew Kiddish, or "blessing over wine" which, in formula, never mentions wine as such, but only the "fruit of the vine." As there are ancient frequently used Hebrew words for wine, grapes, etc., the habitual use of "fruit of the vine" (the word "vine" appears 63 times in KJV of Old and New Testaments) [appears] as a blessing. English WINE and VINE are related—the Hebrew words are not. Some references are intriguing even in raw form, as Psalm 80:8: "You have brought a vine out of Egypt and shall exile the infidel, and planted it "

The complimentary bruchah, or blessing, is over the "bread of the earth." Some discussion was given to vines covering the earth, the drawing of nutrients from the soil, and the alchemical process of making gold from base elements of the earth. Such gold reduces to a white powder, or tincture, using a secret process not suitable for delineation here.

The Hebrew word for VINE, hagufen, or Hey Gimel Peh Nun (final) = 788 in Hebrew qabala. 788 (heb.) = THE SECRET WISDOM, that is to say, the Qabala. Our attention is instant, or should be. VINE in NAEQ6 = 72 and that should get our attention, also. The number 788 yields, in *Liber AL*, AMEN. THIS IS OF THE 4 — THERE IS A FIFTH WHO IS INVISIBLE AND THEREIN AM I. Since English and Hebrew words for VINE are, like Amen, four letter words, it is interesting that, by Theosophical Addition, 788 = 7+8+8=23/2+3=5 the "FIFTH WHO IS INVISIBLE."

788 also produces LOVE/WILL KEY: DO WHAT THOU WILT SHALL BE THE WHOLE OF THE LAW. LOVE IS THE LA W, LOVE UNDER WILL.

788 = ALL RARE SCENTS ARE OF JASMINE AND ROSE; SILVER, GOLD AND LAPIS LAZULI & JASPER ARE THERE, which hits upon our gold theme. Gold, be it noted, is in some sense the "goal of the Great Work" and is a source of both health and wealth. The bruchah or blessings are the closest thing in Judaism to a formal Sacrament comparable to communion. Only it is a communion with a "vine" not a god. Say you so? Jesus, quoted in John 15:1: "1 am the true vine and my Father is the husbandman."

The powdered white gold produced by modern, but alchemica4 processes brought to mind the WHITE TINCTURE. In NAEQ6 WHITE TINCTURE = 231 = SEVENTY TWO FOLD LION and, also HERMETICALLY SEALED. VINE = 72 = I.N.R.I. and all kinds of neat stuff: (Alchemically, WARM ARROW.)

788 = THE SECRET CHIEFS WORK THE KAHN THROUGH SERAPIS BEY, TUITIT BEY. Requires some explanation. Hey Gimel Peh Nun are lines 15, 13, 27 and 24 respectively in *777*. Gimel's magical power is, get this, the WHITE TINCTURE, equal to KHAN in the Taoist system by *777* correspondences. Serapis Bey and Tuitit Bey are two of Madame Blavatsky's "Mahatmas," the Secret Chiefs of the Theosophical System. Actually, these two are modeled on Paolos Metamon, the Coptic magician and adept, and Max Theon, his disciple and successor as Grand Master of the Hermetic Brotherhood of Light in Egypt. You could read the line as "The Secret Chiefs work the white tincture through the HB of L. The HB of L, under Frontal Chief Davidson, moved to North Georgia in the 1880s. Its knowledge and wisdom migrated into the OTO under Grand Master Karl Kellner, an HB of L continental adept.

Examine lines 15, 13, 27, 24 in *777* for further insight.

Love is the Law, love under will.

Bibliography

I believe it was Robert Graves who observed that all translation is a lie. Take the Greek word *Agape*. In English, it means "love"—sort of. Actually, if you truly understand the word, you understand the Great Mysteries.

In the Theosophical literature, the tendency is to use the term "Master" and Mahatma interchangably. In our discussion of the super being concept, I have guardedly used the untranslated German term ubermensch. Nietzsche also used a term usually translated "higher men" and his Nazi "admirers" and corrupters long after his death introduced a term usually translated "subhuman."

Magicians have tended, in the English-speaking world, to refer to the "masters" simply as the Secret Chiefs of the Order.

Ubermensch and Mahatma actually mean the same thing. The Sanskrit root words Maha ("great") and Atman ("being" or "soul") and the German uber ("over" or "super") and mensch ("man" or "human") both carry the sense of "more highly evolved human being." Seen in this light, it can be better understood how Mahatma Ghandi and the Theosophical "Master K.H." may fall in the same category. The reader may wish to compare possible masters of the positive and negative type by trying their hands at Timothy Leary's computer game Mind Mirror. Try Hitler and Christ for starters.

In all cases, I advise one to check sources. Some of the interconnections are startling; Ghandi and the Theosophical Society, the Rite of Memphis and Mizraim, the radical Carbonari, the Socialist Labor Party—all interconnect without the least linkage to conspiracy theo- ries, and explain a lot of subsequent history.

Some suggested sourcebooks:

In Search of the Masters—Behind the Occult Myth by Paul Johnson
UFOs: Operation Trojan Horse by John A. Keel
Passport to Magonia by Jacques Vallee
The lIluminoids by Neal Wilgus
The Nine Unknown by Talbot Mundy
The Morning of the Magicians by Pauwels and Bergier
The Occult Reich by J.H. Brannan
The Spear of Destiny by Trevor Ravenscroft
The Eye in the Triangle by Israel Regardie
The Confessions of Aleister Crowley by Aleister Crowley
The Autobiography of Malcolm X as told to Alex Haley
Magick Without Tears by Aleister Crowley, edited by Regardie
Thus Spoke Zarathustra by Friedrich Nietzche
The Last Testament by Greg Rickman
Valis by Philip K. Dick

The Transmigration of Timothy Archer by Philip K. Dick
Radio Free Albemuth by Philip K. Dick
What Is Enlightenment? John White, Editor
Cosmic Consciousness by Richard Bucke. M.D.
Hitler m'a dit by Hermann Rauschning
The Fellowship by Brad Steiger
The Silencers by Timothy Green Beckley
The Silver Bridge by Gray Barker
The Sirius Mystery by Robert Temple

Also check their sources, if possible. The material on the black lodges in the Nazi era is based on fundamental sources and obscure volumes named in the sourcebooks listed here. Johnson lists his obscure sources in detail. The fictional nature of Mundy's work should be placed in the context of his professional career as a British Colonial Police Officer in India, and P.K. Dick's fiction should be classed as allegory or slightly disguised biography, both by his own account and that of his biographers.

Nephilim Al-Kemy

Nephilim Al-Kemy.

Nephilim Al-Kemy was created after several years of research and intense experiences. In the early 1990s. Ms. Page encountered an authentic Western Adept. Through this person, Ms. Page received the story of the Nephilim, their part in human history. Ms. Page was also shown the progression of the Nephilim's lineage through time — including where it has remained in some level of stability, and where and how it has been corrupted. This story is also a prophecy, and the time of this prophecy is now.

The painting is an unfolding of this prophecy. It is on a 30x40 canvas, with 8 separate panels revealing different aspects of the story. The cover of this text is the central panel, showing the alchemical movement of certain sacred substances, in relation to "The Void", to bring about a specific transformation in the human population. (In popular culture, this has been called "STARFIRE", and the conclusions of this popular stream of thought are incorrect.) Any sincere query regarding this painting can be directed to watcherashera777@yahoo.com.

— *Ms. Debra Page.*

Meeting of the Inner Circle
by Jonathan Sellers.

Afterword
Cipher As Art: Art As Code Language.

This is a book about a secret cipher that exists within *The Book of the Law* (*Liber AL vel Legis*), and which has been found to make some sense of the mysterious and often ridiculous utterances of trance channels and those who have been contacted by the ultra-terrestrials.

This book reveals to a wider public that which Initiates have known, it is fair to say, since at least the 1940s, if not earlier.

There have been ciphers and codes worked into religious and magical teachings since at least the times of the Gnostics. Ciphers and codes have been used to conceal vital information, sensitive data, secret communications. Before Blaise de Viginière's famous table of combinations, used in cryptography, it was known as the Right and Averse Table of Combinations of the Letters, revealed to us in Cornelius Agrippa's seminal magnum opus, the *Three Books of Occult Philosophy*, from Renaissance times. Later it was badly paraphrased by one of the foundation authors of the Western Occult Revival, Francis Barrett, in his *The Magus, or Celestial Intelligencer*. These, in their turn were influenced by Abraham Abulafia's Rational Tables of Ziruph.

While working on the typesetting of the Second Revised edition of *Secret Cipher of the UFOnauts*, I have seen an interesting film, and run across some interesting items elsewhere dealing with the idea of Art being used to conceal messages. In fact, some of the early work presented on the Antiquities of the Illuminati website deals with the concept of "Cipher as Art".

Brief mention must be made (in passing, since a revamped edition of the piece is on the boards) – to the engravings of Pierre Lambert de Lintot. He concealed information in at least three ciphers, one of which was openly revealed, another revealed in the decoded material from THAT cipher, and a third which was not easy to come by, without the information that Speth made available in the *Ars Quatuor Coronati* periodical. Though the encrypted material is rather tame once deciphered, the engravings are captivating, and, in fact, rather haunting at times. *A Curious Masonic Engraving*, published by this reporter on 01 May 2000 c.e., is one such attempt at bringing this material to our online readership.

Also, in passing: the paintings of Nicolas Poussin, who has caught the attention of many people since the franchise cottage industry of *Holy Blood, Holy Grail* came into being in 1982. Upon studying his paintings, I found them to be an example of the first Vector Painting Program that ever existed. Poussin, in his turn, derived a lot of his symbolism from the *Iconologia* of Cesaré Ripa, in the Second Edition (there are three). Some of these are available online. Some aren't. It's really a bit like an ARG (Alternate Reality Game). Using images to convey individual letters, words, and/or ideas is what this kind of thing is all about. What are the messages being conveyed, you ask? Stay tuned.

I recently saw a Sherlock Holmes movie. It was the final pairing of Basil Rathbone and Nigel Bruce, "Dressed to Kill" – and it features a cipher of sorts. This time, the cipher consists of the mistakes intentionally placed in the spikes in the music boxes created by a prison inmate. The mistakes are then compared to the notes on the piano keyboard. There is a method of deriving alphabetical letters (above and beyond the standard seven notes in a scale) – and hey presto! a message appears, and they know where to look for the lost Five Pound Note plates stolen from the Bank of England.

Are these valid things, these days? Of course they are, with such technologies as Steganography being employed by "terrorist cells" and by intelligence agencies. Can encrypted information be transmitted visually that conveys a story? Of course it can!

Really, we humans are conditioned by symbols, codes, ciphers – constantly. We speak and act in code, think in code – particularly when multi-tasking, as most of us are required to do every day.

What the reader, becoming aware of this material for the first time, may need to have background information on in order to grasp the subject matter – some of us can speak of in short-hand.

What may seem like high-weirdness, fringe material, talk of little green men (women and trans-genders too) – to the casual reader, or to the Uninitiated – actually makes perfect sense and can be regarded as a sort of everyday concensus reality among the Illuminati.

As it was written upon parchment – "Solis Sacerdotibus".

Having gained acquaintance, in the Gnostic context, of things – things of which I speak in part, but not in their entirety – in my writings and elsewhere (and I can recognize those who have achieved Initiation into the same or similar mysteries) it is rather amusing (when it isn't just a plain old "damned nuisance") – when people say I speak in enigmas, or in riddles, or in a manner that they cannot understand, when most of the people I communicate with regularly have no such difficulty. It just goes to show ya:

"Behold, I speak in a mystery..."

Cipher as Art: Art as Code Language.

The frontispiece to this book consists of a detail excerpted from a larger picture I did for the Antiquities of the Illuminati website in 2002.

I'd downloaded a narrative of a trip to Tlemcen, Algeria, published in *Tour du Monde*. This was from the 1870s. The image is of a group of Jewish Musicians giving a concert, entitled "Concert Juif à Tlemcen" by D. Maillart....

Concert juif, à Tlemcen. — Dessin de D. Maillart, d'après des photographies de M. Pedra.

There are a number of rather nice engravings in that account. For whatever it's worth, Tlemcen, Algeria, is where Max Theon's facility was – the same facility where he put together *The Cosmic Philosophy*.

At the time I was learning Photoshop skills. I took this engraving (*above*), and decided that I would modify it. I gathered together the images of figures that were important to the Authentic Tradition and placed them over the heads of the Musicians and the other characters in the engraving (*see next page*).

Aleister Crowley was placed in the central position in the grouping of five musicians. I found other heads to place on the other bodies: To Crowley's right, Jacob Frank and Meade Layne. To his left, Mark Probert and Max Theon.

In the foreground, I added a character I'd found in another old French publication. It is a lamp shaped like a rather rotund man, with a flaming penis. I named him "Fire Man" (there was an "inside joke" to this, which had to do with the band Alamantra's song "Lunch Lady Arms".) I later discovered a similar female counterpart, a pitcher, who goes under the name "Tank Girl."

Left: "FireMan"

Right: "TankGirl"

To the left of this assembly are (presumably) the people who live in the villa where these musicians are playing. I placed Allen Greenfield, myself, and the artist who produced the painting used on the cover of the present volume. She is symbolized by the Urartu head. The child morphed into "Father_ACME" aka "LAM 2000".

In the background, on the wall, we see "Do What Thou Wilt" – graffiti taken from a picture of Bobby Beausoleil's house in the Haight, from the 1960s. Also, a "poster" – Antiquities of the Illuminati Tour 2003, featuring the picture which fronts the present article. It, too, is a collage.

Examine the group of musicians: Meade Layne, Jacob Frank, Aleister Crowley, Mark Probert and Max Theon, with "FireMan" in the foreground dancing to the music. Perhaps suggesting the following?

> "I SEE o' nights among the whins
> The Devil walking widdershins. "
> —Aleister Crowley
> — "The Devil's Conversion", from *KONX OM PAX.*

It is this sort of thing we are referring to when we speak of art as cipher. The image here, for us, evokes this poem from *Konx Om Pax.* We recommend the entire poem, but only quote the first line, above.

In the gathering of the musicians, and the "Devil walking widdershins" – we can see a couple of pentagrams. The Right and the Averse. The apex of the Right Pentagram is Crowley. The Apex of the Averse Pentagram is "FireMan". Even the angles of the heads and the directions they point suggest this.

Not only is this a piece of art: it is conveying a very vital teaching, as to how the Illuminati really works. What is this?

A Secret Ritual of the Illuminati?

I was not aware of any of this at the time I created the piece. I was teaching myself Photoshop, as I said, and I was more interested in creating interesting and humorous art pieces to illustrate the Antiquities website.

The work of narrating the past involves a great deal of conjuration – of the characters from the past that we study and write about. Particularly those characters whom we are connected to by sundry associational links – "We are a VERY BIG Organization!"

We do this with our writings, our websites, the information we share, the recordings and the visual art – and so this is how it transpires that the Illuminati can and do arrive on the scene at repeated intervals, usually without any advance notice.

Another thing – consider the elements as glyphs that represent a trigger to the entire body of each "symbol's" work – the works of Layne / BSRF, Jacob Frank, Aleister Crowley, Mark Probert / Yada di Shi'ite, Max Theon – for example, as well as Allen's writings, et al.

I conclude with a short description of the scene that opens this afterword.

I had obtained a copy of *Monuments of Egypt* – the plates from the French "*Description de l'Ègypte*" series commissioned by Napoleon. Here we have a picture of the inside of a tomb. Two of the explorers are in there – or are they locals? One is smoking (dope, probably!), while the other stands in contemplation. We placed Hathor's head above the entry to the alcove. Inside the alcove we placed Father_ACME conceived as a seated Buddha image, a halo of light surrounds his head.

Is this not a Secret Ritual of the Illuminati?

Search and See!

—Jonathan Sellers
—Twin Cedars Lodge
—Fall Equinox 2005, c.e.

ABOUT THE AUTHORS

Timothy Green Beckley

He calls himself "Mr. UFO." Timothy Green Beckley is a UFO & paranormal pioneer. Since an early age his life has more or less revolved around the paranormal. The house he was raised in was thought to be haunted, he underwent out of body experiences at age six, and saw his first of three UFOs when he was ten. Over the years he has written over 50 books on everything from rock music to the secret MJ12 papers. Beckley has made available a total of approximately 250 titles by other authors, such as T. Lobsang Rampa, Brad Steiger, Tim R. Swartz, Sean Casteel, and Maria D' Andrea. Today he is the president of Inner Light/Global Communications and editor of the Conspiracy Journal and Bizarre Bazaar.

www.conspiracyjournal.com

Sean Casteel

Sean Casteel is a freelance journalist who has written about UFOs, alien abduction and related subjects since 1989. His articles have been featured in "UFO Magazine," "FATE Magazine," "UFO Universe Magazine," and "Open Minds Magazine," among many other paranormal-themed newsstand publications. Casteel has also written several books for Global Communications, to include "The Heretic's UFO Guidebook" and "UFOs, Prophecy and the End of Time." In addition, he has co-authored or contributed to numerous other Global Communications books, such as "Disclosure: Breaking Through the Barrier of Global UFO Secrecy" and "The Ark of the Covenant and Other Secret Weapons of the Ancients." He is a frequent contributor to the paranormal website "UFO Digest," as well as the online magazine "Phenomena."

Maria D' Andrea

Maria D'Andrea is an internationally known professional psychic from Budapest, Hungary. Since early childhood she has demonstrated high spiritual awareness and psychic ability. Over her lifetime and as a spiritual leader, she has provided psychic guidance and enlightenment to many people, assisting them on their own personal path of spiritual self discovery. Maria is known for a unique form of divination called Rune Casting. This method was used by Vikings and Europeans to unlock information about the past, present and future by tapping into the Universal Mind. She is also author of such books as: "Heaven Sent Money Spells," "Occult Grimoire And Magical Formulary," and "Your Personal Mega Power Spells."

Allen H. Greenfield, D. D.

Allen H. Greenfield, D.D., is in a unique position to interpret the lore of UFOlogy for occultists and to explain the elusive mythos of Occultism to UFOlogists. A thirty-five year veteran of UFO investigative work, Greenfield has twice been honored with the coveted "UFOlogist of the Year" award by NUFOC (1972 and 1992), and is co-founder of the National UFO Conference, one of the oldest UFO-oriented conventions in the world.

Greenfield edits The Paraufologist and is a Charter Member of the Permanent Organizing Committee of the National UFO Conference. In addition, Greenfield has been an occultist since 1960 and has practiced ceremonial magick since 1969. In 1985, after years of service, he was consecrated a Bishop in the esoteric Gnostic spiritual tradition and has served a substantial metropolitan congregation in this capacity since 1988.

Visit Dr. Greenfield's excelnt website at:
http://www.mindspring.com/~hellfire/bishop/

PLEASE NOTE: THOSE WISHING TO HAVE ALL OF THE SYMBOLS AND CIPHERS IN THIS VOLUME PRINTED OUT ON HEAVY PARCHMENT -- FOR MORE POWERFUL USAGE PLEASE SEND $25.00 + $5 S/H TO

TIMOTHY G BECKLEY
BOX 753
NEW BRUNSWICK, NJ 08903

Or mrufo8@hotmail.com for PayPal Credit Cards 732 602-3407

WATCH AND SUBSCRIBE TO OUR FREE YOUTUBE CHANNEL—MR.UFO'S SECRET FILES

YOUR RECOMMENDED TOOLS FOR SOLICITING AN ANGEL

The Sigillum Dei Emeth

TALISMANS AND SYMBOLS

This book contains a good assortment of talismans and symbols which can be easily duplicated so that you do not have to cut up your copy of this book. Most copy shops can copy the talismans, symbols and tables onto heavy card stock. Maybe make two copies so that you have one as backup.

We do offer copies of all the talismans and symbols printed on heavy parchment. They can be purchased for $25 for the entire set plus $5 shipping and handling.

BLACK-STONE SCRYING BOWL

MIRROR, MIRROR ON THE WALL . . .
LOOK INTO THE DARK MIRROR OF MAGIC TO FIND OUT ALL

Nostradamus Knew Its Powers! Many Prophets Have Used It To Gaze Into The Future! Some Claim That, By Peering Into It, You Can Talk To Spirits Or Tap Into Heavenly Realms To Speak With Your Angel Guide.

Used as a black scrying mirror, our black-stone scrying bowl, is a powerful psychic tool. It can bring the user hidden knowledge and clairvoyant ability and can act as a portal to other planes of existence. History shows its use in many of the traditional mystery schools and oracular temples. Today the serious student of magickal arts can rediscover the ancient rites of the magick mirror, for these techniques are again coming to light. Scrying can be defined as the art of gazing into or upon a crystal, dark mirror or black-stone scrying bowl, allowing the physical eyes to relax, thus letting the inner psychic eyes begin to open and receive desired visions or information. The use of the black mirror is one of the best methods of achieving the state of mind required for entering trance and for scrying work. It not only acts as a focal point for visualization but can become a doorway into other dimensions. It has been adapted as standard fare when engaging unseen kingdoms.

We have Scrying Bowls available for $39.95 plus $12 $hipping

A Black-Stone Scrying Bowl of approximately 4 inches in diameter. Fill this black marble scrying bowl with a shallow pool of water and gaze within to gain the same insights with the scrying methods used by Ancient Greeks, Nostradamus and Enochian magicians John Dee and Edward Kelley.

ARCH ANGEL AMULET

Engraved along its outer edge in Enochian script that reads: "Before me, behind me, to my right and to my left, I am surrounded by protection." No cord. $29.95 plus $5 S/H

7 ARCHANGELES FRAGRANCE STICKS

7 heavenly fragrances of 5 sticks each, in 7 artistically designed packets inside a box. Truly inspired, each scent has a nice sandalwood base with a delicate but distinct flower scent. Each scent is dedicated to one of the 7 Archangels: Michael, Jofiel, Chamuel, Gabriel, Rafael, Uriel, & Zadquiel. Each fragrance has about 5 sticks, totaling 35 sticks in the box. - $10 plus $5 S/H

ANGEL LEATHER BLANK BOOK

Use as your Book of Shadows, Journal or Diary. Angels leather blank book to write down your communication attempts. Hand tooled blank leather journal with embossed angel covers. Border embossing may vary. Sizes vary slightly. Leather, handmade paper. 280 pages, cord closure. 5" x 7" Design and size may vary according to available stock- $39.95 plus $8 S/H

SPECIAL — ALL RECOMMENDED TOOLS FOR CONTACTING YOUR ANGEL GUIDE AS LISTED ABOVE JUST $135.00 + $15 S/H

ORDER FROM:
Timothy G Beckley · Box 753 · New Brunswick, NJ 08903
mrufo8@hotmail.com (we can send PayPal Invoice)
Credit Cards: 732 602-3407

SPELLCRAFT, WISECRAFT, OCCULT, METAPHYSICS
Workbooks And Study Guides From Qualified Instructors

MARIA D' ANDREA

Maria is a gifted psychic, spiritual counselor, and shaman. She has helped those in matters of luck, love and financial concerns. She lectures, holds workshops and does private counseling in NY area. Her books are exclusively published by Tim Beckley.

HEAVEN SENT MONEY SPELLS
IMAGINE RECEIVING MONEY JUST BY USING THE POWERS OF YOUR MIND! Let Maria D' Andrea Tell You How To Turn Your Dreams Into Cash — And Become A Virtual Human MONEY MAGNET. Inspired by the Heavenly Light.Here are spells that anyone can learn to execute. Use herbs, candles and gemstones to create prosperity! Have talismans and amulets help do the work for you!
8.5x11—Workbook format—132 pages—ISBN-13: 978-1606111000—$19.95

SECRET OCCULT GALLERY AND SPELL CASTING FORMULARY
COME UP TO THE "GOOD LIFE" with Maria's top dozen enchantments and occult gallery of mystical and spiritual essentials. Easy to perform spells that could put you on easy street.
8.5x11—Workbook format—152 pages—ISBN-13: 978-1606111284—$21.95

YOUR PERSONAL MEGA POWER SPELLS
A valuable interpretation of blessings, protections, hex-breaking rituals and ceremonies as practiced by the most ardent of Wiccans, alchemists, sages and occultists down through the centuries.
8.5X11—252 pages—ISBN-13: 978-1606111055—$21.95

SECRET MAGICAL ELIXIRS OF LIFE
Explore The Paranormal Vibrations Of Crystals, Gems And Stones For Good Health, Enhanced Psychic Powers And Phenomenal Inner Strength!
8.5X11—150 PAGES—ISBN-13: 978-1606111147—$21.95

HOW TO ELIMINATE ANXIETY AND STRESS THROUGH THE OCCULT
Just utilize Crystals, Gemstones, Meditation, Herbs, Oils, Visualization, Chakras, Music, Prayer, Mandalas, Mantras, Incense, Candles and More.
6x9—150 pages—ISBN-13: 978-1606111383—$19.95

MYSTICAL, MAGICKAL BEASTS AND BEINGS
Come explore the supernatural side of man's best – and worst – "friends" as related in the strangest stories involving beasties of all sorts – seen and unseen. And uppermost learn how to get them to assist in our lives in a positive way. Other contributors include Penny Melis and Sean Casteel.
8.5x11—224 pages—ISBN-13: 978-1606111567—$21.95

OCCULT GRIMORIE AND MAGICAL FORMULARY
10 BOOKS ROLLED INTO ONE! – OVER 500 SPELLS! Reveals the secret of the ages. Manifest your destiny NOW! Most powerful spellcasters deliberately leave out important information. NOT MARIA!
8.5x11—236 pages—ISBN-13: 978-1606111086—$24.00

SUPER SPECIAL: Retail customers get all of Maria's books as listed for $139.00 + $15.00 Postage/Shipping. FREE DVD WITH 3 OF MARIA'S BOOKS OR MORE

WILLAM ALEXANDER ORIBELLO

At an early age, Oribello encountered Angelic Beings. Later in life he was taught by the Masters of Wisdom a variety of occult secrets which he has used to guide many. His teachings combine the Christian Mysteries with the art of Spiritism.

THE MASTERBOOK OF SPIRITUAL POWER—The spells in this sacred text work like a magnet to attract big money, good health, love, freedom from tension and worry...as well as banishing curses and eroding negativity.
8.5x11—116 pages—ISBN-13: 978-1606111109—$18.95

THE SEALED MAGICAL BOOK OF MOSES—Here are arcane secrets of Moses' powers that can now be revealed to series students only. Includes the 21 MAGICAL TALISMANS OF MOSES seldom seen, which can give you the powers of the holy sage.
8.5x11—142 pages—ISBN-13: 978-0938294689—$18.95

CANDLE BURNING MAGIC WITH THE PSALMS—Create life's greatest blessings by combining the power of the Holy Psalms with the magic of burning different colored candles. Best times, days and conditions for spells.
8.5x11—188 pages—ISBN-13: 978-0938294580—$21.95

USING CANDLE BURNING TO CONTACT YOUR GUARDIAN ANGEL
8.5X11—100 pages—ISBN-13: 978-0938294757—$19.95

SACRED MAGIC REVISED—Forbidden knowledge now revealed. . .prosperity for all guaranteed! Includes seven great money secrets.
8.5x11—146 pages—ISBN-13: 978-1606111291—$18.95

DIVINE BIBLE SPELLS—This book proves what you've heard all along – With God All Things Are Possible! Added material from Dragonstar.
8.5x11—142 pages—ISBN-13: 978-1606111499—$18.95

DIVINE MONEY SPELLS—Easy Magickal Spells To Jump Start Your Spiritual Economic Stimulus Package Added material from Dragonstar.Spells to eliminate poverty and to draw abundance.
8.5x11—152 pages—ISBN-13: 978-1606110645—$21.95

THE MEDIUMSHIP OF SPIRIT—The Ascension of William Alexander Oribello. Now an Ascended Master, Oribello has returned to the Earth Plane to continue his great work, assisted by the mediumship of psychic Aurora Thyme...
8.5X11—122 pages—ISBN-13: 978-1606111512—$18.95

GODSPELLS: WRITTEN SPELLS, SPOKEN SPELLS AND SPELL ENHANCERS—Here are the rules laid down thousands of years ago by those who spoke with the Heavenly Host and learned of his TRUE wishes for all of mankind. NOT of the devil. For unselfish use only!
8.5x11—140 pages—ISBN-13: 978-0938294498—$18.95

COUNT SAINT GERMAIN - THE MAN WHO LIVES FOREVER—Let Count Saint Germain — the man who lives forever — help transform your life through his insight into the metaphysical laws that govern the universe. "Strange" bio by Art Crocket. Channelings of the Master by Wm Oribello.
8.5x11—132 pages—ISBN-13: 978-1892062208—$21.95
Add $20 for DVD of Oribello channeling Saint Germain under the purple ray.

CURSES AND THEIR REVERSALS— Plus: Omens, Superstitions And The Removal Of The Evil Eye. Important workbook by Oribello with Maria D' Andrea, Lady Suzanne and others.
8.5x11—182 pages—ISBN-13: 978-1606111406—$21.95

SUPER SPECIAL
Mail Order customers get all of Wm Oribello's books as listed for just $149.95 + $15.00 SH

Mail Order Customers – Book Stores – Wholesalers – Distributors
Order Directly From
TIMOTHY G BECKLEY, BOX 753, NEW BRUNSWICK, NJ 08903
mrufo8@hotmail.com credit card orders 732 602-3407

22360905R00136

Made in the USA
San Bernardino, CA
02 July 2015